SEC REGULATION OF PUBLIC COMPANIES

SEC REGULATION OF PUBLIC COMPANIES

Allan B. Afterman

Prentice Hall, Englewood Cliffs, New Jersey 07632

Afterman, Allan B.
   SEC regulation of public companies / Allan B. Afterman.
      p.   cm.
   Includes index.
   ISBN 0-13-037185-8
   1. Securities—United States. 2. Corporations—Finance—Law and
legislation—United States. 3. Going public (Securities)—Law and
legislation—United States. I. Title.
   KF1439.A73   1995
   346.73′666—dc20
   [347.306666]   94-11319
                                      CIP

Editorial/Production Supervision: Spectrum Publisher Services
Acquisitions Editor: Bill Webber
Cover Design: Rich Dombrowski
Buyer: Patrice Fraccio

© 1995 by Prentice-Hall, Inc.

A Paramount Communications Company

Englewood Cliffs, New Jersey 07632

Printed in the United States of America

10 9 8 7 6 5 4 3 2

ISBN 0-13-037185-8

PRENTICE-HALL INTERNATIONAL (UK) LIMITED, *London*
PRENTICE-HALL OF AUSTRALIA PTY. LIMITED, *Sydney*
PRENTICE-HALL CANADA INC., *Toronto*
PRENTICE-HALL HISPANOAMERICANA, S.A., *Mexico*
PRENTICE-HALL OF INDIA PRIVATE LIMITED, *New Delhi*
PRENTICE-HALL OF JAPAN, INC., *Tokyo*
SIMON & SCHUSTER ASIA PTE. LTD., *Singapore*
EDITORA PRENTICE-HALL DO BRASIL, LTDA., *Rio de Janeiro*

To my almost-four-year-old granddaughter Brittany,
who no doubt someday will be a student of
and a participant in the capital markets.

Contents

Preface

No business education is entirely complete without at least some exposure to the elaborate manner in which publicly held companies are regulated by the Securities and Exchange Commission (SEC). Corporate executives, accountants, and investment bankers are all, to one degree or another, affected by the SEC. Institutional and individual investors alike are also affected, especially on matters of corporate disclosure and shareholders' rights.

SEC Regulation of Public Companies is designed to provide a comprehensive overview of the SEC and the federal securities laws it administers. The book is intended for graduate students and upper-level undergraduates across disciplines. Thus it can be used as a supplemental text in an intermediate or advanced accounting course, in an auditing course, in a business law course, or in a course on corporate finance or investments. It can also stand alone in a course on the SEC or on corporate governance.

Chapter 1 provides an overview of the federal securities laws and the workings of the SEC. This chapter also explores the implications of the efficient market hypothesis on past and future securities regulation. Chapter 2 discusses the pros and cons of going public and explores the roles and responsibilities of the company and the underwriter in a public offering. Chapter 3 covers the registration process and the continuous reporting obligations of public companies. Chapter 4 provides a comprehensive discussion of accounting and financial reporting requirements of publicly held entities.

Chapter 5 covers liability under the federal securities laws, including the latest developments involving the Racketeer Influenced and Corrupt Organizations (RICO) statute. Chapter 6 explains the SEC's scheme for regulating corporate insiders, including insider trading. Chapter 7 discusses the proxy solicitation process, shareholders' rights, and the new executive compensation disclosure requirements. This chapter also explains the complicated rules for regulating takeovers and tender offers.

Chapter 8 provides a comprehensive discussion of the SEC's recent initiatives designed to give smaller companies easier and less-expensive access to the capital markets. Chapter 9 covers the unique problems facing foreign companies that seek to raise funds from U.S. investors or to list their shares on a U.S. stock exchange. This chapter also explains the SEC's far-reaching influence on U.S. companies offering securities abroad.

Actual examples of SEC filings are liberally sprinkled throughout the text, and the full text of the Form 10-K annual report filed with the SEC by Reynolds Metals Company is reproduced and appears after Chapter 9.

Provocative questions at the end of each chapter are designed to stimulate thought and discussion regarding important issues facing regulators, accounting rulemakers, and the financial community at large.

The author wants to acknowledge those who served as reviewers for Prentice Hall: Ehsan H. Feroz, University of Minnesota–Duluth; Douglas R. Kahl, University of Akron; and Edward J. Gac, University of Colorado.

Allan B. Afterman

About the Author

Allan B. Afterman, CPA, Ph.D., has had many years of experience in public accounting. He was Assistant to the National Director of SEC Practice and a member of the Executive Office Research Department at major international CPA firms. Dr. Afterman is the author of numerous professional reference books and treatises on the topics of accountancy, financial reporting, and disclosure under the securities laws in the United States and the United Kingdom. Dr. Afterman is a consultant to governments of emerging nations in the development of accounting and auditing standards and a member of the adjunct faculty of the Graduate School of Business at the University of Chicago.

1

The Institutional Framework of Securities Regulation

THE SCOPE AND PURPOSE OF THE FEDERAL SECURITIES LAWS

The federal securities laws consist of six separate but related statutes; all were enacted between 1933 and 1940. They are

- The Securities Act of 1933
- The Securities Exchange Act of 1934
- The Public Utility Holding Company Act of 1935
- The Trust Indenture Act of 1939
- The Investment Company Act of 1940
- The Investment Advisers Act of 1940

The 1933 and 1934 acts are the most pervasive of the six and are the principal subjects of this book. The 1935 act has a limited focus: regulation of electric and gas utilities to assure geographic integration and corporate simplification. The 1939 act supplements the 1933 act. Among other provisions, it requires an independent trustee to protect the rights of investors that hold an entity's debt securities. The two 1940 acts regulate investment companies and advisers. Under the Investment Company Act, disclosure of the finances and investment policies of mutual funds and other similar entities is required; in addition, sales and promotional literature must conform to specific standards. The Investment Advisers Act requires registration of investment counselors, including those who publish market letters, and it prohibits fraudulent practices by such advisers.

In addition to the foregoing statutes, Congress enacted the Securities Investor Protection Act of 1970. This act insures customers, up to $500,000, against the insolvency of their stockbrokerage firm. Although not formally included within the text of that act, the Securities Investor Protection Act is generally considered to be a part of the 1934 act.

The Securities Act of 1933

The 1933 act, similar to its 1934 counterpart, is primarily a *disclosure* statute. The 1933 act requires that securities offered to the public at large be "registered" before they can be sold. This is accomplished by means of a registration statement filed with the U.S. Securities and Exchange Commission (SEC) containing specified information about

- The securities being offered
- The issuer of the securities
- The means by which the securities are to be sold

As a disclosure statute, registration under the 1933 act is intended to provide potential investors with an adequate and informed basis on which to make a decision regarding the purchase of the securities. Thus the registration process does not involve a review by the SEC of the merits of an offering, nor does the SEC provide a guarantee against loss.

A registration statement under the 1933 act consists of two parts. Part I, the prospectus, includes information relevant to the investment decision and is required to be provided to purchasers of the securities being offered. Part II contains information largely of a procedural or supplemental nature not considered essential to investors; it is usually not furnished to purchasers of the securities.

It is important to understand that registration is necessary under the 1933 act *each* time a company offers securities. Thus, although seasoned public entities may take advantage of a streamlined approach, a registration statement that includes, or provides access to, all required information must be filed whenever capital is sought from the public.

The Securities Exchange Act of 1934

Whereas the 1933 act is concerned with the *distribution* of securities, the 1934 act focuses on *trading* transactions (i.e., the purchase and resale in the marketplace of already outstanding securities). As such, the 1934 act is concerned with the following matters:

- Continuous disclosure by issuers whose securities are registered under the 1933 Act
- Regulation of the securities markets themselves
- Prevention of fraud and market manipulation
- Control of credit for the purchase of securities (i.e., margin trading)

- Regulation of insider trading
- Communication with shareholders (i.e., the proxy solicitation process)

The 1934 act also created the SEC to administer the federal securities laws. Prior to establishment of the SEC, the 1933 act was, for a short time, under the jurisdiction of the Federal Trade Commission (FTC).

Once a company has registered securities under the 1933 act in connection with a public offering, it becomes part of the 1934 act continuous reporting scheme, which requires filing of annual, quarterly, and other periodic reports with the SEC. Unlike a registration statement filed under the 1933 act, which discloses information about the issuer *and* the securities being offered for sale, 1934 act reports include information only about the company itself. This is because in a 1934 act filing no securities are being sold.

ORGANIZATION AND OPERATION OF THE SEC

The SEC has broad powers to administer the federal securities laws. The commission itself consists of five individuals (commissioners) appointed by the president of the United States to five-year terms. The terms are staggered so that only one commissioner's term expires each year. To ensure bipartisanship, not more than three of the commissioners may belong to the same political party. One commissioner is designated as chairman of the commission. Figure 1–1 shows the organization of the SEC.

There are four divisions of the commission. (1) The Division of Market Regulation is responsible for the regulation of securities exchanges. (2) The Division of Enforcement is responsible for the supervision and conduct of enforcement activities and investigations under each of the statutes administered by the SEC. (3) The Division of Investment Management is responsible for the administration of the Investment Company Act and Investment Advisers Act. (4) The Division of Corporation Finance is the primary vehicle for administration of the disclosure requirements and other provisions of the 1933 and 1934 acts through review of registration statements for public offerings and of annual, quarterly, and current reports.

The Office of the Chief Accountant is responsible to the commission for all accounting and auditing matters in connection with administration of the securities acts. In addition, this office is in charge of administering the commission's Rules of Practice among accountants who practice before the SEC.

The Office of the General Counsel represents the commission in litigation matters, provides legal advice to the commission, and assists in the interpretation of statutes, rules, and regulations. The Office of Economic Analysis analyzes data to determine the economic effects of existing and proposed SEC regulations. The responsibilities of the other offices of the commission are largely internal and administrative.

The commission's headquarters are in Washington, D.C. Five regional offices execute the SEC's policies and programs on a regional basis. Most of the actual investigation and enforcement work of the SEC is performed by the regional offices under supervision by the Washington office.

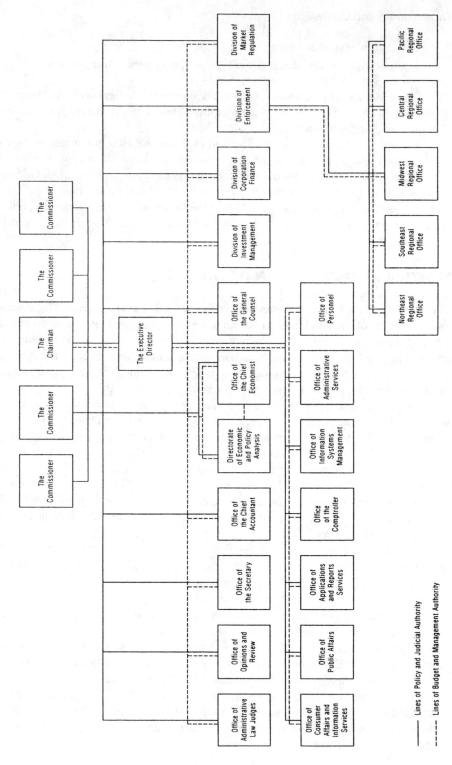

Figure 1–1 Securities and Exchange Commission

— Lines of Policy and Judicial Authority

---- Lines of Budget and Management Authority

In recognition of a developing global securities market, the SEC has created the Office of International Affairs, which is responsible for coordinating enforcement efforts relating to agreements with foreign securities regulators. The Office of International Affairs also consults with divisions and other offices of the SEC regarding the commission's international programs and initiatives.

The Referencing System Under the Securities Acts

Over the years, the SEC has developed a number of rules and regulations applicable to each of the securities acts. The authority to do this is spelled out in the securities acts themselves. The 1933 act and the 1934 act are divided into *sections* for each major topic. Sections constitute *law*. Rules and regulations are promulgated by the SEC for the purpose of carrying out provisions of the law.

Under the 1933 act, rules are assigned three-digit numbers. Certain (but not all) groups of rules form regulations. For example, Rules 400 to 499, developed to administer Section 6 of the 1933 act pertaining to the registration procedure, comprise Regulation C. Similarly, Section 3 of the 1933 act provides for the exemption from registration of certain types of securities. Regulation A, which consists of Rules 251 to 263, relates to the application of one of those exemptions.

Under the 1934 act, rules are numbered to correspond to the section numbers to which they relate. For example, Rules 14a-1 through 14b-2 together form Regulation 14A, which in turn relates to Section 14 of the 1934 act pertaining to proxies.

In addition to rules and regulations that apply only to a specific act, the commission has developed other regulations, primarily Regulations S-X and S-K, which apply to both the 1933 and 1934 acts. Regulation S-X sets forth the requirements for the form and content of financial statements included in registration statements and periodic reports filed under *either* act; Regulation S-K contains the requirements for all other (i.e., nonfinancial statement) information in filings under the 1933 or 1934 act.

In addition to Regulation S-K and S-X, the SEC recently issued Regulation S-B, which applies to entities qualifying as small business issuers. Regulation S-B contains the requirements for both financial statement and nonfinancial statement information included in registration statements and periodic reports filed under either the 1933 or 1934 act.

Means of Communication by the SEC

The SEC communicates to the legal and financial communities at large in the form of releases. Adoption of new or modified rules and proposals that pertain to a specific act is made through sequentially numbered releases under that act (e.g., 1933 Act Release No. 33–6950 or 1934 Act Release No. 34–11259). Information affecting more than one act is published separately under each act to which it applies.

Other types of releases through which the commission communicates are the following:

- *Financial reporting releases* reflect the opinions of the chief accountant and the commission itself regarding accounting and financial reporting matters.
- *Accounting and auditing enforcement releases* cover enforcement-related matters involving accounting, financial reporting, and auditing.
- *International series releases* cover matters specifically related to foreign issuers and internationalization of the securities markets.
- *Staff accounting bulletins* are interpretations and practices of the Division of Corporation Finance in administering the disclosure requirements of the 1933 and 1934 acts. Staff accounting bulletins do not necessarily represent official positions of the commission itself.

Less formally than through these releases, individual commissioners and senior staff members communicate their views about specific topics through speeches to business and financial groups.

The foregoing are vehicles for communicating information to the business community in general. In addition, SEC staff issues "no-action" and interpretive letters to provide guidance to public companies on specific transactions. Such letters are requested by the issuer, its attorneys, or its auditors. A no-action letter is used for a procedure whereby an inquiry is made concerning the SEC staff's view of a prospective transaction.

If the staff agrees with the manner in which the issuer plans to treat the transaction, the staff will state (or imply) that it would not recommend that the SEC take any action under the law; hence the term *no-action letter.* An interpretive letter simply requests the staff's opinion on a specific issue. The no-action procedure is very helpful to public companies and their advisers in complying with the 1933 and 1934 Securities Acts.

A technique similar to the no-action letter is the prefiling conference, which usually includes representatives of the issuer and staff members of the Division of Corporation Finance. Although the staff usually will not formally approve of a proposed course of action, it may indicate that it will not object to what the issuer proposes.

DEVELOPMENT OF THE SECURITIES LAWS

The 1933 act is the direct result of the 1929 stock market crash and the ensuing Great Depression. Passage of the act took place during the first 100 days of President Franklin D. Roosevelt's New Deal. During the decade between the end of World War I and the virtual complete collapse of the market in October 1929, approximately $50 billion of new securities were issued. Eventually, about half (nearly $25 billion) of those securities proved to be worthless.[1] The principal reason for this staggering ratio was, as Congress described it: "The alluring promises of easy wealth . . . with little or no attempt to bring to the investor's attention those facts essential to estimating the worth of any security. High pressure salesmanship rather than careful counsel was the rule in this most dangerous enterprise."[2]

Purchasers of new securities were not the only ones to suffer from the market crash and ensuing economic depression. Indeed, investors holding already outstanding securities took a beating as well. From a precrash high in 1929 to its 1932 postcrash low, the market value of securities listed on the New York Stock Exchange plummeted from approximately $89 billion to about $15 billion, a drop of more than 83 percent.[3]

Congressional inquiry determined the following principal causes of the crash:[4]

- A precrash speculative frenzy that drove prices to artificially high levels
- Uncontrolled credit granting by brokers to investors to acquire stock on margin
- Manipulative practices by brokers and dealers to create false appearances of trading activity
- False and misleading information provided by companies whose securities were listed on the exchange
- The lack of requirements for publicly traded entities to disclose accurate information on a timely basis
- Unabashed trading by corporate insiders who, through access to confidential information, earned profits at the expense of investors at large
- Insufficient responsiveness by corporations to the needs of stockholders due to weaknesses in the proxy solicitation process

Recognizing that the 1933 act addressed only the problems associated with the initial distribution of securities, Congress quickly passed the 1934 act in an attempt to put an end to the myriad problems in the trading markets.

Disclosure versus Merit Regulation

The main objective of the federal securities laws is the protection of investors. Congress opted for "full disclosure" as the central technique by which this is achieved. But it is not the only way to protect the public. The so-called merit process is used by most *states*. Thus in those states, securities regulation may *prohibit* an offering of securities if it is judged not to be "fair, just, and equitable."

State securities laws are referred to as blue-sky laws. The term is derived from an early twentieth-century sentiment that slick and clever investment bankers from Wall Street would attempt to sell securities in entities with not much more substance than the blue sky above to unwitting investors on Main Street.

In theory, registration of an offering under the 1933 act does not automatically entitle those securities to be sold in any given state. In practice, however, registration under the federal securities laws usually enables securities to be offered and sold in most states through processes known as coordination and notification.

In the aftermath of the Great Depression, when deliberating the need for enactment of some federal legislation to regulate the distribution of securities, Congress was faced with the choice of disclosure versus merit regulation. Choosing the disclosure approach, Representative Samuel Rayburn simply stated the following about the bill that would become the Securities Act of 1933:

The purpose of this bill is to place the owners of securities on a parity, so far as possible, with the management of the corporations, and to place the buyer the same plane so far as available information is concerned, with the seller.[5]

An observer would later comment that, in passing the 1933 act, Congress did not take away from the citizen his or her inalienable right to make a fool of him- or herself; it simply attempted to prevent others from making a fool of him.[6]

It should be understood, however, that disclosure and merit, as philosophies, are not completely separate from one another. The very requirement for the presence of full and fair disclosure has a certain policing effect on fraudulent or pie-in-the-sky schemes. As one commentator put it, people who are forced to undress in public will presumably pay some attention to their figures.[7]

The Need for Securities Regulation

A security is an *intangible* item without utility of its own. As such, it has no intrinsic value. To a holder (i.e., an investor), the worth of a security comes from the claim it represents on a company. Thus the decision to purchase or sell a security at a given price requires sufficient, reliable, and timely information about the activities of the issuing entity. It is on this premise that securities regulation is based.

Although there are many variations, essentially a security conveys to its holder an interest either as an owner or creditor of an enterprise. Thus, for example, bondholders, as creditors, are usually entitled to receive interest on their investments and return of principal. Stockholders, as owners, typically have voting rights to choose a firm's directors and to approve major corporate transactions, such as mergers or acquisitions. Stockholders also share in the profits, when declared as dividends, of the entities in which they hold an equity interest. Although the informational needs of these two classes of investors are not identical, they are quite similar.

To impute a value on their entitlements (i.e., the security in which those benefits are embodied), investors must be informed about (1) the nature of the security and the claims it represents; and (2) the issuer's financial condition, past operating performance, and factors that are likely to influence future results. Investors must also have confidence in the securities markets themselves and in the brokers and dealers that execute buy-and-sell transactions. Simply stated, it is toward these ends that the federal securities laws and the scores of rules and regulations thereunder have been established.

From the perspective of issuers of securities, the funds received from investors are used for a multitude of purposes, such as research and development, capital equipment, purchases of raw materials for the manufacturing process, and acquisitions of other entities. For most businesses, even highly successful ones, internally generated funds alone (i.e., through retained profits) are insufficient to finance continued expansion; outside capital is often needed.

Historically, banks were the main intermediaries between savers and users of capital. Banks accumulated funds from customers' deposits and then loaned those funds to businesses. This generally remained the case until the 1960s when corporations began taking greater advantage of the public bond markets. At first, the market for debt capital from outside investors was dominated by investment-grade securities (i.e., those issued by the most creditworthy enterprises). By the early 1970s and through the 1980s, however, speculative-grade companies found that there was growing demand for their securities as well. This trend, which was spurred by the proliferation of sophisticated institutional investors and by the reduction of consumers' use of bank deposits as the primary receptacle for savings, had the effect of diminishing the role of banks as liaisons between providers and users of capital. Since the 1960s many companies have realized that obtaining funds *directly* from public investors was more cost effective than dealing with banks.

Equity capital is the other major source of outside funding for corporate America. In recent years the value of common and preferred stocks registered with the SEC has exceeded $100 *billion* each year. To gain perspective, however, the amount of debt securities registered each year over the past decade has been roughly two and one-half times that amount, and the total value of already outstanding securities traded each year since 1988 has hovered around $3 *trillion*.[8]

For the public securities markets to flourish and thus for corporations to have sufficient capital at a reasonable cost to grow and prosper, investors must feel confident about the regulation of securities, issuers, and the markets themselves. Thus corporations as well as investors benefit from a sound set of laws that are strongly administered and aggressively enforced. It can be argued that the existence of a robust and vibrant public capital market, which can exist only when all participants have faith in the process, has a positive effect on society in general. In support of this argument, a number of countries have sought to set up stock markets in the very early stages of transition to a free-market economy. It is interesting to note that many such countries have resisted laissez-faire. To have adopted such an approach would have been a natural inclination upon emergence from a suppressive hold on free enterprise by the central government. Instead, these countries emulated variations of the U.S. scheme. Officials of these developing nations have apparently concluded that a highly regulated securities market will foster strong investor confidence to provide much needed capital to private enterprise, which, in turn, will use those funds to develop new products and services to benefit the population at large.[9]

The Properties of a Security

In defining a security, the 1933 act provides a laundry list of examples, including obvious instruments such as stocks and bonds and less obvious ones such as puts, calls, options, straddles, and undivided interests in oil and gas rights. Conspicuously missing, however, is a description of the essential characteristics of a security. Not surprisingly, therefore, the definition of a security has largely been determined through case law. Whether a particular financial instrument is a security is not merely an academic issue; a positive determination (especially after the fact) makes the securities laws applicable and could cause legal consequences to the issuer and other parties to the offering.

It is clear that in creating the federal securities laws Congress sought to regulate *investment* transactions, not commercial transactions. Thus, for example, commercial loans by banks that are evidenced by notes are not securities, nor are personal notes

(IOUs) given for the purchase of real or tangible personal property. The securities laws, therefore, do not apply to mercantile or consumer matters.

The courts rely on a number of relevant factors to differentiate investment transactions from commercial ones. An investment transaction—and thus one to which the securities laws would apply—must have the following fundamental elements:

1. It is a contract or scheme calling for capital to be invested in a common enterprise.
2. The investor is led to expect a profit on the investment.
3. The actual profit to be earned is a consequence of the efforts of the entity that issued the security.

From this perspective, it can be further seen that the attributes of an investment transaction (particularly the third attribute) give rise to informational needs for investors and that the securities laws require issuers to provide full disclosure to meet those needs.

Who Are the Securities Laws Intended to Protect?

The answer of course is the buyers, sellers, and holders of securities. But the answer to that question begs another, more substantive question: What is the profile of the "typical" investor? That question is not an unimportant one; indeed, it is of extreme relevance to issuers, their advisers, and securities regulators alike. Decisions about the extent and manner of regulation, including mandatory disclosures, surely should be made with an eye toward the constituency to be served. Thus, if the bulk of investors is made up of individuals who are naive about finance, regulatory choices are different from those that would be made if most investors consisted of highly sophisticated institutions, such as pension funds, insurance companies, foundations, and mutual funds.

Although exact figures are unavailable, it is generally agreed that nearly 50 percent of all the stock (equities) of U.S. public companies is owned by institutional investors, with the heaviest concentration of institutional ownership in the largest corporations.[10] Some have thus argued that institutional investors, who possess both the knowledge of what information is needed *and* the power to obtain that information from issuers, are a more efficient and effective substitute for the ever-growing body of SEC *mandated* disclosures. This group also points out that the costs to society of government-required disclosure exceed the benefits.

The other edge of the sword, however, is that if institutions own about half of the outstanding stock of U.S. public entities, then individuals own the other half. It is estimated that more than 51 million individuals owned shares in publicly traded companies or stock mutual funds in mid-1990, up from 6.5 million in 1952 and 47 million as recently as 1985.[11] Thus nearly 20 percent of all Americans have a *direct* investment in the stock market, and this does not count the millions more who have an indirect stake through pension plans and the like.

But those who would argue for less rather than more required disclosure contend that the complicated maze of financial and other data appearing in a registration statement or periodic report cannot possibly be understood fully by unsophisticated individuals acting on their own. They reason that, in effect, it is the institutional investors that utilize the information they need to establish fair values for securities.

Although this is not an argument that has only recently arisen because of the increase in institutional ownership of securities since the 1960s, it does have a new twist. Indeed, in 1934, just one year after passage of the 1933 act, William O. Douglas (who would several years later become chairman of the SEC) remarked that "those needing investment guidance will receive small comfort from the balance sheet, contracts, or compilation of other data revealed in the registration statement [because] they either lack the training or intelligence to assimilate them and find them useful. . . ."[12] These comments were made when accounting principles and financial statements were relatively simple. In today's environment, as commerce and finance have become exponentially more complex, Douglas' observations would be even more relevant.

Implications of the Efficient Market Hypothesis

The efficient market hypothesis (EMH) is the term used to describe the relationship between movements in prices of securities and *information*. The EMH developed from attempts to explain empirical evidence that stock prices followed a "random walk" (i.e., past price changes cannot be used to predict future price changes). The EMH is thought to exist possibly in one of three different forms:

- *Weak form,* in which the current price of a security reflects all the information embodied in the past prices of that security
- *Semistrong form,* in which security prices reflect all *publicly available* information
- *Strong form,* in which security prices reflect *all* information, including information available only to insiders

Whether markets are efficient with respect to information in any of these forms has not been proven to everyone's satisfaction, although there is a large body of evidence suggesting that, at least for securities traded on the New York Stock Exchange, the market functions in the semistrong form of efficiency.

In an efficient market, the price of a security adjusts so quickly in response to new (previously unavailable) information that possessing the information provides no advantage to buyers and sellers. However, if the market is inefficient, new information is impounded gradually in a security's price, thus giving those who have the information an opportunity to profit from it.

If markets are efficient in either the semistrong or strong form, there are a number of implications for securities regulation, particularly regarding accounting and other mandatory information, including the following:

- The market can distinguish information that is significant from information that is not.
- The market is not tricked by changes in accounting practices or influenced by new

accounting pronouncements that have no substantial economic effect on an enterprise.

- Efforts by accounting rule makers to solve sticky problems of income and asset measurement have largely been for naught; additional disclosure would have sufficed.

- The market effectively evaluates the underlying information prior to an accounting rule change; thus the additional information provided by a new accounting rule is quite limited.[13]

- Concerns about furnishing *too much* information to investors are not valid because the market will sort out what it deems important.

- The form that information takes is not very significant.

- Because the market will already have digested all important accounting information by the time financial statements are issued, the impact of such statements—unless they contain surprises—will be immaterial.

The whole notion of an efficient market in the semistrong form that responds quickly to new information is predicated upon the existence of professional analysts who actively pursue a course of action to obtain such information. Just as important, market efficiency also is the result of skillful investors and their advisers *attempting* to identify misvalued securities. Thus, paradoxically, the very efforts by investors to take advantage of under- or overvalued securities has the effect of narrowing the opportunities for superior (in relation to the market generally) investment returns for everyone.

Although the SEC shows no sign of reducing the volume of required disclosures or even of slowing the pace at which new disclosures are mandated, it has directly responded to at least one important mechanism of the EMH: the information monitoring process by institutional investors and security analysts. As discussed in greater detail in Chapter 3, registration of securities under the 1933 act is simplified for certain companies whose securities are already in the public's hands and that, among other requirements, have been subject to the 1934 act periodic reporting requirements for some time. Thus eligible issuers may offer additional securities without providing *in the prospectus* company-specific information that has been previously included in annual and quarterly reports filed with the SEC. This initiative, which was adopted in 1982, considerably reduces the costly duplication of information for many companies whose securities are widely followed by analysts. It also represents the commission's formal acknowledgment that it is not necessary to require disclosure of data on which the market has already acted.

CHAPTER SUMMARY

The federal securities laws resulted from the 1929 stock market crash, which was followed by the Great Depression. The 1933 and 1934 acts are primarily disclosure statutes. The 1933 act regulates the distribution of securities, whereas the 1934 act focuses on the purchase and resale in the marketplace of already outstanding securities. Registration of securities is required under the 1933 act whenever a public offering is made. Under the 1934 act, once a company becomes publicly held, it has a continuous reporting obligation. The securities laws are administered by the SEC, which consists of five commissioners. The Division of Corporation Finance is primarily responsible for the review of 1933 act registration statements and periodic 1934 act reports filed with the commission.

Although the securities laws themselves do not precisely define a security, the courts have generally held that the two principal characteristics of a security are that (1) the investor is led to expect to realize a profit on the investment and (2) the profit to be earned is largely a result of efforts of the issuing company.

The existence of the EMH has not been conclusively proven, but the SEC has recently streamlined the information dissemination process for large, seasoned public companies on the premise that such companies are already widely followed by security analysts.

DISCUSSION QUESTIONS

1. Distinguish between the purpose of the 1933 act and the purpose of the 1934 act.
2. Do you believe that the right decision was made by Congress in selecting disclosure versus merit regulation? Discuss the advantages and disadvantages of each approach.
3. Based on the attributes of a security, as defined by the courts, name other types of financial instruments that would qualify as securities.
4. Do you believe that mandatory disclosures should be replaced or reduced in light of the arguments that (a) institutional investors know better than the government about what is needed to value a security and (b) individual investors are unable to understand the complex financial and other information included in SEC filings? Explain your answer.
5. Identify other major implications of the EMH on securities regulation. Should accounting rule makers redirect their efforts away from measurement principles toward more disclosure?

ENDNOTES

1. H.R. Rep. No. 85, 73d Cong., 1st sess. (1933).
2. Ibid.
3. James D. Cox, Robert W. Hillman, and Donald C. Langenvoort, *Securities Regulation* (Boston: Little, Brown, 1991), p. 15.
4. Ibid.
5. Louis Loss, *Fundamentals of Securities Regulation,* 2d ed. (Boston: Little, Brown, 1988), p. 32.
6. Ibid., p. 33.
7. Ibid.
8. Cox, et al. *Securities Regulation,* pp. 2–3.

9. This line of reasoning was explained to the author by the chairmen of the Polish and Hungarian securities regulatory agencies, respectively.

10. Cox et al., *Securities Regulation,* pp. 9–11.

11. Loss, *Fundamentals of Securities Regulation,* p. 5

12. William O. Douglas, *Protecting the Investor,* 23 Yale L. Rev., 521 (1934).

13. Although this indeed may sometimes be the case, it can be argued that analysts are limited to evaluating accounting data that management itself accumulates and is willing to provide, even if that data are not required to be disclosed in public filings. Thus, for example, before FASB Statement No. 87 was passed specifying the manner in which an underfunded pension liability should be measured and presented, there was enough information required to be disclosed under prior rules for analysts to estimate the amount of that obligation. However, prior to the passage of FASB Statement No. 106 on accounting for postretirement benefits other than pensions, it was virtually impossible to estimate the amount of that underfunded liability because no disclosures were required, and in the majority of companies, management had not even begun to accumulate the necessary information.

2

The Process of Raising
Capital from the Public

For established companies and start-up enterprises alike, capital is essential for growth and prosperity. As mentioned in Chapter 1, rarely do profits alone generate enough funds for expansion. When outside capital is sought, the decision is three-pronged: (1) the type, (2) the amount, and (3) the source.

Both debt and equity capital can be obtained from a variety of sources, including friends and relatives. Occasionally, even customers and suppliers will provide funding to an enterprise. Their principal reason for doing so, however, often is to ensure a continuing source of supply or an outlet for their products and, thus, may have little to do with traditional return-on-investment considerations.

For development-stage entities in certain "hot" industries (for example, biotechnology companies), initial financing may be available from venture capitalists. For established companies, bank loans, of course, represent a primary source of funds.

Even from these outside sources, however, an enterprise may not be able to raise all the capital it needs or may not be able to obtain it in the form it desires. Thus, although friends and relatives may provide seed capital during a firm's formation stage, they usually cannot be counted on for day-to-day working capital requirements. Customers and suppliers have their own agendas that often do not mesh with the expansion plans of other companies. Venture capitalists, who specialize in providing funds to entities fortuitous enough to operate in certain high-tech industries, normally exact a prohibitive ownership toll from the founders of the company.

Even commercial banks, which are still the major suppliers of outside funding to the overwhelming majority of established businesses, may not be able to satisfy all the needs of all companies all the time. The main reasons for this are as follows:[1]

- Because of the nature of customers' deposits, banks prefer to lend on a short-term basis of one year or less. Although loans for more than one year are common, they almost never extend beyond five years. Thus banks may be unwilling or unable to provide funding for long-term projects.
- Banks are essentially risk-aversive. Thus they are unwilling to fund highly speculative projects, regardless of the interest rate.
- Bank lending practices are very sensitive to economic conditions. As the rate paid for obtaining funds (deposits) and the rate received for lending funds converge (i.e., the spread narrows, yielding a lower profit), the supply of capital otherwise available for loans may be redirected to "safer" investments.
- Banks do not provide equity capital.

For some corporations, the next logical step is to issue securities to the public in exchange for the amount and type of capital that best suits their needs.[2] To be sure, companies that do so are in the clear *minority*. There are roughly *three million* active corporations in the United States. Of these, only about 28,000 have outstanding securities in the hands of the public.[3]

THE DECISION TO GO PUBLIC

When a company issues securities (usually stock) to the public at large for the first time, it is called an initial public offering (IPO). The decision to "go public" is not one that should be made without all the facts. Although equity and debt capital can usually be raised in larger amounts on more flexible terms from the public than from many other sources, there are significant drawbacks to being a publicly held company. Table 2–1 identifies the principal advantages and disadvantages of going public.

Each company must weigh the pros and cons of transformation from a closely held to a publicly held company. As is evident, there are a number or reasons for not going public, but the ones most often cited relate generally to the ongoing burden of continuous reporting under the 1934 act.

WHAT IS A PUBLIC OFFERING?

In the environment of securities regulation, a public offering is distinguished from a private offering (or private placement, as it is often referred to). This is an important distinction: A public offering is subject to the registration provisions of the 1933 act, whereas a private placement is not. Yet, despite their significance, neither the term *public offering* nor *private offering* is defined in the 1933 act. Indeed, what constitutes a public offering is often determined residually, so that an offering is a public one if it does not qualify as a private one.

The offering of securities by an issuer to the *public at large* is considered a public offering. A private offering usually involves the direct placement of securities with one or

TABLE 2–1   GOING PUBLIC

Advantages	Disadvantages
• Capital can usually be raised for a multitude of purposes, because the public is a variety of investor types with different tolerances for risk and demands for reward. Thus highly speculative projects or ventures that otherwise would not see the light of day can usually find a willing group of public investors.	• Preparing for the initial public offering can be quite costly in terms of time, money, and human resources. In addition, each subsequent offering requires registration under the 1933 act.[a]
• A public market for an entity's stock provides a means by which retiring founders may be adequately compensated for their efforts in developing the company.	• New claimants on the company's earnings and assets will be added.
• Talented managerial and technical personnel are more easily attracted to public companies with the lure of valuable stock options. For many previously family-owned enterprises, this may solve the problem of management succession.	• Being a public company subjects the entity to the annual, quarterly, and current ongoing reporting requirements of the 1934 act, which can be expensive and time consuming.
• Acquisitions of another entity may be accomplished through an exchange of stock, thus limiting the drain on cash that would otherwise be needed for the purchase.	• Because of the full-disclosure requirements of the securities acts, information previously considered proprietary will be available to the public (including competitors).
• For well-run, highly profitable entities, the cost of capital may be reduced because the public market is often more sensitive to corporate performance than banks and other private sources of funds.	• The pressures of stock and bond markets may call for a transformation in the way the company is run. Short-term (quarterly) earnings have to be considered, perhaps at the exclusion of long-term, ultimately more profitable projects.
• Although management must answer to the stockholders, owners of a previously privately held business will probably continue to own a controlling interest and thus still be able to control the company's destiny as they did prior to it becoming a public entity.	• Matters that previously were wholly within the purview of the founders will be subject to stockholder scrutiny, including executive compensation.
• Consumer companies whose stock is held by individuals (rather than institutions) may have found new and loyal customers for their products.	• Financial statements must be *audited* and prepared in accordance with generally accepted accounting principles.
	• In terms of cost of capital, poor performance (even in the short term) will be punished just as good performance will be rewarded.
	• Disappointing stock price behavior could cause key employees to leave for a competitor's more lucrative stock compensation program.
	• As public ownership spreads, founders have less and less control over the company's direction.

[a] Some of (but not all) the burden of an IPO has been lightened for "small business issuers" by recent SEC initiatives. These are discussed in Chapter 8.

a limited number of institutional investors, such as life insurance companies or pension funds.

The 1933 act, as a full disclosure statute, is intended to protect investors by requiring issuers of securities to provide information thought necessary for informed investment decisions. The Supreme Court has held that the private-offering exemption hinges on whether the offerees—as a class—need the protection of the 1933 act. The Court concluded that an offering to those who are shown to be able to fend for themselves (e.g., institutional investors) and, therefore, do not need the protection afforded by registration, is not a public offering.

PREPARING THE PUBLIC OFFERING

Once the decision has been made to go public, the issuer and its advisers must begin to prepare for the public offering. Although the process is much the same for already public entities issuing additional securities, the focus of the following discussion is on the IPO.

The Role of the Underwriter

Most public offerings are "underwritten" by investment bankers. Underwriters function as intermediaries between the issuer of securities (i.e., the seller) and buyers. The underwriter's arrangement with the issuing company usually takes the form of either a "firm commitment" or "best efforts," with variations depending on the investment banking house involved.

In a firm commitment, the principal (termed *managing*) underwriter agrees to *purchase* the securities from the issuer to be resold to the public. For large offerings, the managing underwriter typically organizes an underwriting "syndicate" in which each member agrees to buy a specified number of securities for resale. In some offerings, underwriters may resell some of the purchased shares to broker-dealers who are not part of the underwriting group to facilitate the ultimate sale to the public.

The underwriters are compensated for their services through a difference between the price at which the securities are sold to the public (i.e., the public-offering price) and the price paid by the underwriters to the issuer. This difference is known as the "spread," which is normally between 1 percent and 8 percent of the public offering price, depending on the perceived difficulty in reselling the securities.

In a firm commitment, the underwriters—not the issuer—absorb market risk. This is not the case in a best-efforts arrangement whereby the underwriter acts as an *agent* for the issuer. Underwriters' compensation in a best-efforts offering takes the form of a commission rather than a spread. Because the underwriters have not invested their own capital, they usually earn less in a best-efforts arrangement.

There are three basic types of best-efforts offerings: (1) the normal (or straight) deal, (2) the minimum (or mini/maxi) deal, and (3) the all or none deal. The primary difference among the three is the number of shares to be sold before the offering can be considered complete. In a normal deal, there is no threshold number of shares that must be sold. In a minimum deal, a specified number of shares must be placed with investors before the offering is considered successful. If that number is not met, the offering is rescinded and the money received from investors, which was held in escrow, is returned. In an all or none deal, all the shares being offered must be sold; if not, the offering is called off and the funds are returned to investors.

Generally speaking, speculative offerings underwritten by regional or local investment banking firms are done on a best-efforts basis. In contrast, offerings of lesser risk, which are typically underwritten by the large national houses, are the subject of firm commitments. But this is not always true; in some cases, issuing companies that are so seasoned and whose securities usually are placed without much problem prefer a best-efforts arrangement because of the lower cost involved.

The Registration Statement

Under the 1933 act, securities to be sold in a public offering (unless exempt) must be registered. This is accomplished via a registration statement filed with the SEC. For an IPO, Form S-1 must be used.[4] Unlike IRS forms that are filled out line by line, Form S-1 (and other SEC forms, for the most part) is completed in *textual* form in response to specific types of information to be included. Form S-1 consists of two parts. Part I is the prospectus, which contains information thought to be important for an informed investment decision. Part II includes supplementary and SEC procedural data.

Contents of the Prospectus

A Form S-1 prospectus consists of information about three broad categories: (1) the company issuing the securities, (2) the securities being offered, and (3) the method of distribution of the securities.

Specifically, the following is required:

- A description of the entity's business, properties, and pending legal proceedings
- Audited income statements and cash flow statements for each of the last three years, and audited balance sheets for the last two years
- A five-year history of selected key financial data
- If the issuer's independent auditor has resigned or been dismissed, a discussion about disagreements concerning financial reporting, if any, between management of the entity and the former auditor occurring during the previous two years
- Quarterly sales, gross profit, and net income data for each of the past two years
- A comprehensive discussion and analysis covering the latest three years of results of operations, financial condition, liquidity, cash flows, and capital resources, and a discussion of future events known to the issuer that are likely to mean that past results are not indicative of future performance
- The identification and background of officers, directors, and key employees
- Amounts of compensation (including stock options) and pension plans paid to key executives, and a discussion of how executive compensation is tied to corporate performance
- A description of any material interests that officers or directors have in other companies doing business with the issuer
- Information about the market price of the entity's common stock and the frequency and amount of cash dividends declared over the last two years (not applicable to IPOs)

- A discussion of risk factors of which potential investors should be aware (including poor past operating performance, the nature of the entity's business, the existence of substantial competition, the absence of a previous market for the stock, etc.)
- A discussion of management's specific plans for use of the proceeds from the offering
- An explanation of how the public-offering price was determined
- The amount of any significant disparity between the public-offering price and the cost of the entity's stock acquired in the past five years by officers, directors, and other insiders
- Identification of the principal underwriters, the amount of securities to which each underwriter is committed, a description of the underwriting arrangement, and the amount of the underwriters' compensation
- A complete description of the securities being offered, including voting and dividend rights

Filing the Registration Statement

The law is quite clear that sales of securities cannot be made until the registration statement becomes *effective,* which, barring actions by the issuer or the SEC, will automatically occur twenty days after it is filed. As a practical matter, it usually takes considerably longer for first-time issuers and other problem companies.

Once the registration statement is filed with the SEC, it is assigned for review to the branch of the Division of Corporation Finance that specializes in the issuer's industry. Because of human resource shortages and budget constraints, not all registration statements are reviewed. All so-called sensitive transactions, however, including every IPO, is examined by the staff.

Normally, a staff review takes between thirty and sixty days from the date of filing. Note that the SEC does not pass on the merits of the offering; instead the review is undertaken for the purpose of determining compliance with the commission's disclosure requirements. In most cases, SEC staff will have questions or suggestions regarding the registration statement, especially in an initial public offering. These are communicated to the issuer in what is termed a letter of comment.

Because there are stiff legal consequences for a deficient registration statement (discussed in Chapter 5), the issuer will usually amend the registration statement at least once in response to the staff's comments. Even then, the statutory burden of full disclosure rests with the issuer and its advisers. The very existence of a review cannot shift that burden to the staff.

Occasionally, a registration statement is so inadequately prepared that the staff will conclude that a review cannot be justified until the filing has been substantially revised. Such a revision is often termed bed-bugging and is usually associated with IPOs of very small companies and their inexperienced auditors, attorneys, or underwriters.

To prevent a defective registration statement from automatically becoming effective on the twentieth day after filing but before the staff has completed its review, issuers normally utilize a delaying amendment. This postpones the effective date until such time as the registration statement has been revised to comply with the staff's comments.

Just prior to effectiveness of the registration statement (in some instances, literally just one or two hours before), the issuer files what is called the pricing amendment, in which the public-offering price and other data based on that price are inserted in the prospectus. To have filed that information months—even days—before the effective date of the registration statement would have subjected the underwriters to enormous risk of changes in market sentiment.

Underwriter Activities During the Quiet Period

Once the registration statement is filed with the SEC, the so-called quiet period begins; it ends when the registration statement becomes effective. During that period, which takes two months or more for IPOs and other complicated issues, underwriters and dealers may not *sell* (or offer to sell) the securities covered by the registration statement. Such transactions may occur only when the registration statement becomes effective. During the quiet period, however, *selling efforts* may be carried out whereby potential investors are contacted. Prospective purchasers are often furnished with a *preliminary* prospectus that contains substantially the same information required to be included in the final prospectus. The only exception is that the offering price and other information dependent on the offering price may be omitted from the preliminary prospectus.

In addition, the cover page of the preliminary prospectus must contain a legend, printed in red ink, that explains the following:[5]

- The registration statement filed with the SEC has not yet become effective.
- Information included in the preliminary prospectus may have to be changed.
- The securities may not be sold or offered for sale until the registration statement becomes effective.

An example of the cover page of a preliminary prospectus is shown in Figure 2–1. Notice that the required legend is printed along the left-hand margin. Also notice that offering price information and the date at the foot of the page are omitted. This information will be filled in when the final prospectus becomes effective.

During the quiet period, underwriters are permitted to inform prospective investors at large that a public offering is in process and that a preliminary prospectus is available. Typically, this is done through a "tombstone ad" in the *Wall Street Journal* and other financial newspapers. The term itself is derived from the unembellished nature of the announcement. Notice in Figure 2–2 that the tombstone ad contains unequivocal language that the announcement does not constitute an offer to sell the securities or a solicitation of an offer to buy the securities. This is similar to the legend on the cover page of the preliminary prospectus. Recall that, under the law, offers and sales may only take place after the registration statement becomes effective.

SUBJECT TO COMPLETION, DATED MARCH 23, 1993

2,750,000 Shares

IRG TECHNOLOGIES, INC.™

Common Stock

Of the 2,750,000 shares of Common Stock offered hereby, 2,300,000 shares are being sold by the Company and 450,000 shares are being sold by the Selling Stockholders. See "Principal and Selling Stockholders." The Company will not receive any of the proceeds from the sale of shares by the Selling Stockholders.

Prior to this offering, there has been no public market for the Common Stock of the Company. It is currently estimated that the initial public offering price will be between $10.00 and $12.00 per share. See "Underwriting" for a discussion of factors to be considered in determining the initial public offering price. Application has been made to have the Common Stock approved for quotation on the NASDAQ National Market System under the symbol "IRGT."

See "Risk Factors" for a discussion of certain factors that should be considered by prospective purchasers of the Common Stock offered hereby.

THESE SECURITIES HAVE NOT BEEN APPROVED OR DISAPPROVED BY THE SECURITIES AND EXCHANGE COMMISSION OR ANY STATE SECURITIES COMMISSION NOR HAS THE SECURITIES AND EXCHANGE COMMISSION OR ANY STATE SECURITIES COMMISSION PASSED UPON THE ACCURACY OR ADEQUACY OF THIS PROSPECTUS. ANY REPRESENTATION TO THE CONTRARY IS A CRIMINAL OFFENSE.

	Price to Public	Underwriting Discount(1)	Proceeds to Company(2)	Proceeds to Selling Stockholders
Per Share	$	$	$	$
Total(3)	$	$	$	$

(1) *See "Underwriting" for information concerning indemnification of the Underwriters and other matters.*
(2) *Before deducting expenses payable by the Company estimated at $325,000.*
(3) *The Company and the Selling Stockholders have granted to the Underwriters a 30-day option to purchase up to 412,500 additional shares of Common Stock solely to cover over-allotments, if any. If the Underwriters exercise this option in full, the Price to Public will total $, Underwriting Discount will total $, Proceeds to Company will total $ and Proceeds to Selling Stockholders will total $.*

The shares of Common Stock are offered by the several Underwriters named herein, subject to receipt and acceptance by them and subject to their right to reject any order in whole or in part. It is expected that delivery of the certificates representing such shares will be made against payment therefor at the office of Montgomery Securities on or about   , 1993.

MONTGOMERY SECURITIES

KEMPER SECURITIES, INC.

RAYMOND JAMES & ASSOCIATES, INC.

May   , 1993

Figure 2–1   Preliminary Prospectus Cover Page

This advertisement is neither an offer to sell nor a solicitation of an offer to buy any of these securities. The offering is made only by the Prospectus.

New Issue   March 16, 1994

2,000,000 Shares

Common Stock

Price $11.50 Per Share

Copies of the Prospectus may be obtained in any State from only such of the undersigned as may legally offer these Securities in compliance with the securities laws of such State.

McDonald & Company
Securities, Inc.

The Ohio Company

Advest, Inc.	Robert W. Baird & Co. Incorporated	J. C. Bradford & Co.	The Chicago Corporation
Cowen & Company	Crowell, Weedon & Co.	Dain Bosworth Incorporated	Fahnestock & Co. Inc.
First Albany Corporation	Interstate/Johnson Lane Corporation	Janney Montgomery Scott Inc.	Kemper Securities, Inc.
Ladenburg, Thalmann & Co. Inc.	Legg Mason Wood Walker Incorporated		Morgan Keegan & Company, Inc.
Piper Jaffray Inc.	The Principal/Eppler, Guerin & Turner, Inc.		Rauscher Pierce Refsnes, Inc.
Raymond James & Associates, Inc.	The Robinson-Humphrey Company, Inc.		Roney & Co.
Stifel, Nicolaus & Company Incorporated	Sutro & Co. Incorporated	Tucker Anthony Incorporated	Wheat First Butcher & Singer Capital Markets
Cleary Gull Reiland & McDevitt Inc.	Foley Mufson Howe & Company		Hamilton Investments, Inc.
J. J. B. Hilliard, W. L. Lyons, Inc.	C.L. King & Associates, Inc.		Parker/Hunter Incorporated
Pennsylvania Merchant Group Ltd	Raffensperger, Hughes & Co. Incorporated		Scott & Stringfellow, Inc.
The Seidler Companies Incorporated			Spencer Trask Securities, Inc.

Figure 2–2   Tombstone Ad

For all practical purposes, the research department of an investment banking firm that is also an underwriter is precluded from publishing a stock recommendation report about a company during the quiet period.[6]

Issuer Activities During the Quiet Period

Officers and directors of issuers walk a fine line during the quiet period. On one hand, they must continue to provide factual information to the financial community and conduct business as usual. On the other hand, though, issuers and their representatives must be careful not to initiate publicity or to "hype" the securities in such a way that their activities constitute an *offer* during the quiet period. Indeed, the term *quiet period* reflects the notion that as little as possible should be made public about the company during this period and that the issuer should do nothing that could cause the need for a public announcement, lest the announcement be construed as an offer or solicitation in violation of the 1933 act.

But during this quiet period, corporate life goes on. Companies that are already public and thus subject to the 1934 act periodic reporting requirements must, of course, continue to file annual, quarterly, and current reports with the SEC and to communicate otherwise with stockholders. This is not applicable to a first-time issuer whose registration statement covers an IPO. During the quiet period, however, all issuers should refrain from making predictions regarding future earnings or the value of their securities. If information concerning a significant corporate development is released—whether intentionally or inadvertently—during this period, the registration statement must be appropriately revised.

Delivery of the Prospectus to Investors

The 1933 act makes it unlawful for an underwriter or dealer to *deliver* securities to a buyer unless a *final* prospectus accompanies or precedes the delivery. The purchaser's prior receipt of a *preliminary* prospectus does not fulfill the statutory requirement even though the preliminary and final prospectuses contain substantially equivalent information.

For underwriters and dealers who are members of the selling syndicate, the obligation to deliver a final prospectus extends until their respective allotments are fully exhausted. Broker-dealers who are *not* part of the selling group must furnish a final prospectus during the ninety days after the effective date of an IPO registration statement (twenty-five days if the securities either will be listed on a national stock exchange or will be included in the national automated over-the-counter market system). For securities issued by companies that were subject to the 1934 act periodic reporting requirements immediately prior to the offering, no prospectus need be delivered by broker-dealers not included in the selling group.

The requirement that a *final* prospectus be furnished upon the *delivery* of securities to those who already have decided to purchase them seems to weaken the principal intent of Congress in establishing the 1933 act. If the prospectus contains information thought to be vital to investors, shouldn't they be given sufficient time in *advance* of their decision to buy? The answer is, obviously, yes. So why is this not the case? When the 1933 act was written, Congress envisioned that offers would take place after the registration statement became effective, thus enabling prospective investors to pore over material in the *final* prospectus.

But that is not as it was, and giving way to pressures from the industry, the commission permitted underwriters to solicit indications of interest in an offering from potential investors during the quiet period. In doing so, however, the *preliminary* prospectus gained importance as the primary vehicle for informing prospective purchasers.

The SEC has taken steps to ensure that copies of the preliminary prospectus are provided to individuals who may reasonably be expected to purchase the securities being offered, particularly in the case of IPOs. The principal mechanism by which this is accomplished is through a procedure known as acceleration of the effective date of the registration statement (or, more accurately, through *denial* of the acceleration procedure).

Recall that issuers utilize a delaying amendment that postpones the effective date until the SEC has completed its review and the staff's concerns can be addressed. Once the registration statement has been revised to reflect changes required or suggested by the staff, the commission will usually accelerate effectiveness to a date specified by the issuer and the underwriter. This enables the issue to "hit the market" at a time that the underwriter concludes that market conditions will be the most favorable. It is immediately prior to this date that the final public-offering price is set by way of a pricing *amendment*. Without acceleration, another twenty days must pass before the registration statement (now newly revised with offering price data) can become effective. Market factors can change quickly during the intervening period, exposing the underwriter (particularly in a firm commitment) to extreme risk. If acceleration were not available, underwriters would demand exorbitant fees for bearing this risk. In some cases, deals would be killed altogether.

Acceleration of the effective date is not automatic. Although it is the SEC's general policy to accommodate requests for acceleration, such requests will *not* be granted unless both of the following terms are met:

- The preliminary prospectus has been distributed to underwriters and dealers who will participate in the distribution of the securities being offered
- The underwriters and dealers, in turn, have taken reasonable steps to furnish copies of the preliminary prospectus to prospective investors.

SECONDARY OFFERINGS

Up to this point, the discussion has been limited to offerings by the *issuers* of securities. Such offerings are termed *primary* offerings. A *secondary* offering involves the sale of *previously unregistered* securities of an entity held by individuals or institutions. In an IPO, the company itself *and* its stockholders may sell shares to the public. This is termed a combination primary/secondary offering. As discussed earlier in this chapter, one bene-fit of going public is the opportunity for founders of a company to "cash out."[7]

By and large, the registration process in a secondary (or combined) offering is iden-tical to a primary offering of securities. In a secondary offering, however, the prospectus must include information about the selling stockholders, including the amount of shares, if any, and percentage of ownership that they will retain. In addition, the cover page of the prospectus must clearly set forth how the proceeds from the offering will be divided between the company and the selling stockholders as a group.

EXEMPTIONS FROM REGISTRATION

Not all offerings of securities require registration under the 1933 act. Exemptions fall into one of two classes: (1) exempt securities and (2) exempt transactions. In establishing the 1933 act, Congress recognized that, on balance, the burden of full registration is not always necessary when considered in light of adequate state regulation, the relatively small amount of an offering, and the sophistication of a given class of purchasers.[8]

The more common exemptions are the following:

- *In an intrastate offering*, the entire issue of securities is confined to a single state where the issuer and all offerees and purchasers reside.
- *In a small offering*, the aggregate offering price of securities to be sold does not exceed $5 million. (Such an offering is often termed a Regulation A offering; it is named after the group of rules comprising the regulation that applies to the exemption.)
- *In a limited offering*, securities are offered and sold only to so-called accredited investors; this category includes both institutions and individuals who meet mini-mum net worth and income standards.
- *In a private offering*, the offering is not considered a public offering (see previous discussion in this chapter).

Even though registration under the 1933 act is not required for these offerings (nor is periodic reporting under the 1934 act), they remain subject to the antifraud provisions of the securities acts.[9] Also note that securities sold under one of the foregoing exemp-tions cannot be *resold* unless they are registered under the 1933 act or, at the time of resale, another exemption from registration is available.

CHAPTER SUMMARY

When a company issues securities to the public for the first time, the company has "gone public." The decision to become a public company is not an easy one to make. Although there are many benefits, such as an improved access to capital, many companies believe that the economic and human costs of continuous reporting under the 1934 act outweigh the advantages. When securities are offered to the public, a registration statement must be filed with the SEC. Part I of the registration statement is called the prospectus. The prospectus, which is required to be furnished to investors, contains detailed information about (1) the company issuing the securities, (2) the securities being offered, and (3) the method by which the securities will be distributed.

SEC staff reviews a registration statement after it has been filed for purposes of determining whether full disclosure has been made. During the so-called quiet period (i.e., after a registration statement is filed but before it becomes effective), the activities of the issuing company, its officers and directors, and the company's underwriter are severely limited by law. Securities may not be sold during the quiet period, but potential investors may be contacted.

DISCUSSION QUESTIONS

1. Based on the most important advantages and disadvantages, do you think it is a wise decision for a company to go public? What other factors should be taken into consideration?

2. Do you believe that underwriters should be able to make offers during the quiet period? If so, under what circumstances? Or, do you believe that an underwriter's activities should be curtailed during the quiet period?

3. Explain the following statement:

   Delivery of the final prospectus is an exercise in futility. It is the preliminary prospectus that should be required to be furnished to prospective investors.

4. Do you think that guidelines regarding the number of offerees should be established for determining what constitutes a public offering?

5. Some observers believe that the Regulation A small-offering exemption (i.e., one that does not exceed $5 million) should be eliminated on the grounds that investors in such offerings still need the disclosure protection offered by full registration under the 1933 act. Do you believe that this type of an exemption should be repealed? Explain your answer.

ENDNOTES

1. Since the 1970s, commercial finance companies have become an important funding source for established firms. Commercial finance companies specialize in so-called asset-based loans in which funds are advanced against the collection of receivables or the sale of inventory. Although they have existed in one form or another for at least a century, commercial finance companies proliferated in the 1970s when many companies were no longer able to meet the credit requirements for traditional, unsecured bank loans. By providing revolving loans under which additional funds are advanced as new receivables are generated by a borrower, commercial finance companies are able to offer credit for substantially longer periods than banks can offer. In general,

however, commercial finance companies may not be able to satisfy all the needs of their customers for many of the same reasons as banks. In addition, because credit limits are a function of the value of receivables and inventory, funding is usually for the purpose of meeting operating working capital needs and not for long-term projects.

2. Securities may be issued in private transactions that are exempt from many of the provisions of the 1933 and 1934 acts. These transactions are discussed later in this chapter.

3. Benjamin Graham and David L. Dodd, Security Analysis, 5th ed., rev. by Sidney Cottle, Roger F. Murray, and Frank E. Block (New York: McGraw Hill, 1988), p. 12.

4. Other 1933 act registration statement forms are discussed in Chapter 3.

5. Preliminary prospectuses are sometimes referred to as "red herrings" because the warning legend must be printed in red.

6. Under certain limited circumstances, SEC rules permit such research reports before the registration statement becomes effective, but only for companies that are already public. Thus underwriters that will follow the stock of a first-time registrant once the stock begins trading may not distribute investment recommendations about an IPO during the quiet period.

7. Founders and their families need not sell their previously unregistered shares only at the time of an IPO. They may do so subsequently and separately from the company, but those shares must also be registered at the time of sale. Thus it is not uncommon for a registration statement to cover shares being sold to the public after an IPO for which only the shareholders—not the issuing company itself—will receive proceeds from the sale.

8. Exemptions are discussed in greater detail in Chapter 8.

9. None of these offers alone triggers the 1934 act continuous reporting requirements. Companies that are already public and that avail themselves of one of these exemptions, however, must continue to file periodic reports with the SEC.

3

Registration and Reporting under the 1933 and 1934 Acts

As discussed in Chapter 2, when a company wants to raise funds from the public, it must file a registration statement with the SEC under the 1933 act. This is true for an IPO as well as for all subsequent offerings. Because of the severe liability imposed by the 1933 act for the issuance of a defective prospectus,[1] the registration statement must be prepared with painstaking care by persons who are well versed in the registration process.

THE REGISTRATION TEAM

From a company's standpoint, the first step in a public offering is to assemble a team of professionals; each will be responsible for a specific part of the registration statement. Typically, the team is made up of the following principal members:

- The company's attorney
- The company's accountants
- The underwriter

The Company's Attorney

Many smaller public companies (and the majority of small nonpublic companies) do not have in-house counsel; instead virtually all legal matters are handled by an outside law firm. Even though its partners and associates are well versed in general corporate law and taxation, the firm may not have the expertise and experience required to prepare a registration statement and to help guide the company through the registration process. In that case, it will be necessary for the entity to engage a law firm that specializes in SEC work. Such a firm is referred to as special SEC counsel.

A large, seasoned public company that has been through a number of 1933 act offerings (and that must also file frequent periodic reports under the 1934 act) will usually be represented by a firm experienced in securities work as well as in other areas of corporate law. Often, very large, multinational concerns have more than one law firm on retainer, each of whose work is limited to a single corporate legal matter (e.g., securities law, patent law, taxation, contract law).

The Company's Accountants

As with legal counsel, many privately held companies are served by accounting firms without SEC experience. In preparation for an IPO, it will almost always be necessary for the company to replace its present accountants with a firm familiar with SEC rules and regulations.

In many cases, because there is no general statutory requirement for nonpublic enterprises to have their accounts audited, financial statements of privately held entities are unaudited. Even when independent accountants are involved, it is common for the financial statements of such entities only to be reviewed or compiled.[2] Annual financial statements for the latest three years, which are required in a 1933 act public offering (and in subsequent reports filed under the 1934 act), must be audited. There is no exception to this rule; it is required by law and will not be waived administratively by the staff of the SEC. Therefore, preparation for an IPO must be made far enough in advance so that financial statements for each of the most recent three years can be audited.[3]

Although most accounting firms are capable of performing audits, the overwhelming majority do not have SEC expertise.[4] To complicate matters, the SEC's requirements for an accounting firm's independence from its clients are much more stringent than those of the profession in general. Thus it is possible that, under generally accepted auditing standards, a given relationship between an accounting firm and its client would not impair the firm's independence, whereas under SEC rules that same relationship would disqualify the accounting firm from performing audits for that client.

If an IPO is contemplated for the future, the selection of an accounting firm that does SEC work should be made far ahead of the offering itself so that audits can be performed for the requisite number of years.

Although there are hundreds of accounting firms with SEC clients, the financial statements of most publicly held companies, large and small, are audited by a handful of firms known as the "Big Six."[5] These firms are well versed in SEC accounting, auditing, and financial reporting rules and are experienced in the registration process. The internal organization of these firms includes regional and national departments of men and women who specialize only in SEC filings.

An accounting firm's expertise in SEC accounting and auditing and its experience in dealing with SEC staff can often translate into a smoother and quicker journey through the commission's review of a registration statement, especially an IPO. First, when financial statements in an initial offering are audited by an accounting firm whose work is well known to the SEC, the staff will not have to investigate the firm's qualifications. Moreover, based on an SEC study, the commission has concluded that accounting firms with many SEC clients are less apt than other firms to be involved in so-called audit failures resulting from (1) a significant lack of quality controls, (2) a failure to apply basic auditing procedures, or (3) an absence of a working understanding of generally accepted accounting principles.[6]

In addition, underwriters very often will strongly urge that a company offering its securities to the public for the first time engage a Big Six firm. The managing underwriter and members of the underwriting syndicate prefer an experienced accounting firm whose name is familiar to the investment community for two reasons:

- They believe that the firm's expertise in SEC matters will result in fewer queries by the staff of the Division of Corporation Finance during the review process, thus resulting in a more timely effective date.
- The opinion of a Big Six firm on the financial statements of an entity accessing the public markets for the first time will inspire confidence among prospective investors, thereby resulting in a more successful offering.

The Managing Underwriter

The selection of a managing underwriter for an IPO depends on a variety of factors, including the following:

- The industry in which the entity operates and whether its products or services are high-tech or mundane
- Whether the company is an up-start or is established with a history of operations
- Whether the company seeks predominantly institutional or individual investors
- Whether the entity does business locally, regionally, or nationally

It is important that a company select an underwriter that matches its needs. Literally hundreds of firms engage in investment banking activities to one degree or another, but a relatively few firms dominate the industry as managing underwriters of national offerings.[7]

This concentration can be illustrated by studying the tombstone ad in Figure 3–1 for the offering of common stock of Plantronics. The names of Smith Barney Shearson and Prudential Securities, as comanaging underwriters, stand alone at the top of the ad. Managing underwriters earn additional commissions for originating the business. The managing underwriters also select the other investment banking houses that will participate in the offering and determine each house's allotment of securities.

January 24, 1994

3,588,000 Shares

 **PLANTRONICS**

Common Stock

Price $12.50 per Share

Smith Barney Shearson Inc.		**Prudential Securities Incorporated**

Bear, Stearns & Co. Inc.	CS First Boston	Alex. Brown & Sons Incorporated
Dean Witter Reynolds Inc.	Dillon, Read & Co. Inc.	A.G. Edwards & Sons, Inc.
Hambrecht & Quist Incorporated	Lazard Frères & Co.	Lehman Brothers
Montgomery Securities	Oppenheimer & Co., Inc.	PaineWebber Incorporated
Robertson, Stephens & Company	Salomon Brothers Inc	Wertheim Schroder & Co. Incorporated
William Blair & Company	Dain Bosworth Incorporated	Kemper Securities, Inc.
Legg Mason Wood Walker Incorporated	Piper Jaffray Inc.	The Robinson-Humphrey Company, Inc.
Wheat First Butcher & Singer Capital Markets	Advest, Inc. Robert W. Baird & Co. Incorporated	Crowell, Weedon & Co.
Doft & Co., Inc.	Dominick & Dominick Incorporated	First Albany Corporation
First of Michigan Corporation	Gruntal & Co., Incorporated	Interstate/Johnson Lane Corporation
Janney Montgomery Scott Inc.	Ladenburg, Thalmann & Co. Inc.	McDonald & Company Securities, Inc.
Neuberger & Berman	The Ohio Company	Rauscher Pierce Refsnes, Inc.
Scott & Stringfellow, Inc.	Sutro & Co. Incorporated	Tucker Anthony Incorporated
Brean Murray, Foster Securities Inc.	Fahnestock & Co. Inc.	Ferris, Baker Watts Incorporated
First Manhattan Co.	Foley Mufson Howe & Company	Freimark Blair & Company, Inc.
C. L. King & Associates, Inc.	Pennsylvania Merchant Group Ltd	Ragen MacKenzie Incorporated
The Seidler Companies Incorporated		Van Kasper & Company

Figure 3–1. Tombstone Ad

Following Smith Barney and Prudential are the names (in alphabetical order) of firms that are said to be in the "special bracket" of an offering. Such a group usually includes many of the largest houses. Members of this group receive a substantially reduced allotment of shares.

Following the special bracket is the "major bracket" of firms involved in the offering. These firms, for which a new alphabetical order is established (William Blair in the Plantronics offerings), typically include somewhat smaller houses that focus their selling activities in specific regions of the country or specialize in companies operating in certain industries. Major bracket firms receive yet a smaller allotment of shares. Finally, following the major bracket are two "subbrackets" of firms, each beginning with a new alphabetical order (Advest and then Brean Murray in the Plantronics offering). These groups round out the underwriting syndicate. The firms in subbrackets are typically much smaller than those in higher brackets and receive an even further reduced allotment of shares.

As an indication of how shares are allocated among the various groups of underwriters, of the 3,588,000 total shares being issued by Plantronics, Smith Barney and Prudential (the managing underwriters) *each* kept 969,000 shares, or a combined total of 54 percent of the shares being offered. Each of the fifteen firms in the special bracket was allotted 60,000 shares. Each house in the major bracket was allocated 40,000 shares. Firms in the first subbracket were each allocated 20,000 shares, whereas those in the second subbracket each received only 10,000 shares.

Competition among investment banking houses is keen. Although underwriting commissions usually represent only a small fraction of total revenues of such firms, a managing underwriter's relationship with a client can lead to additional *fee-based* services for which the firm's capital is not at stake, as it is in a firm commitment underwriting arrangement. Because it is rare for an established company to change managing underwriters, much of the competitiveness among the top houses centers around *new* clients (i.e., IPOs). Investment banking houses are no different from other types of professional service firms in that status within the industry, as determined by the number and name recognition of clients and the volume of managed public offerings, is the measure of a firm's "success."[8] Because everyone wants to go with a winner, all things being equal, a company planning an IPO is likely to choose a more successful house as its managing underwriter over a less successful house.

THE 1933 ACT REGISTRATION PROCESS

Once the decision has been made to make a public offering and members of the team are in place, the process of preparing the registration statement may begin. The managing underwriter, in conjunction with the company's attorneys, will develop a detailed projected timetable that includes assignments for each member of the registration team. Table 3–1 sets forth an example of such a timetable. The table assumes that all has gone smoothly during the SEC review process and that the registration statement has to be

TABLE 3-1 PUBLIC OFFERING TIMETABLE

Date	Elapsed Number of Days	Item	Responsible Party
April 6	–0–	Meeting of board of directors to act on matters relating to public offering	Company management/ board of directors
April 7	1	Begin writing textual portion of the prospectus	Company's attorney
June 6	61	Receive first proof of registration statement from printer (without) financial statements)	Company's attorney/ printer
June 20	75	Audited annual financial statements and unaudited interim statements sent to printer	Company's accountant
June 25	80	Receive proof of registration statement including financial statements	Printer
		Meeting of board of directors to approve registration statement	Board of directors
June 26	81	Registration statement filled with the SEC	Company's attorney
August 22	138	Receive letter of comments from the SEC	Company's attorney/ company's accountant
August 25	141	File amendment to registration statement reflecting responses to comments by SEC staff	Company's attorney
		Request acceleration of effective date to August 29	Company's attorney
August 27	143	Due diligence meeting	Managing underwriter/ company's attorney/ company's accountant/ board of directors/ principal officers
August 28	144	Meeting of board of directors to approve public-offering price	Board of directors
August 29	145	File pricing amendment; registration statement becomes effective	Managing underwriter/ company's attorney
August 31	147	Closing date (underwriter purchases securities from company)	Managing underwriter/ company management

amended only once in response to the staff's comments. It also assumes that financial statements for the current and two prior years have already been audited.

Notice that the total projected elapsed time is approximately five months, with a duration of sixty-four days between the filing of the registration statement (before amendment) and its effective date. The length of these periods will fluctuate—sometimes considerably—depending on (1) whether the offering is an IPO or is being made by a seasoned public company and (2) the complexity and nature of the entity's operations. IPOs are carefully scrutinized by the SEC; this obviously takes more time. Registration statements of companies that are already public and have thus been filing 1934 act reports are typically not given the same attention as those for first-time offerings. Also, from a practical standpoint, because much of the information in 1934 act filings is the same as in a 1933 act registration statement, the time it takes to actually write the registration statement will be less for a company whose securities are already in the public's hands.

In addition to the greater scrutiny normally given to IPOs, the initial offering of securities of a company in an industry whose revenue-producing or expense-incurring transactions are complicated or are subject to wide fluctuations in amount (depending on the accounting principles applied or the estimates made by management) will receive yet a closer review by SEC staff. Examples of such industries are real estate, franchising, leasing, and insurance.

Not shown in Table 3–1 are preliminary or intermediate steps that may be necessary. For example, if there is a problematic accounting issue or concern regarding the extent or manner in which a specific item should be presented, a prefiling conference with SEC staff is almost always held. Such a conference is desirable for at least two reasons: (1) If issues are not resolved in advance, the SEC review process could take considerably longer, thus jeopardizing the timing of the offering and exposing the underwriter to undue market risk; and (2) by reaching agreement with the staff regarding the treatment of a complicated issue, the parties to the registration statement may have taken a precautionary step against liability for a defective registration statement.

Most of the events in Table 3–1 were discussed in Chapters 1 or 2 or are self-explanatory. One item in particular, however, has not yet been mentioned: the due diligence meeting.

Due Diligence

As explained in more detail in Chapter 5, joint and several liability for a defective registration statement may be imposed upon *each* party to that registration statement under Section 11 of the 1933 act. This includes (1) the entity itself, (2) officers and directors of the entity, (3) the independent accountants, and (4) *each* underwriter. Each defendant to a suit brought under Section 11 (except the issuing company itself), however, has a due diligence defense that provides a possible escape from liability.

Although the extent of this defense depends on the status of a given defendant, reliance on due diligence essentially means that, after a reasonable investigation, the defendant had grounds to believe—and indeed did believe—that the portion of the registration statement alleged to be defective was not.

As a practical matter, extensive due diligence investigations cannot be undertaken for each potential defendant. Just consider the chaos resulting from *dozens* of underwriters interviewing company officials, rummaging through company records, and visiting plant sites around the globe. From the standpoint of the underwriting syndicate, members of the group typically *delegate* to the managing underwriter the investigative work required of all underwriters that will enable them to invoke the due diligence defense.

As part of the managing underwriter's reasonable investigation, a due diligence meeting is almost always held shortly before the expected effective date of the registration statement. Typically, the meeting is attended by (1) the managing underwriter and its counsel; (2) the company's special SEC counsel; (3) the independent accountants; (4) high-ranking executive, legal, and financial officers of the entity; and (5) members of the company's board of directors. A due diligence meeting, normally one of the last steps in the underwriter's investigation process, provides a final opportunity for each party present to inquire of each other regarding the accuracy and completeness of the registration statement.[9]

INTEGRATED DISCLOSURE UNDER THE 1933 AND 1934 ACTS

Although they are now inextricably intertwined, the 1933 act and 1934 act when first passed had separate objectives. The 1933 act was specifically intended to protect investors purchasing securities *directly* from the issuing company, whereas the 1934 act was designed to protect investors in secondary market trading (i.e., transactions between buyers and sellers without participation by the entity whose securities were being traded). Thus the 1933 and 1934 acts, even though their collective goal was to ensure that investors were protected through full disclosure, were administered separately and differently from one another.

In particular, information about the entity, its management, operations, and financial affairs was presented in considerably more detail in a 1933 act registration statement than in an annual report on Form 10–K under the 1934 act, which in turn contained more information than a glossy annual report furnished to stockholders. This difference, among others, stemmed from the basic SEC philosophy that a 1933 act filing should contain more data because investors are infusing capital directly into the company in a public offering. Hence *when* (or if at all) investors were to obtain complete disclosure about a company in a single document depended on the fortuitous circumstance that the entity was making a public offering of its securities.[10]

Responding to commentators' calls for disclosure consistency under the two acts, the SEC adopted the integrated disclosure system (IDS) in 1982. Although the commission continues to fine-tune the system, its two principal features are firmly in place:

1. Virtually the same company-specific information is required in both 1933 act and 1934 act filings such that (a) periodic reports under the 1934 act essentially *update* information about the issuer that was contained in its latest public offering, and (b) even if a public company operates for years without offering additional securities (or never does so), the same information about that company is available through 1934 act documents.[11]

2. Large companies meeting certain criteria can satisfy *1933* act requirements for company-specific disclosures by incorporating the information into registration statements by reference (i.e., by referring readers of a registration statement to the company's *1934* act documents already containing that same information).

By integrating disclosures between the acts, the SEC accomplished two objectives: (1) In requiring the same basic information for filings under both acts, investors in the secondary market were given equal standing with purchasers of securities in a public offering; and (2) if they qualify, seasoned public companies can considerably reduce the cost and time of a public offering by eliminating redundant and overlapping information in a 1933 act registration statement, because that very same information has already been made available to the public in 1934 act reports.

Uniform Disclosure Requirements

The cornerstone of IDS is the requirement for uniform company-related information across the principal 1933 act and 1934 act forms. The source of the required disclosures is Regulation S-K, which governs the *textual* (i.e., nonfinancial statement) information to be included in the various forms. Regulation S-X, discussed in greater depth in Chapter 4, covers the form and content of financial statements contained in 1933 act and 1934 act filings.

The following is a list of company-specific disclosures required in the most-often used 1933 and 1934 act filings.

- A description of the company's business, information about its principal products and services, and details of its foreign and domestic operations by business segment.
- Information about the amount and frequency of cash dividends declared during the past two years, the number of holders of the company's securities, and in what markets (stock exchanges) the securities are traded.
- A summary of selected financial data (e.g., sales, earnings, total assets, working capital, aggregate long-term debt) for each of the latest five years that highlights trends in the company's financial condition.
- Quarterly data about sales, gross profit, and earnings for the past two years (eight quarters). These data are required only of larger companies meeting certain size criteria.
- A discussion and analysis for the latest three years, covering profitability, financial condition, liquidity, cash flows, and capital resources. This item, known as management's discussion and analysis (MD&A) also requires management to focus on events that would cause past performance not to be indicative of future results.
- Audited financial statements prepared in accordance with GAAP and Regulation S-X. (This is discussed in Chapter 4.)
- Information about changes in accountants during the previous two years and, if any, a discussion of disagreements or differences of opinion between management of the company and its accountants. (This is also discussed in Chapter 4.)

The foregoing disclosures comprise what is referred to as the "basic information package" (BIP). The BIP contains information about the entity that the SEC considers vital to all investors and thus must be included in the principal 1933 act and 1934 act forms as well as in the company's glossy annual report furnished to stockholders.[12]

The following *additional* company-specific disclosures, although not part of the BIP, are also required in the principal 1933 act and 1934 act forms and, under certain circumstances, must also be furnished to stockholders as part of a proxy statement.

- A description of the location and character of the entity's principal plants and other important physical properties.
- A description of material pending legal proceedings, other than ordinary litigation in the normal course of business.
- Information about the backgrounds of directors and executive officers and about transactions between them and the company.
- Information concerning compensation of the company's chief executive officer and the four other most highly paid officers. The information provided must include disclosure of salary and bonus, stock options, pensions, and long-term incentive plans. In addition, disclosure must be made of how executive officers' compensation is tied to the company's performance, and a graph must be presented comparing return on the company's equity with returns of the stock market in general and of other entities operating in the same industry as the company.

The S-1-2-3 Scheme

The S-1-2-3 scheme is a three-tier registration system under the 1933 act. This system, in effect, operationalizes IDS through three categories of registration statements. Forms S-2 and S-3 are streamlined forms that rely heavily on the fact that information about the issuing company that otherwise would have to be included in the prospectus is already available in 1934 act forms. Form S-1 must be used for an IPO and by public companies that do not qualify for streamlined registration. Obviously, a company offering its securities to the public for the first time will not have filed annual and quarterly reports under the 1934 act, thus IDS will not apply.

Eligibility to use Form S-2 is based on characteristics of the issuing company. It is available to entities that have been filing periodic 1934 act reports for the previous three years (and have filed each required report in a *timely* fashion). In addition, a company otherwise eligible to use Form S-2 must not have, in the latest fiscal year, defaulted on any obligation (including a dividend payment on preferred stock).

To be eligible to use Form S-3, an issuing company must have been subject to the 1934 act continuous reporting requirements only for the past year (as distinguished from the three-year requirement for use of S-2) and must have filed all required reports timely. As with an S-2 user, the company must not have defaulted on debt or preferred stock. In addition to the foregoing requirements, an S-3 issuer must have a public float (i.e., the market value of its common stock) of at least $75 million. Thus only large public companies are eligible to use this form. Note, however, that this final criterion does not apply if the securities being offered are nonconvertible and are rated as "investment grade" by at least one nationally recognized rating agency.[13] The float requirement is waived because there is evidence that investment-grade debt securities are generally purchased more on the basis of interest rates and ratings than on the basis of a detailed analysis of the issuer.

The differences in eligibility requirements among the three registration forms are reflected in the way each requires information to be *disseminated*.

- In Form S-3, all *company-specific* information from annual and quarterly 1934 act reports may be incorporated by reference into the registration statement. This means that the prospectus itself will include, for the most part, only information related to the offering. Thus, in an S-3 registration, prospective investors must find a way to obtain the relevant 1934 act forms themselves because neither the forms nor the information in them will be furnished with the prospectus.[14]
- In Form S-2, the issuing company may choose either (1) to *deliver* to prospective investors, along with the prospectus containing only information about the offering, a copy of its latest annual and quarterly reports filed with the SEC; or (2) to include company-specific information in the prospectus itself. In either case, in contrast with an S-3 offering whereby investors must secure the information on their own, prospective purchasers of the securities being offered will be provided with company-specific information.
- In Form S-1, all company-specific information must be included in the prospectus; incorporation by reference from 1934 act reports is not permitted.

It is important to remember that (1) information about the *offering* is always included in the prospectus itself, regardless of which form is used; and (2) the company-specific information is virtually identical in all three forms, and the only difference is whether such information is provided to prospective purchasers in the prospectus, along with the prospectus, or in 1934 act reports that investors must obtain on their own. Figure 3–2 illustrates how incorporation by reference is described in a prospectus that is part of a registration statement on Form S-3 (only relevant wording is reproduced).

Form S-3 makes the most use of an important aspect of the EMH: the process by which institutional investors and security analysts follow larger companies (i.e., those with a public float of at least $75 million) whose securities are widely held. That being the case, it is unlikely that the prospectus of such a company would reveal information about which the market is yet unaware.

Form S-2, which can be used by seasoned but smaller public companies (i.e., at least three years of reporting under the 1934 act) also relies, to some extent, on the existence of public information about an entity. Because of their smaller size, however, such companies would not be expected to have the same wide following by analysts. Thus information from 1934 act reports of S-2 issuers must be furnished to prospective investors, although not in the prospectus itself. As with S-3 companies, that information

INCORPORATION OF CERTAIN DOCUMENTS BY REFERENCE

The following documents filed by the Company with the Commission are incorporated herein by reference and are made a part hereof: (i) the Company's Annual Report on Form 10-K for the fiscal year ended July 31, 1992; (ii) the Company's Current Report on Form 8-K dated October 6, 1992; (iii) the Company's Quarterly Report on Form 10-Q for the fiscal quarter ended October 31, 1992; (iv) the Company's Proxy Statement for the Annual Meeting of Shareholders held on November 19, 1992; (v) the Joint Proxy Statement/Prospectus of the Company and Applied Biosystems, Inc. dated January 13, 1993; (vi) the Company's Quarterly Report on Form 10-Q for the fiscal quarter ended January 31, 1993; (vii) the Company's Current Report on Form 8-K dated February 19, 1993; (viii) the Company's Registration Statement on Form 10/A dated June 1, 1993; (ix) the Company's Current Report on Form 8-K dated June 1, 1993; and (x) the Company's Quarterly Report on Form 10-Q for the fiscal quarter ended April 30, 1993.

AVAILABLE INFORMATION

The Company is subject to the informational requirements of the Securities Exchange Act of 1934, as amended (the "Exchange Act"), and in accordance therewith files reports, proxy statements and other information with the Securities and Exchange Commission (the "Commission"). The reports, proxy statements and other information filed by the Company with the Commission may be inspected and copied at the public reference facilities maintained by the Commission at 450 Fifth Street, N.W., Washington, D.C. 20549 and at the following Regional Offices of the Commission: New York Regional Office, 7 World Trade Center, New York, New York 10048; and Chicago Regional Office, Northwestern Atrium Center, 500 West Madison Street, Suite 1400, Chicago, Illinois 60661. Copies of such material may be obtained from the Public Reference Section of the Commission at 450 Fifth Street, N.W., Washington, D.C. 20549 at prescribed rates. In addition, material filed by the Company can be inspected at the offices of the NYSE, 20 Broad Street, New York, New York 10005, and at the offices of the Pacific Stock Exchange (the "PSE"), 301 Pine Street, San Francisco, California 94104. The Common Stock is listed on such Exchanges.

The Company has filed with the Commission a Registration Statement on Form S-3 (together with any amendments thereto, the "Registration Statement") under the Securities Act of 1933, as amended (the "Securities Act"), with respect to the Shares.

Figure 3–2.   Incorporation by Reference

will have been previously filed with the SEC, but because S-2 companies are not widely tracked by analysts, it is *more likely* that the information—although having been available—will be digested, assimilated, and acted upon for the first time.

Smaller, unseasoned public companies and those registering securities for the first time would not, of course, be generally followed by analysts or institutional investors. Thus users of Form S-1 may not rely at all on the existence of already publicly available information. Instead, all required disclosures must be furnished to potential investors in the prospectus.

CONTINUOUS REPORTING UNDER THE 1934 ACT

Although periodic reporting by public companies has always been required, since the development of the integrated disclosure system it has taken on new importance. Indeed, it is the linchpin of IDS. The three principal periodic reports under the 1934 act are

- Annual report Form 10–K
- Quarterly report Form 10–Q
- Current report Form 8–K

Together these forms provide periodic updating of a company's financial and operating situation. All companies, once they have registered securities in a 1933 act public offering, automatically become subject to the periodic reporting requirements of the 1934 act. It must be kept in mind, however, that 1934 act reporting forms, unlike a prospectus in a 1933 act offering, are not routinely provided to investors.[15]

Form 10–K

Form 10–K, the annual report form, is designed to update company-specific information by providing continued disclosure of material facts for the benefit of existing shareholders and prospective investors.

For IDS to work (i.e., for disclosures required in a 1933 act registration statement to be incorporated by reference to 1934 act reports), Form 10–K had to be modified to require the same information that must be included in a prospectus. Thus Form 10–K contains the BIP (and other uniform company-specific information) that is to be filed in a 1933 act registration statement.

Form 10–Q

All companies required to report annually on Form 10–K must also file quarterly reports on Form 10–Q. Only reports for the first three quarters of a company's fiscal year are required; no report is filed for the fourth quarter. Considerably less information is called for in Form 10–Q compared with Form 10–K.[16] Specifically, the only BIP items required are

- *Unaudited* condensed financial statements (discussed in Chapter 4)
- Management's discussion and analysis (MD&A) of financial condition and results of operations

Form 8–K

Form 8–K, the so-called current report, must also be filed by all public companies, but only the occurrence of a designated event triggers the need for filing. Such events are the following:

- A change in control of the company (i.e., when an individual, group of individuals, or another entity obtains the power to control the direction of the company's management)
- The company has bought or sold a significant amount of assets (e.g., the purchase of another entity or the sale of a subsidiary or product line)

- The company has filed for protection under the bankruptcy laws or a receiver has been appointed to manage the company's affairs
- The company has changed its independent accountants
- A director of the company has resigned (or declined to stand for reelection) because of a policy dispute with management

In addition to the foregoing events, which *require* filing Form 8–K, the company may *elect* to report any transaction or event that it feels is of interest to stockholders. Examples include a plant closing due to a fire, flood, or strike; the commencement of material litigation; a significant discovery of mineral resources; or the development or introduction of an important new product.

Timely Filing of 1934 Act Reports

Form 10–K is due ninety days after the end of a company's fiscal year. Forms 10–Q must be filed no later than fourty-five days after the end of each of the first three fiscal quarters. The due date for Form 8–K varies, depending on the designated event that has caused the need for filing. Generally, the due date is fifteen days after occurrence of the event, except that Form 8–K must be filed within five days of either a change in a company's accountants or the resignation of a director. If Form 8–K is filed *voluntarily* to report an event deemed of importance to shareholders, there is no formal due date, although the SEC encourages "prompt" reporting.

Because 1934 act periodic reporting is considered crucial to the continuous flow of information to investors and to the efficient and effective operation of IDS, there can be stiff consequences for late filing. In addition to being subject to a $100 *per day* penalty for each day the document is late, an overdue filer may be subject to SEC enforcement action, which may result in suspension of trading of the company's securities. In addition, in what may be the most potent motivator of all to get 1934 act reports in on time, a company that files late is ineligible to take advantage of the savings afforded from streamlined registration on Form S-2 or S-3 for one year.

REGISTRATION UNDER THE 1934 ACT

Registration under the 1934 act is different from registration under the 1933 act. Unlike the 1933 act, which requires registration of a specified number of securities (e.g., shares of stock) to be made available in a public offering, registration under the 1934 act covers an entire *class* of securities, including shares of that class that will be authorized and issued in the future. Although no further *1934* act registration is necessary when additional shares of the same class are issued, registration under the 1933 act will be required if those additional shares are issued in a public offering. In addition, because a 1934 act registration does not involve the sale of securities, the registration statement (on Form 10) includes only company-specific information and is not distributed to the public.

Registration under the 1934 act is required for a class of securities traded on a stock exchange. Registration is also required for a class of securities traded in the over-the-counter markets, provided that both of the following terms are true:

- They are held by 500 or more stockholders.
- The issuing company has $5 million or more in total assets.

Such registration activates the requirements for continuous reporting under the 1934 act, but so does registration under the *1933* act. One may then ask why, insofar as it relates to periodic reporting provisions, is registration under both acts required?

The answer lies in when and for what purpose the statutory provisions that require periodic reporting were adopted. When the 1933 act was originally passed, it contained no rule or regulation that mandated continuous reporting under the 1934 act after a public offering. Until 1936, a company making a public offering under the 1933 act was under no obligation to join the periodic reporting system under the 1934 act. Such an obligation was triggered only by registration under the *1934* act, which was then only required for *listed* companies (i.e., those whose securities were listed on a stock exchange rather than traded in the over-the-counter market). In 1936, however, the 1934 act was amended to require companies registering securities for the first time under the 1933 act automatically to become subject to the reporting provisions of the 1934 act, regardless of whether the securities were listed or traded over the counter. Thus after 1936, to become part of the periodic reporting scheme, a company had either to have registered securities under the 1933 act or to have been a stock-exchange company and registered its listed securities under the 1934 act. An *unlisted* company that made its IPO before 1936, however, remained free from the 1934 act continuous reporting system.

The scheme stood until 1964. At that time, over-the-counter companies meeting specified size and number-of-stockholder tests were embraced by the 1934 act registration system, thus subjecting those companies to the periodic reporting requirements of the 1934 act. Under the 1964 amendments, all unlisted companies with $5 million or more in assets and 500 or more shareholders had to register under the 1934 act.

By adding such companies, a handful of theretofore *privately held* entities became public companies without ever having made a public offering. In the late nineteenth and early twentieth centuries, when a company fell on hard times creditors were sometimes paid with shares of stock instead of cash. Over the years, holders, upon their deaths, bequeathed those shares to family members, who in turn did the same thing upon their deaths. By 1964, some companies found themselves in the unenviable position of either registering under the 1934 act (and thus be subject to the continuous reporting require-ments of the act) or violating the federal securities laws. Fortunately, not many companies were so affected.[17]

ELECTRONIC FILING

The SEC is now deep in the midst of testing its electronic filing system. The system, elec-tronic data gathering, analysis, and retrieval (EDGAR), is expected to be fully operational in 1996. With EDGAR, all domestic companies filing with the SEC will do so electronically for both 1933 act and 1934 act documents.

According to the SEC, EDGAR will serve three purposes:

- It will provide investors, security analysts, and the public with instant access to corporate disclosure documents, thereby permitting more informed investment decisions.
- Companies will be able to file electronically using their existing equipment.
- SEC staff will be able to process and analyze filings more effectively at computer workstations.

From the standpoint of investors and analysts, information will be available instantly through on-line databases, thus promoting even more efficiency in the market. From a public company's standpoint, specifically in a 1933 act registration statement, the time between the filing and effective dates is expected to be significantly reduced. For both 1933 and 1934 act registration statements and reports, the time and money it now takes to type, correct, print, proofread, and ship documents will also be shortened substantially. Finally, from the commission's perspective, the millions upon millions of pages of paper the SEC receives, logs in, and copies each year will be sharply cut.

CHAPTER SUMMARY

In a public offering, the issuing company's attorneys, accountants, and managing underwriter play key roles. The attorneys are responsible for preparing the textual portion of the registration statement. The independent accountants audit the company's financial statements that are included in the prospectus, and the managing underwriter assembles the selling syndicate. Because the company, its officers and directors, independent accountants, and each underwriter all may be liable for a defective registration statement, an important aspect of the registration process is the performance of a due diligence investigation by each party on which the law imposes liability.

Under the SEC's integrated disclosure system (IDS), virtually the same company-specific information is required in the main 1933 act and 1934 act registration and reporting forms. This information makes up the basic information package (BIP). Also under IDS, there is a three-tier system of registration under the 1933 act. Although the BIP is required in Forms S-1, S-2, and S-3, the latter two forms, which are eligible for use only by seasoned public companies, call for streamlined dissemination of the information. The essence of the S-1-2-3 scheme is the ability to incorporate by reference company-specific information from annual report Form 10–K under the 1934 act into Forms S-2 and S-3 under the 1933 act.

DISCUSSION QUESTIONS

1. Do you feel it fair that IPOs are given a more in-depth review by SEC staff? Do you think that it results from the commission's reliance on the EMH?

2. Some observers believe that there should only be one class of registration statement, an S-1, in which all required information is included for investors. What is your position? Explain your answer in terms of the EMH and the protection of investors.

3. What other types of information do you feel should be part of the BIP and therefore should be required in all principal forms under the 1933 and 1934 act?

4. Do you feel that quarterly reporting is frequent enough (excluding current reports on Form 8–K)? Should monthly reporting be required? Instead of condensed financial statements, should full-blown statements be required to facilitate analysis?

5. Some commentators believe that Form 8–K will be obsolete when EDGAR is fully implemented. They suggest that, because of available technology, "disclosure" about a variety of events should be made daily. Do you agree? In addition to events requiring Form 8–K, what others do you feel should call for mandatory disclosure?

ENDNOTES

1. Actually, the law itself refers to a defective *registration* statement, which contains the prospectus. Because the procedural and supplementary information in Part II of the registration statement is not furnished to prospective purchasers of the securities, however, virtually all actions by investors alleging misleading, inaccurate, or incomplete information involve the prospectus. See Chapter 4.

2. A review of financial statements is not equivalent to an audit conducted in accordance with generally accepted auditing standards. Although it is considered an attest service, the scope and purpose of a review are considerably less than those of an audit. A typical review consists mainly of inquiries of company management and analytical procedures applied to the financial statements. A review does not usually entail gathering and evaluating corroborating evidence in support of amounts contained in the financial statements. A compilation of financial statements is *not* an attest service. The outside accountant's purpose in a compilation is to determine that the financial statements are in the appropriate form and are free from obvious material error.

3. In rare cases, audits may be conducted retroactively. That is, when the company maintains very good records and has an airight internal control structure, it may be possible for audits of *prior* years to be conducted currently. Even in such cases, however, it will usually not be practicable for the auditor to verify inventory quantities on hand in past years or to confirm accounts receivable balances outstanding in earlier years.

4. Indeed, because of the enormous liability imposed on accountants under the 1933 act (and to a somewhat lesser extent under the 1934 act), most accounting firms purposely *avoid* involvement with public companies. See Chapter 5.

5. These firms are (in alphabetical order) Arthur Andersen, Coopers & Lybrand, Deloitte & Touche, Ernst & Young, KPMG Peat Marwick, and Price Waterhouse. Two other firms have relatively large numbers of SEC clients: Grant Thornton and BDO Seidman. In light of recent initiatives by the SEC that enable small companies to have easier and less-expensive access to the public markets, additional accounting firms serving such companies may be forced to develop SEC expertise to protect their relationships with these types of clients. See Chapter 8.

6. Securities Act Release No. 6695, April 1, 1987.

7. These firms are (in alphabetical order) Bear, Stearns; CS First Boston; Dillon, Read; Donaldson, Lufkin & Jenrette; Goldman, Sachs; Lazard Freres; Lehman Brothers; Merrill Lynch; Morgan Stanley; Paine Webber; Prudential Securities; Salomon Brothers; and Smith Barney Shearson.

8. At least two independent companies (IDD and Securities Data Company) keep a semiannual score, on a firm-by-firm basis, of the number and dollar value of managed offerings. Utilizing these sources, the *Wall Street Journal, Forbes,* and other financial publications periodically publish this information. In addition, at least once each year many of the leading investment banking houses place advertisements in the financial press boasting of their own records.

9. Actually, the final step in the managing underwriter's due diligence investigation is receipt of a so-called comfort letter from the company's independent accountants. Such a letter provides "comfort" to the underwriter that there have been no material adverse changes in the issuer's financial condition from the date of the latest financial statements contained in the prospectus to the effective date of the registration statement. Comfort letters are explored in greater detail in Chapter 4.

10. Harold S. Bloomenthal, Securities and Federal Corporate Law, (Deerfield, Ill.: Clark Boardman Callaghan, 1993), p. 2A-2.1

11. Under IDS, only information about the *entity* is the same in 1933 and 1934 act filings. Information relating to the *offering* (e.g., a description of the securities, use of the proceeds, and the underwriting arrangement) appears only in a 1933 act registration statement; in a 1934 act document, no offer of securities to the public is being contemplated.

12. Proxy rules, including annual reports to shareholders, are discussed in Chapter 7.

13. Currently, the SEC will accept ratings by Standard & Poor's, Moody's, Duff & Phelps, and Fitch Investor Services. Using the Standard & Poor's system, securities rated AAA, AA, A, or BBB are considered investment grade. Securities rated BB, B, or below are noninvestment grade (or "junk", as they are often called).

14. Virtually all companies using Form S-3, however, offer to provide without charge, upon request, any document incorporated by reference into the registration statement.

15. This is an important point. Investors must specifically request to be furnished with a Form 10–K (and other periodic 1934 act reports) or must obtain such reports themselves from the SEC. Much of the same information, however, is provided to shareholders in the glossy annual report, which is *required* by the commission's proxy rules. See Chapter 7.

16. Incorporation by reference is also permitted in Forms 10–K and 10–Q. Thus to the extent that a company's annual or quarterly reports to stockholders contain information required to be included in Form 10–K or Form 10–Q, such stockholder reports may be referred to in the company's 10–K or 10–Q, respectively, filed with the SEC. Stockholder reports are discussed in Chapter 7.

17. Through experience, the author is aware of at least one such company in the Midwest that had been operating since the eighteenth century. Under just the scenario described, the company's attorney recognized that registration under the 1934 act was required. When faced with the situation of having to file documents with the SEC every quarter of every year, management instead chose to close the doors.

4

Accounting and Financial Reporting under the Securities Laws

STATUTORY AUTHORITY

Legislators deliberating what would eventually become the 1933 and 1934 acts believed early on that financial statements represented the cornerstone of the full-disclosure approach to securities regulation. In recognition of that belief, lawmakers bestowed sweeping powers upon the SEC regarding accounting and financial reporting. Specifically, the 1933 and 1934 acts authorize the commission to prescribe

- The form in which required information should be presented
- The items to be shown in the financial statements
- The accounting methods to be used in preparation of the accounts

RELIANCE ON THE PRIVATE SECTOR

Despite the obvious significance of financial statements (and thus of accounting practices followed in measuring items in the statements), the SEC has never taken upon itself the task of formulating accounting principles, even though it has the statutory authority to do so. Instead, throughout the years the commission has, by and large, relied on private sector standard-setting organizations to establish generally accepted accounting principles (GAAP).

The commission's role in the standard-setting process was established early in its history. In what is the antithesis of its position today (and the position of the current private-sector rule-making body), the SEC, in 1934, did not object to financial statements that were *incorrect on their face* as long as the notes to the statements and the accompanying accountants' certificate (as it was then referred to) pointed out the errors and explained the effects of applying another method of accounting.[1]

Although this approach may seem strange in the present environment of "cookbook" accounting rules,[2] (1) it reflected the manner in which financial statements were prepared and presented during the immediate postcrash era, and (2) it was then thought not to violate the doctrine of full disclosure.

After an internal struggle among the five commissioners, the SEC concluded that, given the fluctuating state of accounting, rule making was a job best left to the profession. The practical consequence of this decision was to place the burden of standard setting on the accounting profession but subject to SEC review.[3] In 1938 the American Institute of Certified Public Accountants (AICPA) created the Committee on Accounting Principles (CAP) for the purpose of establishing a comprehensive set of uniform accounting principles. Although the SEC was not in the rule-making business per se, it wanted to stay involved. Thus also in 1938 the SEC authorized the chief accountant of the commission to issue releases periodically that "interpreted" accounting principles, thereby *contributing* to the development of a set of uniform standards.[4] In 1959 the CAP was replaced by the Accounting Principles Board (APB), which continued its work.

But all did not go smoothly after that. Beginning in the middle of the 1960s and lasting through the early 1970s, many within the accounting profession were dissatisfied about the ad hoc way in which the APB was establishing accounting rules. The major criticism centered around the board's lack of progress in reducing the number of alternative ways in which GAAP could be applied to the same or similar transactions.

In reality, the APB was unable to narrow the different (indeed, sometimes contradictory) accounting principles that were used for a host of reasons. The prevailing notion at the time, however, was that three factors contributed most to the problem:

- Many members of the APB were also partners in large accounting firms. This was thought to constitute a conflict of interest because client interests might stand in the way of sound accounting.
- Instead of developing a conceptual framework, the APB addressed key issues of the moment in a "firefighting" manner, often closing loopholes only after they had already been exploited and abused by corporate management.
- APB opinions (as they are called) were *nonbinding*. Under SEC policy, all that was necessary to comply with the commission's requirements was that financial statements need only be prepared in accordance with accounting principles having "substantial authoritative support."[5] The low threshold for this test could be met just by finding a handful of leading accounting firms that supported a particular principle, even if that principle differed from an opinion of the APB.

In 1970 the AICPA, sensing that the APB was about to crumble, appointed a committee led by former SEC Commissioner Francis Wheat to review the operations of the APB and the way that accounting principles were being made. Not surprising to anyone, the Wheat Committee's report issued in 1972 recommended that the APB be abolished.

CREATION OF THE FINANCIAL ACCOUNTING STANDARDS BOARD

In 1973 the Financial Accounting Standards Board (FASB) was set up as the successor private-sector body to the APB. Unlike the APB, however, the FASB would consist of seven *full-time* members having no other business affiliations. Concurrent with creating the FASB, the AICPA amended its code of professional conduct, making it an *ethical violation* for an accountant's opinion to state that an entity's financial statements were in compliance with GAAP if the statements contained a departure from an accounting principle promulgated by the FASB.[6] Thus, whether or not supported by corporations, their accounting firms, or academics, FASB pronouncements (and APB opinions that were not superseded) had to be followed by companies in the preparation of financial statements; if not, accountants were ethically bound to issue a *qualified* opinion on those financial statements.

To round out the process, in 1973, just after the FASB was formed, the SEC issued a release endorsing the FASB and reaffirming the commission's position to look to the private sector for the establishment of accounting principles.[7] In that same release, however, and even more firmly in another release seven years later, the SEC confirmed to the financial community that it was still in the business of "contributing" to the promulgation of accounting standards. It warned:

> The Commission does not believe . . . that a decision to require a particular method of accounting . . . conflicts with the [SEC's] basic policy of relying on the FASB for leadership in establishing financial accounting and reporting standards. . . . While there is, of course, always the possibility that the Commission may conclude it cannot accept a FASB standard in a particular area, such events have been rare.[8]

Establishment of the FASB Emerging Issues Task Force

During the early years of the FASB's existence, the accounting profession and the business community at large remained cautiously optimistic about the board's ability to make the rule-making process effective. By the early 1980s, however, the honeymoon was over. This time, critics charged (among other things) that the FASB could not get important issues resolved in a timely fashion. As fodder for their contention, critics cited a number of key topics that languished on the board's agenda for years without resolution.

To counter this criticism, the FASB created an Emerging Issues Task Force (EITF) in 1984 to identify and define emerging accounting issues. From task force proceedings, the FASB would learn whether there was a divergence of views among practitioners on how a particular transaction should be accounted for. The inability of task force members to agree would indicate that official guidance in the form of an FASB pronouncement was necessary. On the other hand, a consensus among EITF members presumably represented evidence that an issue had already found a resolution in practice.

Officially, consensuses of the EITF merely reflected practice; they were not intended to establish new accounting principles. In reality, the EITF, which continues in existence at this time, accomplished the following:

- It provided guidance to practitioners, on a timely basis, regarding the *implementation* of complex pronouncements of the FASB (and of its predecessor, the APB).
- It addressed industry-specific topics and general-interest topics of a somewhat narrower nature than the FASB typically addressed.

Although many issues considered by the task force were (and still are) practice-related interpretations of *existing* GAAP, on some key issues EITF consensuses represent the only authoritative guidance. For example, various EITF consensuses in the late 1980s still constitute the only comprehensive discussion of how to account for a leveraged buy-out (LBO). Officially, these LBO consensuses simply *interpreted* an existing pronouncement: APB Opinion No. 16 on business combinations. As a practical matter, however, many accountants, who were nonetheless thankful for the task force's timely guidance on this critical accounting issue of the day, recognized these consensuses as the promulgations of *new* GAAP.

To put the EITF's work in perspective, as of mid-1993, nine years after it was formed, the Task Force had addressed 256 issues. Of those, only about 10 percent remain unresolved. In contrast, during that same period the FASB has issued only 59 pronouncements, and 5 of those were just for the purpose of delaying the effective dates of other pronouncements.

Almost immediately, the SEC too recognized the advantages of the EITF. The commission adopted task force consensuses as its own and used task force meetings as a forum to express its views. At one of the first meetings, the SEC chief accountant, who to this day remains an "observer with floor privileges," stated that the application of EITF consensuses will be expected of public companies.

Given the power and influence of the commission's chief accountant, it was unlikely that the EITF would reach a consensus with which the SEC disagreed. Thus, by utilizing task force consensuses as its own policies, the commission remained true to its word of letting the private sector set accounting standards while managing to incorporate its views into new rules and into interpretations of existing ones.

Because the ostensible original objective of the EITF was to provide the FASB with information about what was going on in practice, it made sense to stock the task force with practitioners. Although the number has varied slightly from time to time, the EITF currently has fourteen members, of which nine are partners in large accounting firms and four are high-ranking financial executives of Fortune 100 companies. The chairman of the task force is the FASB director of research and technical activities. This composition is frighteningly similar to that of the APB, whose demise attributed in part to having consisted of practitioners whose client interests may have conflicted with those of conceptually sound accounting principles.

Rejection of Certain Private-Sector GAAP

For the most part, the SEC and the FASB (and its predecessors) have worked harmoniously. The commission's part in the rule-making process has largely been devoted to (1) making suggestions regarding major topics to be added to the FASB's agenda, (2) commenting on proposed FASB pronouncements, (3) interpreting issues that are not sufficiently explicit in the authoritative accounting literature, and (4) fine-tuning Regulation S-X with the occasional inclusion of additional or expanded disclosures not called for by GAAP in general.[9] Every so often, though, the SEC will flex its statutory muscle regarding accounting standards as if to caution the private sector against taking the commission's congressional-imposed power too lightly. Although there have been others, the most celebrated occasions of defiance involve the following:

- Accounting for the investment tax credit
- Accounting for oil and gas producers

In 1962, to stimulate capital, Congress provided businesses with a tax credit of up to 7 percent of the cost of certain depreciable assets acquired and placed in service. In December 1962 the APB issued Opinion No. 2, which concluded that for financial reporting purposes the investment credit should be accounted for as a reduction of depreciation expense of the asset to which the credit was related (the deferral method), not as a reduction of income tax expense in the year the property was acquired (the flow-through method). The APB reasoned that since earnings arise from the *use* of facilities, not from their acquisition, the benefit of the investment credit should be spread over the asset's useful life.

In January 1963, without warning, the SEC issued Accounting Series Release (ASR) No. 96, permitting public companies to account for the investment credit *either* as a reduction of depreciation over the life of the property or as a reduction of income tax expense in the year in which the credit arises.[10] The commission's action was a real setback for the APB. It had, after all, only been in existence for three years and had only issued one other opinion up to that time. Some observers contend that ASR No. 96 was, in effect, the blow that killed the APB a decade before it was officially pronounced dead.

In response, the APB was forced to issue Opinion No. 4 in March 1964. That opinion, while stating that the deferral method remained the preferable treatment, also permitted use of the flow-through method. Of the twenty board members, eight assented with qualification and five dissented completely to the issuance of Opinion No. 4.

The dissenters expressed anger at the commission's intervention, with one board member writing:

> This opinion illustrates the accounting profession's complete failure . . . to establish accounting principles that are comparable among companies and industries. . . . There is no justification for sanctioning two contradictory practices to accommodate the SEC.[11]

A member who assented with qualification stated that the commission's actions simply left the board with no other practical choice but to approve a method of accounting that the SEC allowed.[12]

Some fifteen years after the investment credit debacle and well into the FASB's tenure as the private sector's rule-making body, the SEC and the profession locked horns again. This time the issue involved accounting by oil and gas producers. In December 1977, the FASB issued Statement No. 19, which required the use of the so-called successful efforts (SE) method of accounting for oil and gas reserves. Under SE, all expenditures related to exploration are written off as expenses in the year incurred. Prior to Statement No. 19, some oil and gas producers used SE while others used a method known as full-cost (FC) accounting. Under this method, all costs of drilling and funding oil and gas are capitalized and then subsequently depleted or depreciated. Either method was acceptable under GAAP.

In August 1978, however, before the effective date of Statement No. 19 (which was for calendar year *1979* financial statements), the SEC issued ASR No. 253.[13] Although it adopted certain *disclosure* standards of Statement No. 19, ASR No. 253 continued to permit public companies to use *either* SE or FC as a comprehensive measurement method. Embarrassed, the FASB was forced to issue Statement No. 25, which delayed the effective date of Statement No. 19. Echoing the sentiments of the dissenters to APB Opinion No. 4 in 1964, two FASB members objected to the issuance of Statement No. 25. They felt that by suspending Statement No. 19, the board had abdicated its standard-setting responsibility and stepped aside while the SEC attempted to resolve the issues.[14]

Actually, the SEC believed that neither SE nor FC provided sufficient information to investors about an oil and gas producer's assets and earnings. Thus it saw no reason to demand the use of one unacceptable method at the exclusion of the other.

Meanwhile, the SEC was attempting to develop its own method of oil and gas accounting, which it referred to as revenue recognition accounting (RRA). After three years of uncertain test results, however, the SEC abandoned RRA. Subsequently, the SEC supported the FASB's efforts to develop a comprehensive set of *disclosures* for oil and gas producers. That effort resulted in the issuance of FASB Statement No. 69 in 1982. Note, however, that to this day the SEC still permits use of either SE *or* FC as a measurement method.

Notwithstanding these two well-publicized situations, Regulation S-X, the commission's principal accounting regulation, explicitly requires that financial statements filed with the SEC be prepared in conformity with generally accepted accounting principles.

UNIFORM FINANCIAL STATEMENT REQUIREMENTS

As discussed in Chapter 3, the operation of the integrated disclosure system (IDS) is dependent upon uniform disclosures between the 1933 and 1934 acts. The major benefit of IDS to investors is that they get the same kind of company-specific information under both acts and thus may keep abreast of an entity's progress on an ongoing basis. For public companies, the principal advantage is the mechanism of incorporation by reference of company-specific information from 1934 act reports into 1933 act registration statements.

Recall that the information about an enterprise that the SEC considers vital is contained in the basic information package (BIP). Obviously, a very important element of the

BIP is a company's financial statements. Prior to IDS, a number of discrepancies concerning financial statement requirements existed between 1933 and 1934 act filings. As with other such inconsistencies, these differences were eliminated when IDS was introduced. The result is that financial statements required to be included in 1933 act registration statements on Forms S-1, S-2, and S-3 are *identical* to those that are to be included in an annual report on Form 10–K and a registration statement on Form 10 under the 1934 act. Financial statements in filings under both acts must conform to Regulation S-X, which in turn requires compliance with GAAP.

Annual Financial Statements

The following annual financial statements are required in Forms S-1, S-2, and S-3 under the 1933 act and in Forms 10–K and 10 under the 1934 act:[15]

- Balance sheets as of the end of the entity's *two* most recent fiscal years
- Income statements and cash flow statements for each of the entity's *three* most recent fiscal years
- Changes in the individual components of stockholders' equity for each of the entity's *three* most recent fiscal years

(This last requirement may be met either by presenting a separate statement of stockholders' equity or by presenting the same information in a note to the financial statements.)

In addition to complete conformity with generally accepted accounting principles (both the measurement and disclosure aspects of GAAP), Regulation S-X requires certain additional information to be disclosed either on the face of the financial statements themselves or in the notes thereto. This additional information is thought to be of value to investors. The main disclosures not called for by GAAP but required of publicly held companies are the following:

- Information about formal and informal compensating bank balances. A compensating balance is the amount on deposit with a bank to support an existing borrowing arrangement. The amount maintained to assure future credit availability must also be disclosed.
- Information regarding third-party restrictions on a subsidiary's ability to transfer, loan, or advance funds or pay dividends to its parent.
- Information about the amount and terms of unused lines of credit available to the company.
- Information about preferred stock that is mandatorily redeemable or redeemable at the option of the holder. On the face of the balance sheet, redeemable preferred stock may *not* be included in stockholders' equity; instead it must be shown between liabilities and equity. This required presentation differs from GAAP, which has no prohibition against showing redeemable preferred stock as a component of equity.

- Separate identification of the amounts of inventory attributable to finished goods, work in process, and raw materials.
- The amount of income realized due to the liquidation of a substantial portion of an entity's last in, first out (LIFO) inventory.
- Separate financial statements of significant companies acquired or to be acquired.

In addition, Regulation S-X is very precise about materiality thresholds for the purpose of separate disclosure of certain items. As an example, any intangible asset that by itself exceeds 5 percent of total assets must be shown separately on the face of the balance sheet. Similar thresholds exist for "other current liabilities," "deferred credits," and "other current assets." For the most part, GAAP has no such quantified presentation guidelines.

Interim Financial Statements

Financial statements are also required in Form 10–Q, the quarterly reporting form under the 1934 act. The financial statements to be provided are as follows:

- A condensed balance sheet as of the end of the most recent fiscal quarter.
- For comparative purposes, a condensed version of the balance sheet as of the entity's most recent fiscal year. A condensed balance sheet as of the end of the corresponding quarter of the previous fiscal year is ordinarily not necessary. It need be presented for comparative purposes only if it assists in understanding the seasonal nature of the entity's business.
- A condensed year-to-date income statement and a condensed year-to-date cash flow statement as of the end of the most recent fiscal quarter and for the corresponding period of the preceding year.

Compared with annual statements, interim financial statements may be significantly condensed. Only major captions must be presented on the balance sheet, income statement, and cash flow statement. Moreover, footnotes need not disclose information contained in the notes to the latest annual financial statements. Although quarterly reporting is obviously better than no interim reporting at all, analysis of quarterly financial statements is, to a large extent, limited by the very nature of severely aggregated data.

The Age of Financial Statements

The age of financial statements (i.e., how old are the statements of the most recent period) is obviously of consequence. The older they get, the less value they have. Assuming that Forms 10–K and 10–Q are filed on a timely basis, the statements contained therein will be as current as practicable.

The same cannot be said, however, for 1933 act registration statements for which there is no "due" date. For example, if a registration statement is filed on February 15,

1994, and the effective date is April 12, 1994, the *latest* financial statements (presumably for the year ended December 31, 1993) will be fifty-six days old. But what if the registration process is prolonged and the effective date extends to, say, July 10, 1994? Under these circumstances, the latest financial statements will be 145 days old. A later effective date will make the statements even older.

To prevent outdated financial information in a 1933 act registration statement, Regulation S-X requires that the latest financial statements in a prospectus not be, on the effective date, older than 134 days. If they would be older, they are considered "stale" and must be updated to meet the 134–day rule. For a company that is already public, updating can easily be accomplished by including condensed quarterly financial statements from its latest Form 10–Q. This option, of course, is not available to a company making an initial public offering. Alternatively, so-called stub-period financial statements may be provided. These are full-blown statements presented in columns comparative to and in the same detail as the annual financial statements. In either case, interim statements for the current period and for the corresponding period of the prior year must be included.

OTHER FINANCIAL INFORMATION IN THE BASIC INFORMATION PACKAGE

In addition to the financial statements themselves, the BIP contains other financial and financial-related information as follows:

- Selected financial data
- Quarterly data
- Management's discussion and analysis
- Information about changes in and disagreements with accountants

Together with the financial statements, the foregoing items constitute the "heart" of the BIP.

Selected Financial Data

At a minimum, the following items must be presented, in tabular form, for each of the latest five years:

- Net sales
- Income from continuing operations
- Earnings per share
- Total assets
- Long-term obligations (including capital leases and redeemable preferred stock)
- Cash dividends declared per common share

The purpose of this item in the BIP is to present information extracted or derived from the financial statements that highlight certain significant trends in a company's financial condition and operating performance. Thus other data, in addition to the required minimum, that would enhance an investor's understanding or highlight other trends may be provided. In practice, this item often includes much data not specifically required. Figure 4–1, taken from the prospectus of International Imaging Materials, Inc., illustrates the type of information provided and how it is presented.

Quarterly Data

Quarterly data (not to be confused with condensed quarterly financial statements filed on Form 10–Q) are required only of companies meeting certain size tests regarding (1) the number of shareholders and shares outstanding, (2) the number of dealers making a market in the shares, (3) the market value of the outstanding shares, (4) net income for each of the latest three years, and (5) total assets as of the end of the most recent fiscal year.

If an entity qualifies, it must disclose the following amounts for each quarter within the latest two years:

- Net sales
- Gross profit
- Net income
- Earnings per share

The value of quarterly data is questionable, considering that much more information (except for that of the fourth fiscal quarter) is available from an entity's Forms 10–Q. Figure 4–2, taken from the 1992 annual stockholders' report of Digital Equipment Corporation and incorporated by reference into its 1992 Form 10–K, illustrates how quarterly data are often presented.

Management's Discussion and Analysis

Management's discussion and analysis (MD&A) is one of the most meaningful portions of the BIP. Its primary objective is to provide investors with management's *own* analysis of the financial statements and other financial data as they relate to (1) liquidity, (2) capital resources, and (3) results of operations. Although no longer a problem in today's economic environment, the impact of inflation on a company's business, when applicable, must also be described. In general, the discussion should enhance the understanding of a company's financial condition, operating results, and cash flows by giving the investor the opportunity to look at the company through the eyes of management.

Because financial statements comprise historical data, the SEC requires that the analysis focus on events, trends, and uncertainties *known to management* that could cause past results *not* to be indicative of future performance. This includes a discussion of matters (1) that would have an impact on future operations but that did not have an impact in the past and (2) that have had an impact on past performance but that are not expected to affect the future. Note that information *known* to management is different from a forecast

SELECTED FINANCIAL DATA

The following selected financial data for each of the years in the five-year period ended March 31, 1993 have been derived from the financial statements of the Company, which financial statements have been audited by KPMG Peat Marwick, independent auditors. The data presented below should be read in conjunction with "Management's Discussion and Analysis of Financial Condition and Results of Operations" and the Financial Statements, including the notes thereto, appearing elsewhere in this Prospectus.

	Fiscal Year Ended March 31,				
	1989	1990	1991	1992	1993
	(In thousands, except per share amounts)				
INCOME STATEMENT DATA:					
Revenues:					
Color ribbons	$ 1,835	$ 4,123	$ 5,969	$ 8,683	$16,463
Bar code ribbons	6,321	13,539	14,387	17,693	25,480
Other ribbons	956	1,945	3,359	5,948	6,495
Total revenues	9,112	19,607	23,715	32,324	48,438
Cost of goods sold	6,930	13,685	16,663	24,958	36,892
Gross profit	2,182	5,922	7,052	7,366	11,546
Operating expenses:					
Research and development	366	593	916	845	1,121
Selling	717	1,160	1,322	1,498	2,251
General and administrative	796	1,123	1,360	1,548	2,024
Total operating expenses	1,879	2,876	3,598	3,891	5,396
Operating income	303	3,046	3,454	3,475	6,150
Interest and other expense, net	222	298	488	1,192	1,433
Income before income taxes and extraordinary item	81	2,748	2,966	2,283	4,717
Income taxes (1)	1	864	489	739	1,706
Income before extraordinary item	80	1,884	2,477	1,544	3,011
Extraordinary item (2)	—	824	72	—	—
Net income	$ 80	$ 2,708	$ 2,549	$ 1,544	$ 3,011
Net income per share of common stock (3)	$ .01	$ .47	$ .48	$ .29	$ .50
Weighted average common shares outstanding (4)	5,666	5,804	6,079	6,417	6,442
BALANCE SHEET DATA (at end of year):					
Working capital	$ 7,477	$ 6,198	$ 5,442	$ 3,342	$ 4,243
Total assets	21,288	26,363	36,917	45,975	57,483
Note payable and long-term debt	8,754	8,091	15,367	20,004	24,745
Stockholders' equity	$11,152	$14,780	$17,329	$18,887	$21,838

(1) Reflects benefits from investment tax and general business credits of $504,000 and $3,000 in fiscal 1991 and 1992, respectively.

(2) Reflects the utilization of net operating loss carryforwards.

(3) Calculated as described in Note 1(g) to the Financial Statements.

(4) Adjusted to give retroactive effect to the reclassification of each authorized and issued share of Common Stock, without par value, into 1,000 shares of Common Stock, par value $.01 per share, that occurred on April 22, 1993.

Figure 4–1   Selected financial data

or projection about the future based upon *hypothetical* assumptions. Only the former is required.

The SEC has purposely left vague the specific details about what items should be discussed and how the analysis should be framed. This was done because the commission believes that it is management's responsibility to identify and address the key quantitative

(in millions except per share data)	Total Operating Revenues	Gross Profit	Income/ (Loss) Before Income Taxes	Income/ (Loss) After Income Taxes[5]	Net Income/ (Loss)	Net Income/ (Loss) Per Share[1]
For the year ended June 27, 1992						
First Quarter[2]	$ 3,293	$ 1,490	$ 40	$ 12	$ (474)	$ (3.80)
Second Quarter[2]	3,479	1,441	(153)	(155)	(155)	$ (1.25)
Third Quarter[2]	3,253	1,268	(291)	(312)	(312)	$ (2.50)
Fourth Quarter[3]	3,906	1,600	(1,674)	(1,855)	(1,855)	$ (14.76)
Total Year	$13,931	$ 5,799	$ (2,078)	$ (2,310)	$ (2,796)	$ (22.39)
For the year ended June 29, 1991						
First Quarter	$ 3,093	$ 1,435	$ 35	$ 26	$ 26	$ .21
Second Quarter	3,353	1,606	156	111	111	$ .92
Third Quarter	3,520	1,671	179	117	117	$ .94
Fourth Quarter[4]	3,945	1,921	(890)	(871)	(871)	$ (7.08)
Total Year	$13,911	$ 6,633	$ (520)	$ (617)	$ (617)	$ (5.08)

[1] *Earnings per share is computed independently for each of the quarters presented and therefore do not sum to the total for the year.*
[2] *Restated to reflect the adoption of SFAS No. 106–Employers' Accounting for Postretirement Benefits Other Than Pensions.*
[3] *Includes restructuring charges of $1,500M.*
[4] *Includes restructuring charges of $1,100M.*
[5] *Before cumulative effect of change in accounting principle.*

Figure 4–2   Quarterly financial data

and qualitative factors that represent the crux of its business. Flexible requirements, in the commission's view, elicit more meaningful disclosure and help to avoid "boilerplate" discussions.

Figure 4–3 includes an excerpt of a particularly good example of the kind of insightful discussion the SEC expects in MD&A. It is taken from the 1992 Form 10–K of Dexter Corporation.

Analysis of Financial Condition and Operations

Principles of Consolidation   The consolidated financial statements include the accounts of all majority-owned subsidiaries. All consolidated subsidiaries are wholly owned except Life Technologies, Inc. (LTI) (55% owned) and a few other subsidiaries, primarily outside the United States, in which aggregate minority interests are not significant. Intercompany accounts, transactions and profits have been eliminated in the consolidated financial statements. Companies owned 20% to 50% are accounted for by the equity method. Certain amounts for prior years have been reclassified to conform to and be consistent with the 1992 presentation.

Acquisitions and Divestitures   In June 1992, Dexter completed the sale of its Water Management Systems Division operations in North America to Diversey Corporation, a Canadian-based multinational subsidiary of The Molson Companies Limited. The sale resulted in a capital gain in the second quarter of 1992.

Effective June 1992, Dexter completed the sale of its Composites Division to Hycomp, Inc.

In September 1992, Dexter sold its polyurethane release agent business in Germany to Air Products and Chemicals Pura GmbH & Co.

In October 1992, Life Technologies, Inc. acquired certain assets from Telios Pharmaceuticals, Inc. which were used in its manufacture and sale of research products.

In December 1992, Dexter completed the sale of its plastisols business to Florida Capital Partners. The transaction involved the sale of 100% of the capital stock of Dexter's subsidiary company, Rutland Plastics, Inc. for cash. The sale resulted in a capital gain which was recorded in the fourth quarter of 1992.

In December 1992, Dexter signed a letter of intent to enter into a global alliance in the aerospace coatings business with Akzo Coatings International B.V., The Netherlands. The transaction involves the transfer of Dexter's U.S.-based coil coatings business to Akzo in exchange for cash plus Akzo's U.S.-based aerospace coatings business. Also, Dexter and Akzo will enter into a 60/40 Akzo majority-owned joint venture based in Europe to supply aerospace coatings to the worldwide market outside the Americas. Technology exchange agreements will be established between Dexter and the joint venture to form a global alliance.

In December 1992, Dexter signed a letter of intent for the sale of its Pultrusions Division. The cash proceeds of the sale are expected to approximate the book value of the business. The transaction is expected to be completed during the first quarter of 1993.

In January 1993, Dexter announced its decision to divest its automotive headliner business located in West Unity, Ohio.

In February 1993, Dexter announced that it had signed a contract with Jallut S.A. for the purchase of all of the shares of its subsidiary, Vernicolor A.G., a leading technology food can coatings manufacturer located in Gruningen, Switzerland. The acquisition is expected to close in the first quarter of 1993.

Figure 4–3   Excerpts from MD&A

Events, Trends, and Vulnerabilities Dexter is subject to a multitude of events and trends which influence its business prospects, profitability and liquidity. Many of these events and trends are outside the control of the company. Furthermore, the relative importance of any one such force or trend varies from time to time with one force bearing more influence today, another tomorrow and the possible reemergence of the first along the way.

Of immediate concern are the recessionary pressures facing the United States and spreading to other parts of the world. While the United States appears to be slowly struggling out of its recession, Europe appears to be heading straight into one. The U.S. recovery, if indeed there is one, is sporadic, uneven, and regional. Such a recovery may not benefit the businesses of Dexter in 1993. Since approximately 50% of Dexter's profits arise from products produced outside the United States, a worsening recession in Europe will negatively affect Dexter's business. To a lesser extent, economic conditions in Japan appear to be weakening and Japan's economy can influence those of other Asian nations. While the extent cannot now be determined, sales to the automotive, electronics, medical and construction markets could be adversely affected. Further, a possible failure of a GATT Treaty or the apparent trend toward protectionism could further restrict international trade with negative implications on the economies involved.

In recent months the currencies of Western Europe have decreased in value vis-a-vis the U.S. dollar resulting in an adverse translation impact on Dexter's dollar-denominated financial statements. The decrease has been most pronounced for the pound sterling, Swedish krona and Italian lira. While exposure in the Italian lira is small, Dexter has substantial business emanating from Great Britain and Sweden. The adverse impact is to some degree ameliorated by the invoicing of a majority of Dexter's British and Swedish sales in stronger continental currencies. The impact on profit margins is not ascertainable at this time and depends on the extent to which prices and costs readjust to the new exchange rates. Further, margins have been enhanced by currency hedging taken to reduce the impact of devaluation on the future purchase of imported raw materials. Dexter sales which are vulnerable to currency fluctuations principally fall into the international food packaging, electronics, and medical markets.

The general aging of the U.S. population will create challenges with respect to the availability of employees as well as amplifying trends in increased health care costs. By adopting SFAS No. 106 in the first quarter of 1993, Dexter expects to account for the liability of medical benefits of retirees through an accumulated charge of $25 million (before corresponding tax benefits) and an ongoing estimated annual pretax charge of $3.3 million. Should Dexter fund this obligation, the ongoing charge would be expected to be reduced to $0.8 million, or about the same amount as is currently being charged on the pay-as-you-go basis. Such funding will depend upon the outcome of a revenue ruling request presently under consideration by the IRS.

Undoubtedly, there will be increasing costs necessary to respond to heightened regulatory pressures throughout the whole spectrum of industrial life. Although we expect such increased costs might be moderate in areas of corporate governance and securities regulation, we expect such increases to be significant in such areas as environmental, health, social and administrative regulation. Heightened worldwide environmental concerns will lead to greater capital requirements and increased operating expenses. While the company, based on known facts and circumstances, has provided substantial environmental reserves as shown at year-end in the "Statement of Financial Position" and discussed below, the ultimate cost of compliance and remediation cannot be ascertained and, therefore, there is no assurance that such reserves will prove to be adequate over time.

The future trend of taxation is hard to predict. Substantial national and local deficits dictate the need for greater tax receipts. The current recession has given rise to the possibility of tax incentives or reduced tax rates. How these two conflicting pressures will affect Dexter cannot now be ascertained. Changes in tax rates, the incidence and method of taxation, all have an impact on economic recovery and inflation. These factors in turn have an impact on currency exchange rates as does the political atmosphere in each country. The change in the Administration in the United States will undoubtedly have an impact on all these factors, but when, in which direction, to what degree, and with what kind of melded result is uncertain at this time.

As always, Dexter is vulnerable to management error. The execution of the restructuring plans over 1993 and 1994 calls for the closing of nine factories and distribution centers in the United States. Of these, only one small product line which is operating at a loss will be sold or discontinued. The remainder will be consolidated into six world class facilities. In addition, a strategic product line swap with another company is planned. In Europe we expect to integrate an important acquisition and form a significant joint venture. These restructuring activities are to be carried out in a highly competitive, global environment amidst economic uncertainty. Although Dexter has been steadily building its management expertise to deal with these issues, we are vulnerable to mistakes in the execution of this plan.

Other areas which will no doubt have important impact on the future of the company will be the increasing rate of technological change, a universal move toward higher quality products and the globalization of our customers and competitors. It will be necessary for the company to devote greater resources to research and development, the training of its financial, marketing and administrative personnel and the acceleration of the company's progress toward world class manufacturing. All of these factors will entail increased costs, placing pressures on margins in the near term. The heightened degree of competition throughout the world will continue to make price increases to our customers difficult to obtain. We may therefore experience cost increases without commensurate price increases.

In addition, the company's Life Technologies, Inc. subsidiary is subject to the fluctuation in the prices of raw materials, particularly fetal bovine serum which stems from a fundamental limit to supply, and national funding of medical research in several countries. Further, there is a severe competition to develop substantive products for cell culture which do not depend upon traditional raw materials.

The complexities of the ever-changing worldwide events and trends, the emergence of the global marketplace, and the advancement of technology generate numerous vulnerabilities and challenges. The company believes, however, that it will face these challenges with vigor, innovation and productivity.

Liquidity The company has ample lines of credit currently available and its liquidity is strong. Cash provided from operations exceeded cash needed for investments by $56.6 million. Financing activities used funds of $30 million, resulting in an increase in cash and short-term investments of $26.6 million. Excluding LTI, cash provided from operations and investments totaled $50.3 million. Financing activities used funds of $28.6 million, resulting in an increase in cash and short-term investments of $21.7 million. The company plans to meet its future working capital and capital expenditure needs with funds provided from operations and, as needed, short-term and long-term borrowings.

Figure 4–3   Excerpts from MD&A (*continued*)

In contrast to Dexter's MD&A, the SEC determined that the 1989 Form 10–K of Caterpillar, Inc., failed to adequately disclose *known* developments relating to the firm's Brazilian operations.

Caterpillar Brazil (known as CBSA) enjoyed an exceptionally profitable year in 1989, accounting for 23 percent of Caterpillar's consolidated net income while only contributing 5 percent of consolidated revenue. CBSA's operating results for 1989 were in line with operating earnings for prior years, but certain *nonoperating* items contributed significantly to overall net income. These items included (1) currency-translation gains, (2) export subsidies, (3) interest income, and (4) tax-loss carryforwards.

In December 1989 Brazil elected a new president to deal with the country's hyper-inflation. In 1990, when the president substantially reduced the amount of currency in circulation and initiated a plan to devalue the Brazilian cruzado, the country was immediately thrust into an economic crisis.

Early in 1990 (before the 1989 Form 10–K was filed) Caterpillar's management informed the board of directors that CBSA's situation was volatile. In June 1990 Caterpillar issued a press release announcing that consolidated profit for 1990 would be significantly reduced because of a dramatic decline in CBSA's results.

The SEC charged that the MD&A portion of Caterpillar's 1989 Form 10–K contained no disclosure about the disproportionate impact of CBSA's profit on consolidated net income and did not indicate that a decline in CBSA's future results could have a material adverse effect on Caterpillar's 1990 net earnings.

The SEC concluded that Caterpillar's MD&A should have discussed uncertainties regarding CBSA's future operations and the impact of CBSA on overall results. The SEC noted that investors were left with an incomplete picture of Caterpillar's financial condition and results of operations and were denied the opportunity to see the company through management's eyes.[16]

Changes in and Disagreements with Accountants

The final piece of accounting-related information in the BIP involves an entity's accounting firm. When a publicly held entity changes accountants, the following information must be disclosed:

- Whether the former accountant's reports on the company's financial statements covering the latest two fiscal years contained a qualified or adverse opinion or whether the former accountants disclaimed an opinion
- Whether the change in accountants was approved by the entity's board of directors or the board's audit committee
- Whether there were any unresolved disagreements between the former accountants and the entity's management during the past two years regarding (1) accounting principles, (2) disclosures, or (3) auditing procedures

Figure 4–4, excerpted from the 1992 Form 10–K of Allergan, Inc., illustrates the form of the required disclosure.

The disclosures required when a company changes its accountants represent the outgrowth of the commission's concern regarding so-called opinion shopping. The SEC acknowledges that companies may, of course, change accountants at their discretion. The commission believes, however, that full disclosure should be made of a change that results from an entity's desire to engage an accounting firm that is willing to interpret GAAP in a manner that frustrates the true economic substance of a transaction or event.

Opinion shopping is no longer as prevalent as it once was. Its presence has been significantly diminished since the early 1980s due largely to stiff disclosure requirements and the commission's stepped-up detection and enforcement efforts.

INDEPENDENT AUDITORS

On September 22, 1992, the Company engaged the accounting firm of KPMG Peat Marwick, as independent auditors to audit the Company's financial statements for the fiscal year ended December 31, 1992, replacing the firm of Coopers & Lybrand, which were the principal independent auditors for the Company's most recent financial statement. The decision to change independent auditors was made by the Audit Committee of the Board of Directors after soliciting bids from a number of auditing firms, including Coopers & Lybrand. There have been no disagreements with Coopers & Lybrand on any matter of accounting principles or practices, financial statements disclosure, or auditing scope or procedure, which disagreements if not resolved to the satisfaction of Coopers & Lybrand would have caused Coopers & Lybrand to make reference in connection with its report on the Company's financial statements to the subject matter of the disagreement. Coopers & Lybrand issued an unqualified opinion on the financial statements of the Company for 1990 and 1991. Representatives of KPMG Peat Marwick are expected to be present at the stockholders' meeting, will have the opportunity to make a statement if they desire to do so and will be available to respond to appropriate questions. Independent auditors for the fiscal year ending December 31, 1993 will be selected by the Board of Directors after a review and recommendation to the Board by the Audit Committee.

Figure 4–4   Changes in accountants

THE SEC AND AUDITING

In the commission's view, an audit of a public company's financial statements by independent accountants is just as important as the financial statements themselves and the accounting principles on which they are based. The SEC believes that the federal securities laws underscore the primary role of the auditor as that of protecting public investors. Thus virtually all *annual* financial statements called for in the principal 1933 act registration forms and 1934 act reports must be audited in accordance with generally accepted auditing standards (GAAS). Quarterly financial statements on Form 10–Q and stub-period statements required in 1933 act registration statements to comply with the 134–day rule need not be audited, although they must be prepared in conformity with GAAP.

As with the promulgation of accounting principles, the SEC has statutory authority to regulate the auditing process. For the most part, as with GAAP, the commission has left the establishment of auditing standards to the private sector.[17]

ACCOUNTANT'S INDEPENDENCE

The SEC has historically considered the independence of accountants as central to the effective implementation of the securities laws. Of course, the accounting profession itself recognizes the importance of independence in monitoring public confidence. Thus, under GAAS as well, an accountant must be independent of the entity whose financial statements are being examined, although the commission's rules are somewhat more stringent than those of the accounting profession in general (see Chapter 3).

Independence is defined as the ability to act with integrity and objectivity. To *actually* be independent, an accountant must be intellectually honest. To be *recognized* as independent, the accountant must be free of any relationship that could lead others to question whether such independence indeed is present. Thus independence in *both* fact and appearance are essential for the public to view the audit process as an unbiased examination of an entity's financial statements.

Independence *in fact* is a state of mind, and as such it cannot be regulated. Thus the best that can be done by the SEC (or by the profession in general, for that matter) is to regulate the *appearance* of independence. Indeed, that is what has been done. Both GAAS and the commission's separate rules of independence, by and large, are made up of a series of relationships, which if any exist would be deemed to impair an accountant's independence with respect to a given entity.

Although not every possible set of circumstances can be anticipated, over the years the SEC has published literally hundreds of examples of actual and hypothetical situations regarding the independence of accountants. They are not intended to be all-inclusive but rather to put accountants and their clients on the alert for relationships that could cause the loss of independence. They can be broadly categorized as situations including one or more of the following:

- Financial interests in a client or in an entity related to a client
- Family and personal or business relationships with members of a client's organization
- The performance of accounting, bookkeeping, or other nonaudit services for a client
- Conflicting occupational interests (e.g., acting as a client's attorney or stockholder as well as the client's accountant)

Obviously, any significant financial interest, and personal or business relationship is ruled out, as is a conflicting occupational interest. The SEC is unwavering in its strict enforcement of these situations. When it comes to performing other nonaudit services, however, the commission's views may be described as inconsistent.

Accounting and Bookkeeping Services

Financial statements are representations of management who are responsible for their propriety and accuracy.[18] As such, financial statements are not *prepared* by the independent accountant, whose only responsibility is to express an opinion on them regarding their conformity with GAAP after conducting an audit in accordance with generally accepted auditing standards.

As part of this rationale, under SEC rules independence would be considered impaired if accountants were to perform a managerial or decision-making function, which, according to the commission, includes maintenance of the basic accounting records and preparation of the financial statements. Such functions would differ only in degree—but not in kind—from that of an employee. In effect, accountants would be auditing the results of their own work.

Management Consulting Services

In contrast to its stand on bookkeeping and accounting services, the SEC, in recognizing the financial realities of many large accounting firms, is much more philosophical about management consulting services (MCS). Since the 1970s the scope of MCS has proliferated to range from the traditional type of work such as designing and setting up accounting systems, both manual and computerized, to the exotic, such as executive search, psychological testing, and developing an executive compensation plan. For some major firms, MCS fees approach those for auditing and tax work.

According to the SEC, the distinction between bookkeeping services and MCS hinges on establishing where advice ends and managerial responsibility begins. In making this determination, the basic consideration is whether the client appears to be substantially dependent upon the accountant's skill and judgment or reliant only to the extent of the customary type of consultation or advice.

Even though Congress and other public oversight bodies made a number of starts and stops to regulate the type of MCS that accountants could perform for their SEC clients, no service is specifically prohibited. Nevertheless, the commission's overall policy for nonaudit services still applies: Independence will be impaired if through performance of consulting services an accountant's role is viewed as a part of management.

ACCOUNTANTS' SELF-REGULATORY PROGRAM

In response to congressional concerns about the quality of auditing services, in 1977 the AICPA established the Division for CPA Firms, a self-regulatory organization. The division is divided into two sections, one for firms without SEC clients and another for firms that conduct audits of public companies.

The two sections have similar memberships requirements, the most important of which is a triennial peer review to determine whether a firm has in place an effective system of quality control that meets established standards and contributes to the performance of quality accounting and auditing work.

In addition to peer review, members of the SEC section must adhere to the following requirements:

- All partners and professional staff must obtain a minimum of 120 continuing education (CPE) credits over a three-year period.
- Rotation of the partner in charge of an SEC audit engagement must be made no less frequently than every seven years.
- Each audit report for an SEC client must be subjected to a concurring review by a partner not otherwise associated with the engagement.

- The partner in charge of an SEC audit engagement must meet at least annually with the client's board of directors or audit committee regarding certain accounting and audit matters arising during the course of the engagement. In addition, the audit committee or board of directors must be informed of the fees earned from the client for MCS and the type of consulting services performed.
- Each member firm must provide specific information that is available to the public about its operations, including gross fees earned for MCS and tax services from all SEC clients as a group.

Finally, members of the SEC section must refrain from performing the following types of MCS for SEC audit clients:

- Psychological testing
- Public opinion polling
- Merger and acquisition assistance for a finder's fee
- Executive recruitment
- Actuarial services to insurance company clients

It is important to remember, though, that there is no SEC rule or policy formally requiring an accounting firm that audits a public company to belong to the SEC section of the Division for CPA Firms. Thus while membership in the AICPA itself requires a firm that has SEC clients to belong to the SEC section, the commission does not prevent firms that are not members of the AICPA from auditing publicly held entities. As a practical matter, this does not seem to be a serious problem. More than 90 percent of the public enterprises accounting for better than *99 percent* of the aggregate sales volume of *all* publicly traded entities are audited by members of the AICPA SEC section. Although a small gap still exists, the commission seems satisfied with private-sector efforts to subject all accounting firms with SEC clients to peer review and other quality-control standards eventually.

CHAPTER SUMMARY

Although the SEC has statutory authority to set accounting standards, for the most part it has relied on the private sector to do so. Financial statements included in filings with the SEC must comply with GAAP and must also conform to Regulation S-X, which requires certain additional disclosures beyond what is called for by generally accepted accounting principles. In addition to the financial statements themselves, other information required in SEC filings includes (1) selected financial data, (2) quarterly data, (3) MD&A, and (4) the circumstances surrounding a change in and disagreements with an entity's accountants, if applicable.

The SEC requires annual financial statements to be audited in accordance with GAAS. As with accounting principles, the commission relies on the private sector to establish auditing standards. In addition to compliance with the accounting profession's standards in general, accounting firms that audit financial statements of public companies are also subject to the SEC's more stringent rules regarding independence.

DISCUSSION QUESTIONS

1. Considering the importance of accounting and financial reporting to the operation of the federal securities laws, do you believe that the SEC should play a more active role in promulgating accounting principles? One consequence of doing so would be to permit the FASB to continue to make rules for privately held companies but that publicly held entities would have to follow GAAP made by the SEC. Is this a reasonable approach? Do you feel that there should be two sets of GAAP, one for private companies and one for public companies?

2. The SEC and the private sector disagreed on how the investment tax credit should be reported and on the required method of accounting for oil and gas producers. In both instances the private-sector body (i.e., the APB regarding the investment credit and the FASB concerning oil and gas accounting) was forced to give in to the SEC. Describe other choices that may have been available to the APB and FASB and what their consequences might have been.

3. The principal 1933 act and 1934 act forms require balance sheets as of the two most recent fiscal years and income statements and cash flow statements for the three latest years. Is this sufficient? Do you feel that financial statements for more years should be required? If so, how many? Explain your answer.

4. Some observers believe that accounting firms should not be allowed to perform any consulting service whatsoever (including tax compliance and planning) for an SEC audit client. What risks to independence do you believe are caused by giving corporate tax planning advice?

5. Some observers feel that highly condensed quarterly statements as required by Form 10–Q are of little analytical value because they do not provide sufficient detail. Do you feel that complete full-blown quarterly financial statements should be required? Explain your answer.

ENDNOTES

1. This position was expressed in Securities Act Release No. 254 (November 21, 1934).

2. The term *cookbook* refers to very precise criteria contained in recent accounting standards. If a recipe is followed to the letter by every chef, all broths should taste the same. Under the cookbook approach, there is little room for judgment in the application of accounting principles.

3. Louis Loss and Joel Seligman, *Securities Regulation*, (Boston: Little, Brown, 1989), p. 702.

4. These releases, termed Accounting Series Releases (ASRs), continued until 1982. In all, 307 ASRs were issued, although many of them pertained to commission enforcement actions against accountants, not to accounting policy issues. In 1982 the SEC discontinued publishing

ASRs. They were replaced by two new categories of releases: (1) Financial Reporting Releases (FRRs), which are concerned only with accounting and auditing matters; and (2) Accounting and Auditing Enforcement Releases (AAERSs), which relate to enforcement and disciplinary proceedings.

5. Accounting Series Release No. 4 (April 25, 1938).

6. Rule 203 of the AICPA's Code of Professional Conduct.

7. Accounting Series Release No. 150 (December 20, 1973).

8. Accounting Series Release No. 280 (September 2, 1980).

9. Although the two are often inextricably intertwined, the SEC draws a distinction between the measurement and disclosure aspects of GAAP. The commission views measurement (i.e., quantification of data) to be the primary concern of the private sector and disclosure (in *addition* to what must be disclosed under GAAP) to be its principal concern. Thus the SEC believes that the existence of financial statement disclosures mandated by Regulation S-X above and beyond those required by GAAP does not violate the letter or the spirit of its policy to rely on private-sector bodies for the establishment of accounting principles. Over the years, as the FASB addressed most of the pressing accounting issues that were not previously resolved by the CAP or the APB, the number and substance of SEC incremental disclosures has diminished.

10. Accounting Series Release No. 96 (January 10, 1963).

11. This view was expressed by Leonard Spacek, a partner in Arthur Andersen. Although more to the point than other opinions, it summed up the views of the other dissenting members.

12. This view was expressed by Walter Frese.

13. Accounting Series Release No. 253 (August 31, 1978).

14. The dissenters were John March and David Mosso.

15. Note, however, that Forms S-2 and S-3 permit financial statements and other information to be incorporated by reference (see Chapter 3). Also note that financial statement requirements are different for so-called small business issuers (see Chapter 8).

16. Accounting and Auditing Enforcement Release No. 363 (March 31, 1992).

17. Auditing standards are set by the AICPA, not the FASB. Under the present structure, the Auditing Standards Board (ASB), a senior technical body of the AICPA, establishes GAAS.

18. To drive this point home, the auditor's standard report was recently modified to include explicit wording to that effect.

5

Liability under the Federal Securities Laws

SECTION 11 LIABILITY UNDER THE 1933 ACT

As briefly explained in Chapter 3, Section 11 of the 1933 Act imposes liability for any material misrepresentation or omission in a registration statement (whether as part of the original distribution or in the open market). Any person acquiring securities covered by a defective registration statement may file suit against (1) the issuing company itself, (2) the issuing company's directors, (3) the issuing company's principal executive and financial officers, (4) each and every underwriter, and (5) the accounting firm whose opinion on the company's financial statements appears in the prospectus.

To file suit under Section 11, a plaintiff need only meet the following conditions:

- The suit must be brought within one year after the defect has been (or should have been) discovered, but in any case not later than three years after the security was offered to the public.
- The plaintiff must not have known of the material misstatement or omission.
- The securities acquired must have been covered by the defective registration statement.

A plaintiff need *not* prove *reliance* on the defect or even on the registration statement itself in making the decision to purchase the securities; an exception to this is the unlikely case in which the security was acquired after the issuer made available an earnings statement covering at least a period of twelve months from the effective date of the registration statement. A plaintiff also need not show privity (i.e., a direct contractual relationship) to any of the defendants, scienter (i.e., intentional reckless conduct), causation, or even *injury*.

At first glance it seems that just about anyone may file a Section 11 suit. One limiting factor, however, is the statutory requirement that the securities acquired must have been covered by the defective registration statement. This may be a significant impediment to a potential plaintiff who purchased the securities in the open market. Thus, in a public offering of *additional* securities of a class already outstanding, the buyer must prove that the acquired shares were specifically covered by the registration statement in question and not by an earlier registration statement. In today's environment in which securities are often held in "street name" by or for the account of a broker (i.e., the purchaser does not take physical delivery), it may be next to impossible to identify which securities applied to which public offering. Although there does not appear to be any sound conceptual reason for this provision of Section 11, the courts have unanimously interpreted the specific identification requirement on a literal basis.

Damages under Section 11 are expressly provided for as the difference between the amount paid for the securities and the price of the securities at the time the suit is brought. The maximum amount recoverable, however, is limited to the original public-offering price. Liability under Section 11 is joint and several. Thus any one defendant is liable for the full measure of damages but with a right of contribution from co-defendants.[1]

The issuing company's liability under Section 11 is absolute. Thus an issuing company's only defense is that (1) the plaintiff knew of the misstatement or omission or (2) the reduced value of the security was not due to the defect. The most common defense available to all other defendants is the "reasonable care" (often referred to as the due diligence) defense. Such a defense may be invoked if it can be established that, after reasonable investigation, a defendant had reasonable grounds to believe—and indeed did believe—that the registration statement did not contain a material error or omission.

The Reasonable Care Defense of Experts

Section 11 distinguishes between expertized and nonexpertized portions of a registration statement. An expertized portion of a registration statement is included upon the authority of an expert. The most common example is financial statements, which are included in a registration statement upon the authority of the accounting firm as experts in accounting and auditing matters. Other examples include the reports of engineers, geologists, or appraisers.

Experts have no liability on any portion of a registration statement other than those portions they have expertized. Thus an accounting firm is only liable for errors and omissions in the financial statements on which it has expressed an opinion. As an expert, an accounting firm may raise the reasonable care defense if, after a reasonable investigation, it had reasonable grounds to believe and did believe that the financial statements were not defective. The burden for conducting a reasonable (i.e., due diligence) investigation of the audited financial statements rests entirely with the accounting firm; other Section 11 defendants are not required to perform any due diligence procedures on an expertized portion of a registration statement. Thus insofar as it relates to the audited financial statements (and to other information included upon the authority of experts), other defendants may rely solely on the work of those experts.

Accountants' Due Diligence

Under generally accepted auditing standards, accountants must consider events that may have occurred after the date of the financial statements through the completion of the audit. Under Section 11 of the 1933 act, however, the accounting firm may be culpable for errors or omissions in the financial statements as of the *effective* date of the registration statement. In performing a reasonable investigation, the accounting firm must keep current of events that may have taken place after the date of the financial statements through the effective date, which may be several or more months later.

Accountants refer to the process of keeping current as an SEC subsequent events or (postaudit) review.[2] The objective of such a review is to determine whether, between the date of the audited financial statements and the effective date of the registration statement, there have been any transactions or events that require recognition in the financial statements or disclosure in the notes thereto so that at the effective date the financial statements are free from material misstatements, misleading information, or omissions. The scope of an SEC subsequent events review depends on the facts and circumstances of each offering, but the procedures generally performed are in the nature of inquiry and review, rather than of testing, checking, or corroborating.

Virtually all accounting firms that have SEC clients have a subsequent events program or checklist, and generally accepted auditing standards contain a separate standard that addresses the steps to be taken in an SEC subsequent events review.

In a landmark 1968 case involving (among other defects) materially incorrect audited 1960 financial statements, the Court found that an accounting firm did not sustain its *due diligence defense* because the senior accountant assigned to conduct the SEC subsequent events review did not perform some of the procedures that the accounting firm's own written program had prescribed. Acknowledging that a subsequent events review is not intended as a complete audit, the Court nonetheless determined that, under the circumstances, the scope of the accounting firm's review was inadequate.[3]

Due Diligence of Others

Officers, directors, and underwriters may also raise the due diligence defense if they have made a reasonable investigation of the *nonexpertized* portions of a registration statement. Thus every defendant (except the issuing company itself for which the reasonable care defense is unavailable) must take *some* investigative steps to determine that, at the effective date, the registration statement contains no material defects.

In another case pertinent to 1933 act due diligence, the Court stated that what constitutes an adequate reasonable investigation will vary with a given defendant's involvement, expertise, and access to relevant information. Insiders (i.e., officers and inside directors) with intimate knowledge of corporate affairs will be held to a higher standard of due diligence than outsiders.[4]

Both the commission itself and the courts have held underwriters to a very high standard of reasonable care. The SEC has indicated that failure to make an appropriate investigation is not only a basis for Section 11 liability but also for possible revocation of the underwriter's privileges as a broker-dealer. Indeed, the SEC believes that an underwriter has an obligation to make a reasonable investigation not just for the purpose of its own due diligence defense in a Section 11 action but also as a duty to the investing public.[5]

Tacit reliance on management's assertions is unacceptable; instead, one court noted that an underwriter must play the devil's advocate.[6]

The Due Diligence Meeting

The actual procedures performed in an underwriter's reasonable care investigation, like those of an accountant, depend on the nature of the issuer's operations and the relative complexity of the offering. In all cases, however, a due diligence meeting is held shortly before the effective date of the registration statement. All potential Section 11 defendants usually attend.

At the meeting, participants have the opportunity to inquire of each other regarding current conditions and recent developments that may affect information included in the registration statement. The issues typically discussed at a due diligence meeting relate to the issuer's products and markets, competitive conditions, and the company's current financial situation. Although important because it is held just before the effective date and thus provides participants with a final chance to consider late developments, the due diligence meeting represents but one step in a reasonable care investigation. To one degree or another, depending on the status of a given party, each potential Section 11 defendant should have performed other due diligence procedures prior to the meeting.

Accountants' Comfort Letters

As part of an underwriter's reasonable care investigation, a "comfort letter" will almost always be requested from the accounting firm. Such a letter, which is not part of the registration statement nor is it filed with the SEC, is intended to assist underwriters in discharging their due diligence requirement.[7] Typically, a comfort letter provides the underwriter with the following assurances:

1. *Positive* assurance that the accountant is independent of the issuing company
2. *Positive* assurance that the *audited* financial statements comply with the commission's accounting requirements
3. *Negative* assurance that the *unaudited* financial statements conform to GAAP and comply with the commission's requirements[8]
4. *Negative* assurance that from the date of the latest *unaudited* financial statements contained in the registration statement to the effective date of the registration statement there have not been any substantial increases in the company's long-term debt or decreases in its equity

5. *Negative* assurance that for the period from the date of the latest unaudited financial statements contained in the registration statement to the effective date of the registration statement there has not been a significant decrease in sales or earnings when compared with the corresponding period of the prior year

In a sense, assurances concerning items 1 and 2 are already implied or expressly stated in the accountant's report on the audited statements included in the registration statement. Such assurances are also included in a comfort letter to provide a formal basis for the underwriter's reliance on the work of the accountant as an *expert* in a Section 11 action. Assurance regarding item 3, however, helps the underwriter document a reasonable care investigation on the *unaudited* financial statements, which constitute *nonexpertized* information in the registration statement. Items 4 and 5 assist the underwriter concerning the possibility that last-minute developments may require disclosure to keep the registration statement from being misleading as of the effective date.

Materiality

Only misstatements or omissions that are material within the meaning of Section 11 can predicate liability. As would be expected, what is material must be determined in the context of a given situation. In general, the courts have interpreted materiality to mean the omission or misstatement of an item to which a reasonable investor would attach importance in determining whether to purchase the securities being offered.

In deciding whether an error or omission is material, the courts, by and large, have considered alleged misrepresentations in the context of the entire document. This has given rise to what is referred to as the "bespeaks caution" doctrine. Under this doctrine, *specific* misstatements that might be material if they stood alone are not considered significant when the prospectus *as a whole* contains sufficient cautionary statements regarding the risks and speculative nature of the investment.

One court, in a relevant case, refined the definition of materiality by stating that a fact is material when it is more probable than not that a significant number of investors would have wanted to know about it before deciding to purchase the securities at that time and at that price.[9]

The U.S. Supreme Court has held that a fact is material if there is substantial likelihood that a reasonable investor would consider it in an investment decision. The Supreme Court noted that this standard of materiality does not require proof that knowledge of the error or omission would have resulted in a *different* decision, only that it would have assumed actual significance in the investor's deliberations.[10]

Very few Section 11 cases have comprehensively addressed the issue of materiality. One case, however, has shed some light on how one court has interpreted the materiality of erroneous financial information.[11] Table 5–1 lists items that the court said constituted material errors or omissions. Many observers feel that because the misstatements were clearly of large magnitude, the real benefit of this case is the systematic approach the court took in determining materiality rather than the determinations themselves.

TABLE 5-1

Item	As Shown in the Prospectus	As Determined to be Correct	Difference of Error
Annual sales for the latest year	$9,165,320	$8,511,420	7.7%
Earnings per share for the latest year	$0.75	$0.65	15.4%
Current assets as of the end of the latest year	$4,524,021	$3,914,332	15.6%
Sales for the latest interim quarter	$2,138,455	$1,618,645	32.1%
Unpaid officers' loans outstanding	-0-	$ 386,615	100.0%
Sales backlog	$6,905,000	$2,415,000	185.9%

SECTION 12 LIABILITY UNDER THE 1933 ACT

Under Section 12 of the 1933 act, any party that offers or sells securities that are covered by a defective registration statement may be liable to the purchasers of the securities. The most common example of a potential Section 12 defendant is a member of the selling group who is not an underwriter. The only defense (other than the lack of materiality or the absence of the alleged defect) is that the defendant did not know—and in the exercise of reasonable care could not have known—of the misstatement or omission.

By and large, Section 12 has not given rise to as much litigation as Section 11 has. The principal purpose of Section 12 is to subject to liability sellers of securities that are not covered under Section 11 of the 1933 act.

RULE 10B-5 LIABILITY UNDER THE 1934 ACT

Known as the antifraud provision of the 1934 act, Rule 10b-5 bars intentional deceit in connection with the sale of securities. Specifically, Rule 10b-5 makes the following acts unlawful:

- To employ any device, scheme, or artifice to defraud
- To make any untrue statement of a material fact or to omit stating a material fact necessary to make the statements made, in light of the circumstances under which they were made, not misleading
- To engage in any act, practice, or course of business that operates or would operate as a fraud or deceit on any person in connection with the purchase or sale of any security

Suits are often filed under Rule 10b-5 of the 1934 act when Sections 11 and 12 of the 1933 act are unavailable because of their short statutes of limitations or because securities were purchased in the open market rather than directly from the issuer and thus cannot be specifically traced to the defective registration statement. Although Rule 10b-5 primarily applies to misstatements or omissions in periodic reports under the *1934* act, it may also be the basis for a suit relating to a defective *1933* act registration statement. The premise for the latter is that the false registration statement had an adverse impact on the *secondary* market at large for the issuing company's securities. In addition, because Rule 10b-5 covers reports under the continuous disclosure scheme of the 1934 act (e.g., Forms 10–K and 10–Q), actions under 10b-5 apply to both defraud buyers *and* sellers in the trading of a company's securities. This is in contrast to Sections 11 and 12 of the 1933 act, which apply only to the distribution of securities and therefore are limited to purchasers of securities.

Compared with Section 11, under Rule 10b-5 a greater burden falls on the plaintiff. To prevail under 10b-5, a plaintiff must establish (in addition to the existence of a material error or omission) the following:

- That the defendant acted with scienter (i.e., intentional misconduct with a deliberate disregard of the consequences)
- That the plaintiff relied on the misstatements or omissions and that such misstatements caused the loss

Damages in a 10b-5 action are not expressly stated in the statute. The courts have generally calculated them, however, as the difference between the price of the purchase or sale and the actual value of the securities (had the misrepresentation not been made) at the time of purchase or sale.[12] There is no federal statute of limitations specifically applicable to Rule 10b-5, which may partly account for its position as one of the most frequently employed antifraud provisions of the securities laws (including its use as an alternative to Section 11 of the 1933 act, which has a three-year statute of limitations).[13]

Because Rule 10b-5 is an antifraud provision, the only defense is that a defendant's actions were performed in good faith. The U.S. Supreme Court has stated that the legislative intent of Section 10(b) (and thus Rule 10b-5 thereunder) was not to make anyone liable who acted in good faith.[14]

Scienter

To prove a Rule 10b-5 violation, a plaintiff must establish that a defendant acted with scienter. This does not mean, however, that the plaintiff must prove that a defendant intended to defraud or injure the plaintiff. Indeed, proof of a defendant's *knowledge* of the error or omission is sufficient to establish scienter. Although not all circuits agree, most courts that have addressed the issue have found that reckless conduct constitutes scienter.

Reliance and Causation

Rule 10b-5 plaintiffs also bear the burden of proving that they relied on the misstatement or omission. Unlike a Section 11 action, then, the plaintiffs must be familiar with the document that contained (or omitted, as the case may be) the falsity.

Although inseparable from reliance, causation must also be proved. In this regard, the courts have required plaintiffs to establish two types of causation if they are to prevail:

- *Transaction causation* (i.e., but for the defendant's fraudulent conduct, the purchase or sale of securities would not have taken place or would have been on different terms)

- *Loss causation* (i.e., that the defendant's fraudulent conduct actually produced the plaintiff's loss)

The Fraud on the Market Theory

The fraud on the market theory has as its underpinning the premise that, in an open and developed market, the price of a company's securities is determined by the available information about the company. The Supreme Court, in accepting that notion, has stated that misleading statements will defraud purchasers of stock even though the purchasers (or sellers) do not *directly* rely on the errors or omissions.[15] Thus, even though reliance is required in a Rule 10b-5 suit, a *presumption* of reliance arises—based on the fraud on the market theory—even in the absence of proof that a plaintiff *actually* relied on a defendant's misstatement.

Rule 10b-5 Actions against Accountants

Accountants are frequently named as defendants in 10b-5 lawsuits.[16] That an accountant's work is merely inadequate does not in itself establish scienter. Thus mere *negligence* by an accountant will not support liability under Rule 10b-5. If, however, performance of an audit falls so short of professional standards that it constitutes *reckless* conduct, a plaintiff will usually be able to sustain an allegation of scienter.

A specific court case helps distinguish between recklessness and negligence. In a Rule 10b-5 action against an accounting firm, the Court of Appeals found that despite the existence of an error in the financial statements—about which the accountants were informed *before* the document was sent to stockholders but that remained uncorrected—the accounting firm's conduct did *not* constitute recklessness.

The court concluded that failure to correct the error or to otherwise call the mistake to the attention of stockholders and the SEC clearly indicated negligence on the accountant's part. Nevertheless, the court found nothing to indicate that the accountant had a motive to deceive, manipulate, or defraud. Thus in spite of the accountant's negligence, lack of scienter defeated the plaintiff's claim.[17]

The rule that negligence does not constitute scienter remains sound, although the distinction between negligence and recklessness is fact-sensitive. Thus it could be argued that in the foregoing case negligence was transformed into reckless conduct when the accounting firm became aware of the error in time to correct the financial statements but chose not to do so. The court, however, did not see it that way.

In general, accountants have not been held to standards above those recognized by the accounting profession. In evaluating an accountant's conduct, courts have almost always relied on GAAP and GAAS, although one court has noted that the fair presentation of financial statements—not mere compliance with GAAP—is the more appropriate standard.[18] Thus accountants will not be protected solely by complying with GAAP and GAAS if they are aware that by doing so the financial statements will not be fairly presented.

Other Types of 10b-5 Actions

In addition to its use for errors and omissions in 1933 act and 1934 act registration statements and reports, Rule 10b-5 is also commonly relied upon in the following circumstances:

- When an officer or director (or other party having a fiduciary relationship) trades in the company's securities on the basis of material nonpublic information
- When an insider selectively discloses material nonpublic information to another party who trades in the company's securities
- When a company issues misleading information to the public or keeps silent when there is a duty to disclose

All three of these situations are covered in Chapter 6.

THE RACKETEER INFLUENCED AND CORRUPT ORGANIZATIONS (RICO) STATUTE

In 1970, Congress passed the Racketeer Influenced and Corrupt Organizations Act (RICO) as a means of slowing the infiltration of organized crime into legitimate businesses. Specifically, RICO prohibits

- Using income derived from a pattern of racketeering activity to acquire, establish, or operate an enterprise
- Acquiring or maintaining an interest in an enterprise through a pattern of racketeering activity
- Conducting or participating in the affairs of an enterprise through a pattern of racketeering activity

The use of RICO in securities litigation spawns mainly from the inclusion of "fraud in the sale of securities" as part of a long list of racketeering activities contained in the statute.

RICO includes a host of potent civil remedies for plaintiffs, including the recovery of attorney's fees and *treble* damages. Criminal remedies include fines, imprisonment, and mandatory forfeiture of property acquired through a RICO violation.

The principal common thread running through RICO is the phrase "pattern of racketeering activity." To sustain a RICO violation, a plaintiff must prove, among other things, that the defendant engaged in such a pattern. The RICO statute itself defines a pattern of racketeering as the commission of a minimum of *two* acts of racketeering within ten years. It is important to keep in mind that no evidence that the defendant is a racketeer or is even connected with organized crime need be provided.

Although two acts of racketeering are necessary, they may not be sufficient under a recent interpretation of RICO by the U.S. Supreme Court. In 1985 the High Court noted that the legislative history of RICO supports the view that two *isolated* acts of racketeering activity do not constitute a pattern.[19] After this 1985 case, lower courts began developing their own formulations of what constitutes a pattern. This added to the confusion, prompting the Supreme Court's 1989 clarification that a pattern required both continuity (i.e., multiple illegal acts within a single scheme) and relationship (i.e., the illegal acts must be related through common characteristics, such as similar methods of commission, participants, results, or purpose).[20]

In a much-publicized case in which investors asserted a civil RICO claim against Jim and Tammy Bakker for the systematic fraudulent sale over a number of years of "lifetime partnerships," the Court concluded that the Bakkers' scheme, which defrauded more than 55,000 people, met the Supreme Court's two-pronged test of continuity and relationship.[21]

Although infrequently used in its early years, by the 1980s the lure of treble damages and the recovery of lawyers' fees proved irresistible. As a result, RICO actions have become quite popular by purchasers and sellers in all types of securities litigation, notwithstanding attempts by some courts to limit RICO's reach. Indeed, the Supreme Court, while acknowledging that the primary concern of Congress in enacting the law was mobsters, has rebuffed recent efforts by lower courts to curb RICO's application.

CHAPTER SUMMARY

Liability for a material misstatement or omission in a 1933 act registration statement may be imposed under Section 11 on (1) the issuing company, (2) the issuer's officers and directors, (3) each underwriter, and (4) the accounting firm. All parties having Section 11 liability may raise the so-called reasonable care defense. Such a defense means that, after a reasonable investigation, the defendant had reasonable grounds to believe—and did believe—that the registration statement was not defective. Thus, even though each party with Section 11 liability must perform some form of due diligence to determine that the registration statement is not defective, an expert (e.g., an accountant) is only responsible for the expertized portion of the registration statement. Conversely, nonexperts with Section 11 liability need only perform due diligence on nonexpertized portions.

Rule 10b-5 of the 1934 act prohibits fraud in connection with the sale of securities. Unlike Section 11, under which a plaintiff need not establish reliance on the material error or intentional deceit on the part of the defendant, under Rule 10b-5 both of those allegations must be proved.

In recent years RICO has been used as a basis for securities litigation. Under RICO, fraud in the sale of securities is but one in a long list of racketeering activities. To sustain a RICO violation, the plaintiff must prove that the defendant has engaged in a pattern of racketeering activity.

DISCUSSION QUESTIONS

1. Some have observed that Congress enacted Section 11 of the 1933 act more as a preventative measure against defective registration statements than as a punishment. Do you agree with the open-ended provisions of Section 11, or do you feel that a plaintiff should have to prove reliance on the defect in the decision to purchase securities?

2. Do you believe that in bringing securities to the market underwriters should be held to a higher standard of reasonable care than others? Comment on the SEC's assertion that an underwriter's due diligence is a duty to the investing public.

3. To sustain a Section 11 action, a defect in a registration statement must be proved material. Attempt to formulate your own definition of materiality that includes quantitative guidelines.

4. Attempt to explain why Rule 10b-5 of the 1934 act requires a plaintiff to prove reliance, whereas no such proof is necessary in a Section 11 action under the 1933 act.

5. Does the fraud on the market theory apply to public companies whose securities are thinly traded or to companies whose fates and fortunes are not widely followed by analysts? Explain your answer.

ENDNOTES

1. For example, in the case of a $20 million public offering in which the stock ends up being worthless, the accounting firm, whose fees may have been less than 1 percent of the total offering, or the underwriter, whose commission may have been 5 percent, could be held *individually* liable (subject to possible contribution from other defendants) for the full $20 million (plus legal fees).

2. Sometimes such a review is referred to as an "S-1" review, although an SEC subsequent events review is performed on financial statements included in other 1933 act forms (e.g., S-2 or S-3).

3. *Escott v. BarChris Construction Co.,* 283 F.Supp. 643 (S.D.N.Y. 1968).

4. *Feit v. Leasco Data Processing Equip. Corp.,* 332 F.Supp. 544 (E.D.N.Y. 1971).

5. *Richmond Corp.,* 41 S.E.C. 398, 406 (1963).

6. *Feit v. Leasco Data Processing Equip. Corp.*

7. Comfort letters are also often furnished to other parties (e.g., directors) having a statutory due diligence defense under Section 11.

8. Negative assurance differs from positive assurance. Regarding compliance of unaudited statements with GAAP and the SEC's requirements, for example, a statement providing negative assurance might be phrased as follows: "[Based on limited procedures . . .], nothing came to our attention that caused us to believe that any material modifications should be made to the unaudited financial statements for them to be in conformity with generally accepted accounting principles and in compliance with the accounting requirements of the 1933 act."

9. *Feit v. Leasco Data Processing Equip. Corp.*

10. *TSC Industries v. Northway, Inc.,* 426 U.S. 438, 449 (1976).

11. *Escott v. BarChris Construction Co.*

12. Thus even if plaintiff-sellers have realized a gain, they may recover damages based on the amounts they would have received had they not been defrauded.

13. There are more than 4,000 reported cases that at least mention Rule 10b-5, per Larry D. Soderquist, *Understanding the Securities Laws* (New York: Practicing Law Institute, 1990), p. 257.

14. *Ernst & Ernst v. Hochfelder,* 425 U.S. 206 (1976).

15. *Basic Inc. v. Levinson,* 485 U.S. 224 (1988).

16. When fraud does indeed occur, bankruptcy of the perpetrating company often follows. Thus accounting firms (whether or not culpable), fortified by enormous malpractice insurance coverage, are frequently attractive targets in 10b-5 and other securities litigation.

17. *Adams v. Standard Knitting Mills, Inc.,* 623 F.2d 422 (6th Cir. 1980), cert. denied, 449 U.S. 1067 (1980).

18. *In re Commonwealth Oil/Tesoro Petroleum Corp. Securities Litigation,* 467 F.Supp. 227, 255 (W.D. Tex. 1979).

19. *Sedima S.P.R.L. v. Imrex Co.*, 473 U.S. 479, 496 (1985).

20. *H.J. Inc. v. Northwestern Bell Tel. Co.,* 492 U.S. 229 (1989).

21. *Combs v. Bakker,* 886 F.2d 673 (4th Cir. 1989).

6

The Regulation
of Corporate Insiders

Prior to enactment of the federal securities laws, profiting from insider trading was thought to be an emolument to which corporate executives were entitled. As explained in Chapter 1, congressional inquiry determined that trading by corporate insiders at the expense of outside investors was one of the main causes of the 1929 stock market crash. To deal with this problem, Congress wrote the 1934 act to include rules (Section 16) that require reporting by insiders of transactions in the issuer's securities and that prohibit short-swing trading by insiders (i.e., the purchase and sale or sale and purchase within a six-month period) in the issuer's securities. Clearly, however, these specific mechanisms fall far short of embracing the full range of potential insider-trading situations.

Although concern about insider trading grew after the securities laws were passed, Congress chose not to amend the 1934 act. Instead, it was left to the plaintiffs' bar and the courts to find existing provisions of the 1934 act that could be applied to the wide range of trading abuses not encompassed by Section 16. Not surprisingly, Rule 10b-5, the antifraud rule, has become the most important regulatory tool in such cases based on the theory that actions by insiders to trade on information known only to them constitute a scheme to defraud public security holders.[1]

DISCLOSE OR ABSTAIN

The courts have interpreted Rule 10b-5 to impose an affirmative duty on corporate insiders to disclose *material* nonpublic information or refrain from trading in or recommending the company's shares as long as the information remains undisclosed. This has given rise to the disclose-or-abstain rule.[2]

Insiders are not precluded generally from trading in their company's securities. The disclose-or-abstain rule simply requires that such trading not be done on the basis of information not known to the public at large. Because insiders are frequently faced with situations whose *premature* disclosure could be harmful to the company, corporate insiders often have no viable alternative but to abstain.[3] Similarly, the disclose-or-abstain rule does not *always* prevent insiders from trading in their company's securities just because they, as a matter of obvious fact, are more familiar with the entity's operations than outside investors are. An insider's duty to disclose or abstain arises only when there is extraordinary information that is reasonably certain to have a substantial effect on the market price of the company's securities.

The Duty to Disclose in General

If insiders do not trade on the basis of inside information, mere possession of such information does not, of itself, trigger a duty to disclose it.[4] This is true even if the financial markets are laden with misimpressions, untruths, or rumors, provided that the erroneous information has not been spread by the issuing company.

The absence of a duty to make affirmative disclosure is qualified in two instances:

- When disclosure is necessary to update or correct earlier information released by the company
- In response to questions by security analysts and reporters

It is generally agreed that a company has an obligation to modify or correct prior disclosures upon which the public may still be relying. When responding to questions by analysts or the press, an issuer may state "No comment" but is precluded from uttering half-truths or providing incomplete information.

In addition to the aforementioned exceptions, two additional situations could cause the need for affirmative disclosures:

- When the issuer itself (as distinguished from corporate insiders) is buying its own securities (as in a stock repurchase program)
- When the issuer is aware that insiders are trading in the company's stock on confidential information

These are both insider-trading issues. Although not yet definitively settled by the courts, there is some evidence that each triggers the duty to disclose.

The Materiality of Inside Information

Various courts have described the materiality of inside information in different ways. In examining the concept of materiality, the U.S. Supreme Court has stated that a fact is material if it would have taken on actual significance in an investor's deliberations.[5]

If the impact of a corporate development is clear and certain, its materiality is generally not an issue. If, however, the development is preliminary or highly contingent on future developments, whether an investor would have considered it is subject to debate. The Supreme Court has held that the materiality of preliminary merger discussions depends on both the probability of consummation and the potential significance to the issuer.[6] Thus the materiality of a speculative development must be analyzed in terms of the likelihood that it will come to fruition and the magnitude of its impact.

The Timing of Insider Trades

At what point after disclosure of material information may insiders trade in their company's securities depends on how quickly the information makes its way through newswire services and on the nature of the information. In an important insider-trading case, the Court of Appeals held that, at a minimum, an insider should not have placed an order to purchase securities until the information could reasonably have been expected to appear over the news service with the widest circulation.[7]

The SEC itself has taken a stiffer position, requiring that in addition to dissemination through recognized channels of distribution, public investors must be afforded a reasonable waiting period to react to the information. The American Stock Exchange recommends that insiders wait from twenty-four hours to forty-eight hours after general publication of information, depending on how widely spread dissemination has been.

Who Are Corporate Insiders?

In general terms, corporate insiders may be defined as persons who, by virtue of their relationships with the issuer, are aware of material information about the entity that is not available to the public at large. Over the years, the courts have held the following parties to be corporate insiders:

- Officers and directors
- Controlling persons (i.e., those that have the power to influence the activities of the entity such as a shareholder with a significant voting interest)
- Members of the immediate families of officers, directors, and controlling persons

In addition, the U.S. Supreme Court has stated that an underwriter, accountant, lawyer, or consultant engaged by an issuer takes on the role of "temporary insider" if the issuer expects the outsider to keep undisclosed information confidential and if the relationship with the issuer is of such a nature that it implies confidentiality.[8] For the most part, case law has established that individuals having a *fiduciary* relationship with an issuer clearly must adhere to the disclose-or-abstain rule.

Tipping

In addition to not trading on undisclosed information to their own advantage, corporate insiders may not "tip" the information to outsiders. Tipping is viewed as a means of *indirectly* circumventing the disclose-or-abstain rule. Tippees who know or should reasonably have known that the information they received from an *insider* was confidential are also precluded from trading on such information. Thus if the *tipper* has breached a fiduciary duty, the *tippee* inherits the responsibility to disclose or abstain.

Not every tip of material undisclosed information breaches an insider's fiduciary obligation. In a landmark case, the Supreme Court held that the test is whether the insider will benefit from disclosure to the tippee.[9] A typical example of such a benefit may be a *quid pro quo* relationship in which the tippee is expected to reciprocate in one form or another to the tipper. Of course, if the tippee chooses not to trade, mere disclosure of the confidential information is not, of itself, a violation of the securities laws because the public at large has no specific rights to the undisclosed information.

SHORT-SWING LIABILITY

Section 16 of the 1934 act provides that profits realized by officers, directors, and beneficial owners of more than 10 percent of an entity from so-called short-swing trading in that entity's stock *inure* to the *entity itself*.[10] The purchase and sale (or sale and purchase) of equity securities within a *six-month* period is considered a short-swing transaction.

The application of Section 16 is absolute and does not depend on the possession or use of inside information. Thus it is different from Rule 10b-5, under which insiders are prohibited from trading on material confidential information without first disclosing that information to the public. Also, for Section 16 purposes, insiders are limited to officers, directors, and 10 percent or more shareholders. For Rule 10b-5 purposes, outsiders may take on the role of temporary insiders.

Section 16 has a different legislative focus from the prohibition of trading on inside information. Specifically, Section 16 was intended to eliminate much of the temptation for corporate executives to profit from short-term fluctuations at the expense of the long-term financial health of their companies. Presumably, it prevents insiders from concerning themselves more with trading in their company's securities than with their managerial and fiduciary responsibilities. Section 16 was also designed to remove the temptations for insiders to manipulate corporate events and enter into transactions solely for the purpose of maximizing their own short-term trading profits. In contrast, trading by insiders based on information known only to them is prohibited because such activity is thought to be detrimental to the outside shareholders of an issuer and to the public at large.

Recovery of Short-Swing Profits

Unlike many other provisions of the federal securities laws, the SEC has no explicit authority to enforce Section 16 short-swing transactions. Instead, suit to recover profits must be instituted by the issuing company itself or by stockholders of the company on behalf of the issuer.

To facilitate enforcement by the issuing company or its shareholders, Section 16 also contains a reporting requirement. Officers, directors, and beneficial owners of more than 10 percent of an entity's equity securities must file reports with the SEC within ten days of the end of a month in which there has been a change in the number of securities held. For small transactions, however, reporting may be deferred until the end of the year.[11]

Determining Profit from Short-Swing Transactions

In a situation involving a single purchase and a single sale (regardless of which occurs first), the amount of profit that an insider must *pay to the company* is calculated simply as the difference between the purchase and sale prices.[12] If the transaction does not result in a profit, recovery under Section 16 is not applicable.

When multiple purchases and sales have taken place, profit is determined by the "lowest in/highest out" method under which the highest sales price is matched with the lowest purchase price within the six-month period. The next highest sales price is then matched with the next lowest purchase price, and so on, until all shares have been accounted for.

Short Sales

Section 16 also prohibits so-called short sales by insiders. In a short sale, stock that is not owned is sold in hopes of purchasing it at a lower price before delivery is required. In addition, "sales against the box" by insiders are also prohibited. In such a transaction, the seller already owns at least enough shares to cover the short sale (i.e., the sale of shares not owned) but chooses to deliver different shares to be purchased before settlement is required. A sale against the box does not constitute a violation if the shares ultimately delivered already belong to the seller.

The prohibitions against short sales and sales against the box are necessary to round out the gamut of possible short-swing transactions. They presumably also serve to deter insiders further from *intentionally* entering into transactions that are harmful to the issuer (thus causing the stock price to decline) solely for the purpose of reaping personal benefits.

Derivative Securities

Because of the proliferation of derivative securities (e.g., puts, calls, options, warrants), in 1991 the SEC adopted a comprehensive regulatory framework to deal with such securities in the application of Section 16. Under the rules, derivative securities are considered functionally equivalent to the underlying equity securities because the value of a derivative is related to or is a function of the securities from which they derive.

In general, for purposes of short-swing profit recovery under Section 16, transactions in derivative securities are matchable with transactions in the same and other derivatives and with the underlying equity securities themselves.

THE ARGUMENTS FOR AND AGAINST INSIDER TRADING

Among the arguments in support of the prohibition against insider trading, the principal one involves the doctrine of fair play in the markets. Proponents of this argument reason that individuals and institutions will be loathe to enter or remain in the capital markets if the rules of the game place them at a serious disadvantage. This, of course, they contend will ultimately result in an inefficient—and perhaps even *insufficient*—allocation of capital.

A related argument is that corporate insiders in positions of authority will not be able to overcome the temptations to make business decisions that might be harmful to their companies just so that they may reap the benefits of their market activities.

There is also the argument for the appearance of morality. Proponents of this argument believe that because most individuals simply feel that insider trading just "can't be right," it is important for Congress, the SEC, and the courts not merely to make the playing field level but to *appear* to be doing so as well.

As convincing as these arguments sound, not everyone agrees that insider trading is evil. The principal arguments against the prohibition of insider trading, mostly espoused by economists, are the following:

- The exploitation of valuable information is essential as a method of compensating entrepreneurs; by permitting insider trading, entrepreneurs who might otherwise not be willing to enter the business arena will do so.
- Insider trading is a victimless crime. Insiders' gains do not result in outsiders' losses.
- Insider trading is not harmful to the securities markets; instead, it is actually helpful because it results in more, not less, efficient allocation of resources.
- For the most part, the markets are dominated by institutions that, while not technically falling into the statutory categories of true insiders, have the clout to obtain—and indeed do obtain—information not known to the general public. Those who advance this argument thus contend that a form of insider trading goes on in the market every day by large institutional investors. It is these investors, acting on information not known to small individual investors, that set the prices of securities at efficient levels. Without this insider knowledge, some economists assert, the markets would be in a shambles.

The SEC and Congress seem unimpressed by calls for the abolishment of the insider-trading prohibitions. If anything, they have acted in recent years to tighten the rules.

It might be interesting to note that virtually every major industrialized country (including Germany and Japan, which had heretofore held out) has rules that, to one degree or another, prohibit trading on inside information. An important step in this direction was the adoption of a directive by the European Economic Community that required every member country to have in place by mid-1992 a statutory scheme for the regulation of insider trading. On the other hand, because most countries do not specifically proscribe short-swing transactions, foreign companies with securities registered in the United States are *exempt* from Section 16 of the 1934 act.

CHAPTER SUMMARY

Under the securities laws, corporate insiders may not trade in a company's shares on the basis of material information that has not been disclosed to the public at large. In general, corporate insiders are (1) officers and directors, (2) immediate family members of officers and directors, and (3) shareholders with significant voting interests. In addition to not trading on material undisclosed information, insiders are prohibited from tipping the information to outsiders. A tippee who knows or should have known that information received from an insider was confidential inherits the responsibility from the tipper to refrain from acting upon the information if it has not been disclosed to the public.

Profits earned by officers, directors, and beneficial owners of more than 10 percent of an entity from short-swing trading in the entity's shares must be turned over to the entity itself. A short-swing transaction is one in which a purchase and sale (or sale and purchase) of equity securities have taken place within a six-month period. Insiders are also prohibited from engaging in short sales of the entity's stock.

DISCUSSION QUESTIONS

1. In addition to underwriters, accountants, and lawyers, what other types of outsiders can take on the role of a temporary insider?

2. The courts have slowly expanded the categories of individuals who can become temporary insiders for Rule 10b-5 purposes, yet for Section 16 purposes insiders are limited to officers, directors, and 10 percent or more shareholders. Do you feel that outsiders who become temporary insiders under Rule 10b-5 should also be subject to the Section 16 short-swing provisions? Explain your answer.

3. Do you believe that it is fair that officers, directors, and 10 percent or more shareholders of foreign issuers whose securities are registered in the United States are exempt from Section 16? What are the arguments for and against such exemption?

4. Based on the arguments advanced for and against the prohibitions against insider trading in general, do you believe that such prohibition should remain, be abolished, or be modified? Explain your answer.

5. If short-swing transactions are prohibited in general by Section 16, why was it necessary for Congress to specifically preclude insiders from engaging in short sales and sales against the box?

ENDNOTES

1. Rule 10b-5 bars intentional deceit in connection with the sale of securities. See Chapter 5 for a discussion of the specific provisions of Rule 10b-5.

2. The issuer (i.e., the company itself) does not make disclosures. Information is provided by or upon the authorization of management. Not all insiders have the authority to make disclosures on behalf of the company. Thus, as a practical matter, the disclose-or-abstain rule really means that insiders may not trade in the entity's securities unless the information has been made public based on a management decision to do so. It does not mean that a corporate insider acting on his or her own must blurt out the information so that he or she may buy or sell the company's securities.

3. As examples, disclosure of preliminary merger negotiations or the early promise of a drug that could cure or prevent cancer might be detrimental to the entity if it does not materialize.

4. The duty to disclose in this context is, of course, different from mandatory disclosures called for in 1933 act and 1934 act forms including Form 8–K, which requires current reporting on the occurrence of one or more specific events or transactions (see Chapter 3). The duty to disclose material inside information in such situations is often explicitly required to ensure that the disclosures are complete and not misleading. The most common example of this duty arises in connection with management's discussion and analysis (MD&A), which requires disclosure of information *known to management* that could cause past results not to be indicative of future performance.

5. *TSC Industries v. Northway, Inc.,* 426 U.S. 438, 449 (1976). See Chapter 5.

6. *Basic Inc. v. Levinson,* 485 U.S. 224 (1988).

7. *SEC v. Texas Gulf Sulphur Co.,* 401 F.2d 833, 848 (2d Cir. 1968).

8. *Chiarella v. United States,* 445 U.S. 222 (1980), 463 U.S. at 655 n.14. On the other hand, the Supreme Court made it clear that not everyone who obtains confidential information is prohibited from acting on it without first having disclosed such information. Chiarella was a mark-up man in the composing room of a New York financial printer. Among the documents he handled were announcements of separate takeover bids for five companies. Although the names of the companies involved were concealed (until the night of the final printing), Chiarella was able to identify the target entities accurately before their names were revealed. Without disclosing his knowledge, Chiarella purchased shares of the target companies and then sold them immediately after the takeover attempts were made public. Over the course of approximately fourteen months, Chiarella realized a gain of just over $30,000. Chiarella was convicted of violating Rule 10b-5, and his conviction was upheld upon appeal. The U.S. Supreme Court, however, overturned the conviction, stating that the duty to disclose or abstain does not fall on everyone. Indeed, the Court ruled that the element to make silence fraudulent—the duty to disclose—was not present. Because Chiarella was not a person in whom the selling shareholders of the target companies had placed their trust and confidence (i.e., he was *not* a fiduciary), the Supreme Court held that to affirm his conviction of having committed fraud in violation of Rule 10b-5 would radically depart from the well-established doctrine that the disclose-or-abstain obligation arises from a specific (fiduciary) relationship between the parties.

9. *Dirks v. SEC,* C463 U.S. 646 (1983). Dirks was a security analyst specializing in investment analysis of insurance companies. In March 1973, Dirks was informed by Secrist, a former officer of Equity Funding of America, that the life insurer's assets were overstated as a result of a massive fraud. Dirks investigated the allegations and found corroboration for Secrist's story. Dirks discussed the information he had obtained with a number of his firm's clients, many of whom sold large holdings in Equity Funding. Neither Dirks nor his firm owned or traded Equity Funding stock. Within weeks of Secrist's original allegations, the California insurance authorities uncovered the fraud, and Equity Funding was placed in receivership. Shortly thereafter, the SEC began investigating Dirks' role in the exposure of the fraud and found that he had

violated rule 10b-5 by informing clients and others of Secrist's allegations. The SEC contended that Dirks was a tippee who was in possession of material nonpublic information and thus had inherited the duty to disclose or abstain. Notwithstanding Dirks' position as an investment analyst, the SEC maintained that he had no special license to ignore the insider-trading rules of the federal securities laws. The U.S. Supreme Court took a different position, however, stating that Dirks (the tippee) did *not* inherit an obligation to disclose or abstain because the tipper (Secrist) did not directly or indirectly derive a personal benefit from having tipped the information to Dirks. The Court determined that Secrist was motivated only by a desire to expose wrongdoing. Hence, since the tipper breached no fiduciary duty to disclose or abstain, the Court reasoned, no such obligation attached to the tippee.

10. Although not defined in the 1934 act, the commission and the courts regard a person as a beneficial owner if the securities are held in the name of a spouse or child or in the name of any other person or entity whose relationship would indicate that the individual in question obtains benefits substantially equivalent to those of direct ownership.

11. A number of publications, including the *Wall Street Journal*, regularly report changes in insider holdings. The information is obtained directly from SEC Form 3, on which insiders report their initial holdings, and from Form 4, on which changes in the number of shares held are reported. In addition, on the premise that insiders know best about their company's upcoming fates and fortunes, some investment advisory services use the information from Forms 3 and 4 as a basis for making recommendations regarding a company's stock.

12. The actual term used to describe the give-up of profit by an insider is *disgorge*. The rather vivid dictionary definition of this term is to discharge by mouth, as in vomit.

7

Proxy Rules and Takeover Regulation

The term *proxy* means the authority or power to act for another. In the context of the securities laws, proxies are security holders's votes on corporate matters requiring their authorization or consent. In physical form, a proxy is typically a card on which shareholders cast their ballots "for" or "against" one or more matters up for vote.

Proxies are solicited by company management for any number of matters. The most common are for (1) the election of directors and (2) the ratification of the selection of the company's auditors. Other matters include authorization for[1]

- The adoption or modification of an executive compensation or retirement plan
- The issuance of a new class of security
- A merger or acquisition
- Amendment to the articles of incorporation or bylaws
- The adoption of defensive measures designed to make it more difficult for the company to be acquired in a hostile takeover (see discussion later in this chapter)

THE ANNUAL MEETING

The annual meeting of shareholders represents the focal point of most proxy solicitations. State corporation laws require annual meetings, and large, publicly held corporations with thousands of shareholders usually cannot satisfy quorum requirements unless most shareholders are represented by proxies.[2]

In addition to the business at hand, annual meetings can often be lively affairs sprinkled with pointed questions by attending shareholders, especially when earnings have not met expectations or when the company's share price has languished or dropped.

From management's standpoint, the annual meeting often presents a public relations opportunity. Usually the chairperson, president, and certain other officers and directors will speak to the gathering, thus "personalizing" an otherwise impersonal entity.

SHAREHOLDER PROPOSALS

Not all matters for which proxies are solicited are initiated by the management of a company; proposals may be made by so-called qualified shareholders. A qualified shareholder means being a shareholder for at least one year and owning at least 1 percent of the entity's voting stock (or stock with a market value of $1,000). Under the SEC's proxy rules, a qualified shareholder may present an issue to management for shareholder approval, and the company, whether or not it agrees with the proposal, is required to circulate it to all shareholders for a vote.

Recently qualified shareholders have presented various issues of political or social importance for consideration, such as a proposal to stop a company from manufacturing chemicals known to be destroying the earth's ozone layer. Another proposal sought to ban a company from expanding its South African operations until that country establishes a representative government that will lead it into a nondiscriminatory constitutional democracy.[3]

There have literally been thousands of proposals by shareholders. In the overwhelming majority of cases, these proposals are opposed by management. Only a handful of such proposals have received enough votes to prevail against a contrary management recommendation. Indeed, it is unusual for a shareholder proposal not favored by management to get more than 5 percent of the votes cast. In light of the informal investment rule either to "support management or sell the stock," this should not be surprising.[4]

THE PROXY STATEMENT

The solicitation of proxies is regulated by Section 14 of the 1934 act. Consistent with the overall philosophy of the federal securities laws, the cornerstone of proxy regulation is full disclosure, the focal point of which is the proxy statement.

Under Section 14, shareholders must be furnished with a proxy statement that contains information concerning the matters upon which they are being asked to vote. In addition, every proxy statement must include the following information:

- The date, time, and location of the annual shareholders' meeting
- The identity of the persons on whose behalf the solicitation is being made and the estimated cost of the solicitation (usually the solicitation is made by the board of directors and the cost is borne by the company, even when a shareholder's proposal is included)

- A statement regarding proxy revocability (i.e., whether proxies may be withdrawn after they have been cast)
- A statement regarding the rights, if any, of dissenters on any matter to be voted upon
- The number of shares of the issuer's stock held by each director and executive officer

The Commission's Review of the Proxy Statement

Proxy statements are required to be filed with the SEC ten days prior to distribution to shareholders. As with other 1934 act documents, not all proxy materials are examined by the commission. Although the securities laws do not bestow specific authority on the SEC to comment on a proxy statement before it is sent to shareholders, the staff of the Division of Corporation Finance usually does. Typically, staff comments are communicated informally to the issuer by telephone or fax. Because of the stiff legal complications, the issuer will usually respond to the commission's inquiries and suggestions by modifying the proxy statement.

The Relationship of the Annual Report to Shareholders to Form 10–K

If, as is the case each year for most publicly held companies, directors are to be elected at the annual meeting, shareholders must also be furnished with the company's annual report. This requirement serves two purposes: (1) When electing directors, shareholders are entitled to be informed about the company's financial situation so that they can evaluate the past performance of incumbent management; and (2) without regard to suffrage, shareholders, as investors, are entitled to annual information about the entity in which they have invested their funds.

The annual shareholders' report is the central disclosure document for investors. Recall from Chapter 3 that unlike a 1933 act prospectus a company's annual report on Form 10–K under the 1934 act is *not* routinely furnished to investors.

As part of IDS, however, much of the same information called for in Form 10–K is also required in the annual shareholders' report, thereby closing the integrated disclosure system's loop. Thus virtually the same company-specific information is required (1) in a prospectus covering a 1933 act offering, (2) in annual report Form 10–K filed with the SEC pursuant to the 1934 act continuous reporting scheme, and (3) in an annual report provided to shareholders. In addition, from the issuer's standpoint, the other principal feature of IDS (i.e., incorporation by reference) is complete as well: Company-specific information from Form 10–K may be incorporated by reference into 1933 act registration Form S-2 or S-3, and the same company-specific information included in the annual shareholders' report may simply be incorporated by reference into Form 10–K.

THE ELECTION OF DIRECTORS

A preponderance of proxy solicitations involves the election of directors. Obviously, information regarding the qualifications and backgrounds of such persons is essential to an informed shareholder decision. When directors are to be elected, the following must be included in the proxy statement:[5]

- The names and ages of all directors and director-nominees and the positions and offices they hold with the issuing company
- The business experience and background of directors and director-nominees and their involvement as directors of other publicly held companies
- Family relationships among directors, director-nominees, and executive officers
- Information concerning criminal proceedings against directors and director-nominees during the past five years
- The names of any incumbent directors who failed to attend more than 25 percent of meetings of the board of directors and meetings of committees on which the directors served

In addition, when directors are to be elected *or* when action is to be taken regarding compensation, profit sharing, bonuses, or stock-option plans involving executive officers or directors, information about the manner and amount of compensation for such individuals must also be provided. This information, which is quite elaborate, is generally referred to under the umbrella term *executive compensation*. Thus, besides the annual report, which provides information about the overall financial condition of an entity and which reflects *generally* about management's past performance, investors must also be furnished with *specific* information about incumbent directors and those who have been nominated for directorship.

Executive Compensation

Details about management's remuneration have been required in proxy statements for some time, presumably to enable shareholders to judge for themselves whether they—as investors—were getting their money's worth, so to speak. In 1992, responding to growing concern by investors, particularly institutional investors, that existing rules did not adequately reflect the changing nature of executive compensation, the SEC adopted new disclosure requirements.

The new rules are responsive to recent trends in executive compensation design and practices that focus on long-term compensation packages that provide corporate management with incentives to create shareholder value. Previously, executive compensation emphasized so-called current pay delivery (i.e., a fixed salary plus bonus).

In addition, the revised requirements call for explanations of the manner in which executive compensation is determined and of the relationship between compensation and corporate performance.[6] Specifically, the following information is required about an issuer's chief executive officer (CEO) and each of the four most highly compensated executive officers (other than the CEO). Together these officers are referred to as "named executive officers."

- A summary table detailing the amount and form of current and long-term compensation
- Individual tables supporting the summary table that provide details about each type of long-term compensation
- A discussion of the entity's executive compensation policies generally and of the relationship between the CEO's compensation for the latest year and the company's performance specifically
- A line graph comparing, over the last five years, the cumulative total shareholder return of the company's common stock with corresponding returns of the market in general and of the industry in which the company operates

Figure 7–1, an excerpt from the 1993 proxy statement of Great Lakes Chemical Corporation, illustrates the required summary compensation table, line graph, and discussions concerning executive compensation policies.

EXECUTIVE COMPENSATION AND OTHER INFORMATION

Summary Compensation Table

The following table sets forth certain information regarding compensation paid during each of the Company's last three fiscal years to the Company's Chief Executive Officer and each of the Company's four other most highly compensated executive officers.

| | | Annual Compensation | | | Long Term Compensation | | | |
| | | | | | Awards | | Payouts | |
Name and Principal Position	Year	Salary ($)	Bonus ($)(1)	Other Annual Compensation $ (4)	Restricted Stock Award ($)	Options/ SARs (#)(5)	LTIP Payouts ($)	All Other Compensation ($)(2)(4)
Emerson Kampen,	1992	790,529(3)	280,000	—	—	60,000	—	4,364
Chairman, President, and	1991	650,230(3)	400,000	—	—	100,000	—	—
Chief Executive Officer	1990	585,750(3)	360,000	—	—	80,000	—	—
Robert T. Jeffares,	1992	231,231	50,000	—	—	9,000	—	3,562
Vice President, Finance and	1991	201,154	75,000	—	—	16,000	—	—
Chief Financial Officer	1990	183,204	65,000	—	—	14,000	—	—
Robert B. McDonald,	1992	238,173	48,000	—	—	8,000	—	3,562
Senior Vice President	1991	203,942	70,000	—	—	16,000	—	—
	1990	177,285	70,000	—	—	14,000	—	—
John B. Talpas,	1992	210,923	25,000	—	—	7,000	—	2,810
Vice President, Manufacturing	1991	177,769	45,000	—	—	12,000	—	—
	1990	155,692	35,000	—	—	10,000	—	—
David A. Hall,	1992	194,654	42,000	—	—	8,000	—	3,016
Vice President, Development	1991	156,808	65,000	—	—	14,000	—	—
	1990	129,231	55,000	—	—	12,000	—	—

Figure 7–1

REPORT OF THE COMPENSATION AND STOCK OPTION COMMITTEES
OF THE BOARD OF DIRECTORS ON EXECUTIVE COMPENSATION

The Compensation and Stock Option Committees recognize that the Company's success in the years ahead is dependent on being able to attract and retain executives who have made our past success possible and attracting new executives with the ability to lead the Company into the future. We believe that the executives of the Company are a group of employees committed to maximizing shareholder values through the production of high quality products which meet the needs of our diverse customer base and global markets. Compensation programs consist of base compensation, annual incentive compensation, and long term incentive compensation in the form of stock options.

The Compensation Committee reviews the base compensation of the Executive Officers. In determining individual base salary, the Committee considers the individual's scope of responsibility, experience, individual performance, and compensation surveys of comparable companies. Incentive compensation levels are based on Company and individual performance using measures such as return on equity and earnings per share.

Stock options are another important component of executive compensation. Stock awards are based both on a combination of an individual's contribution to the Company's performance and on the executive's individual performance.

To further align Stock Compensation with shareholder interests, the Board is recommending shareholder approval of the 1993 Employee Stock Compensation Plan ("1993 Plan"). The 1993 Plan will give the Stock Option Committee the flexibility to tailor stock compensation to encourage stock ownership over the long term. See Proposal 3 for more information on the 1993 Plan.

Emerson Kampen's compensation may best exemplify the performance-oriented aspect of the Company's compensation policy. Dr. Kampen was named CEO in 1977. As shown on the enclosed performance graph, the value of $100 invested in Company stock on December 31, 1987 increased to $534.61 by December 31, 1992. This compares to $208.91 and $191.59 for similar investments in the S&P 500 Composite or S&P 500 Specialty Chemical Index. Dr. Kampen's compensation package has been designed to encourage performance in line with the short and long-term interests of the Company's shareholders. We believe that Dr. Kampen's total compensation which is composed of base salary, incentive bonus, and stock option awards is competitive in the marketplace and in line with his and the Company's performance. The Committee used the same factors to determine Dr. Kampen's compensation package as those described for other executive officers.

The Compensation Committee is composed of four members including Dr. Kampen. He is not present when matters concerning his compensation are discussed. The Stock Option Committee is composed of three members, none of whom is or has been an employee of the Company. This report is submitted by the members of the Compensation and Stock Option Committees.

Compensation Committee	Stock Option Committee
Emerson Kampen	John S. Day
John S. Day	Leo H. Johnstone
Leo H. Johnstone	Wesley H. Sowers
Wesley H. Sowers	

Figure 7–1 (*continued*)

Stock Price Performance Graph

The graph below compares the cumulative total shareholder return on the common stock of the Company for the last five years with the cumulative total return on the S&P 500 Composite Index and the S&P Specialty Chemical Index over the same period.

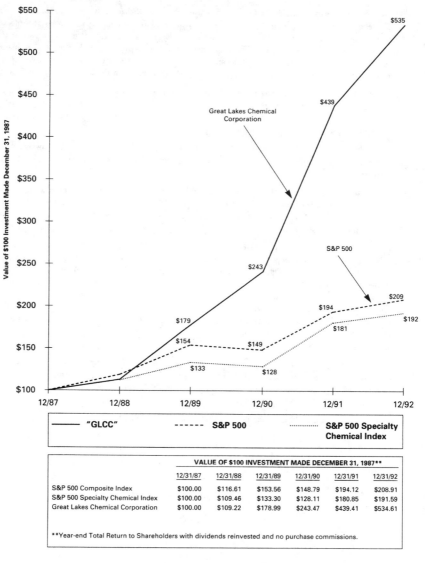

GREAT LAKES CHEMICAL CORPORATION ("GLCC") vs. STOCK INDICES
Five Year Cumulative Total Return to Shareholders

	VALUE OF $100 INVESTMENT MADE DECEMBER 31, 1987**					
	12/31/87	12/31/88	12/31/89	12/31/90	12/31/91	12/31/92
S&P 500 Composite Index	$100.00	$116.61	$153.56	$148.79	$194.12	$208.91
S&P 500 Specialty Chemical Index	$100.00	$109.46	$133.30	$128.11	$180.85	$191.59
Great Lakes Chemical Corporation	$100.00	$109.22	$178.99	$243.47	$439.41	$534.61

**Year-end Total Return to Shareholders with dividends reinvested and no purchase commissions.

Figure 7–1 (*continued*)

APPROVAL OF THE SELECTION OF AUDITORS

The bylaws of many publicly held companies require shareholder ratification of management's selection of auditors. Although neither state statutes nor the federal securities laws mandate such ratification, the SEC believes that involving shareholders in the auditor selection process enhances recognition of the independent accountant's role.

When proxies are solicited for the purpose of approving management's choice of auditors, the following information is required to be disclosed in the proxy statement:[7]

- The name of the accounting firm that has been selected to audit the financial statements of the current year and, if different, the name of the firm that audited the financial statements of the most recently completed year
- A statement regarding whether representatives of the accounting firm will be in attendance at the annual meeting of shareholders and whether the representatives of the firm will be available to answer shareholders' questions

Figure 7–2 illustrates the form of required disclosure for ratification of the selection of auditors. It has been excerpted from the 1993 proxy statement of the Kroger Company. Notice that, although not required, information about audit and nonaudit fees has also been included.

Additional information is required when there has been a change in auditors during the past two years. The circumstances surrounding the change must be described, along with a discussion of unresolved disagreements, if any, between management of the company and the former auditors concerning accounting principles or auditing procedures.

The purpose of these disclosures is to provide shareholders with information about what the SEC terms *opinion shopping* and whether management has sought to engage an accounting firm that is willing to "bend" GAAP to meet the client's desires.[8] (See Chapter

---

SELECTION OF AUDITORS
(ITEM NO. 2)

The Board of Directors, on February 11, 1993, appointed the firm of Coopers & Lybrand as Company auditors for 1993, subject to ratification by shareholders. This appointment was recommended by the Company's Audit Committee, comprised of directors who are not employees of the Company. If the firm is unable for any reason to perform these services, or if selection of the auditors is not ratified, other independent auditors will be selected to serve. Ratification of this appointment requires the adoption of the following resolution by the affirmative vote of the holders of a majority of the shares represented at the meeting:

"RESOLVED, That the appointment by the Board of Directors of Coopers & Lybrand
as Company auditors for 1993 be and it hereby is ratified."

Fees for all audit services provided by Coopers & Lybrand in 1992 totaled $786,545. In addition, fees totaling $47,789 were charged for non-audit services.

A representative of Coopers & Lybrand is expected to be present at the meeting to respond to appropriate questions and to make a statement if he desires to do so.

THE BOARD OF DIRECTORS AND MANAGEMENT RECOMMEND A VOTE FOR THIS PROPOSAL.

Figure 7–2

4 for more discussion of opinion shopping and Figure 4–4 for an example of the required disclosures when there has been a change in accountants.)

The Audit Committee

Every company whose securities are listed on the New York or American Stock Exchange or traded through NASDAQ (the national over-the-counter market) is required to have a standing audit committee composed of a majority of directors who are independent from management.[9] In general the audit committee has oversight responsibility for the financial reporting process, including selection of the entity's independent auditors, subject to ratification by shareholders.

Generally accepted auditing standards (GAAS) require communication with the audit committee concerning the following matters:

- Management's initial selection of or changes in significant accounting policies affecting recognition and measurement of assets, liabilities, revenue, and expenses
- The process used by management in formulating sensitive accounting estimates
- Significant adjustments to the accounts or financial statements resulting from the audit
- Disagreements with management regarding the application of accounting principles
- Consultations between management and other auditors (i.e., potential opinion shopping)
- Difficulties with management encountered during the audit
- Material intentional or unintentional errors or omissions in the financial statements
- Illegal acts by client personnel
- Material weaknesses in the client's internal accounting control structure

The SEC considers the existence of an independent audit committee to be an important part of the overall corporate governance of public companies. Such a committee provides shareholders with an added element of assurance regarding an entity's financial statements.

PROXY CONTESTS

To be sure, not all proxy solicitations are friendly. A proxy contest between one or a group of shareholders on one hand and company management on the other may involve the following:

- The election of directors
- Assistance in a takeover attempt
- Opposition to management's proposals

In a contested election of directors, shareholders dissatisfied with the company's performance seek to elect their own candidates for board membership by attempting to persuade other shareholders that their nominees will do a better job of maximizing the entity's value.

A proxy contest is often combined with a *hostile* takeover bid (i.e., the takeover attempt is opposed by management). Some companies have in place in their bylaws anti-takeover measures that are triggered when an unfriendly bid is made. A proxy contest may be utilized to eliminate one or more of these defensive tactics so that the bidder may proceed with the takeover. (Takeovers and tender offers are discussed in more detail later in this chapter.)

The number of institutional investors holding equity interests in public companies has grown dramatically since the late 1970s. With this growth has come a diminishing willingness of such institutions to blindly support management unquestioningly, especially if past performance has been disappointing. Thus, if management's proposals are perceived as potentially detrimental to shareholder value, institutional investors with large holdings are more likely than ever to oppose such proposals in a proxy contest.

The regulatory scheme for contested proxy solicitations is quite complicated and outside the scope of this book. Suffice it to say that the rules and regulations, which were substantially modified in 1992, are intended to promote—to the extent reasonably possible—equal standing between management and insurgent shareholders and to facilitate the linkup among shareholders to discuss how they might vote on specific matters.[10]

THE INFORMATION STATEMENT

As previously discussed, a proxy statement, together with the company's annual report, must be furnished to shareholders only when proxies are solicited. Thus, if proxies are not solicited for one reason or another, no such statement need be provided to shareholders.[11] Under Section 14 of the 1934 act, however, management is still required to furnish information to shareholders substantially *similar* to that called for when proxies are being solicited, except that the information pertaining to voting procedure is obviously not applicable. The vehicle for communicating to shareholders in the absence of a proxy solicitation is termed the *information statement,* and among other data it must contain (1) full disclosure regarding executive compensation and (2) information on matters that will be acted upon at the annual meeting but on which proxies are not being solicited. In addition, the information statement must be accompanied by the company's annual report. The requirement to provide an information statement thus keeps *nonmanagement* shareholders adequately informed even when their votes are not being sought.

TAKEOVERS

A takeover bid (or tender offer, as it is often called) is an attempt to capture control of what is usually an *unwilling* target company. Typically, a takeover involves an offer by a bidder to purchase shares of a target company directly from the target's shareholders at a premium over the prevailing market price. Quite often a bidder will publicly announce in the financial press its intentions to purchase enough shares to give it control of the target.[12]

A bidder, on one hand, and management of the target company, on the other hand, are natural enemies. A takeover bid typically results from the perception that a target company's stock is undervalued and its earning power unfulfilled. This perception, accurate or not, casts a dark shadow on the performance of a target company's management.

In 1968 Congress passed the Williams Act to provide a framework for the regulation of corporate takeovers.[13] The principal objective of the Williams Act is to protect the investors in a company that is the target of a hostile takeover attempt. The regulatory scheme is a fine-line approach whose purpose is to equalize the positions of the bidder (sometimes referred to as the suitor) and the target company's management, which is trying to prevent the takeover.

The Regulatory Scheme

At the heart of takeover regulation is the so-called early warning system in which a suitor that becomes the beneficial owner of more than 5 percent of the stock of a public company must file disclosure documents with the SEC and also furnish them to the target company's management. In addition, a bidder must provide information about the offer to the target company's shareholders. Among other information, the suitor must reveal its identity and the source of funding for and purpose of the takeover.

The reason for such disclosure presumably is to notify the target company's shareholders of a possible change in control. Thus a shareholder might postpone a planned sale of stock with the expectation of getting a higher price, perhaps as other bidders enter the picture. In addition, if it is not already aware of the bidder's intentions, the target company's management will heed the suitor's early warning and prepare to halt its takeover efforts.

To protect shareholders from having to act hastily, the Williams Act requires that tender offers be held open for at least twenty business days (i.e., four weeks) from the announcement date and an additional ten business days if there is an increase in the offering price. An increase might be necessary, for example, if a sufficient number of shares has not been tendered to give the suitor control or if a competitive suitor emerges. Shareholders that tender shares before a price increase are entitled to receive the same price as those who tender after the increase.

To avoid the herd effect of a first-come, first-served offer, the Williams Act requires a pro rata allocation of shares tendered during the first ten days of a bid if less than 100 percent of the outstanding shares will be purchased. Finally, as a protective measure, shareholders are permitted to withdraw tendered shares for as long as the offer remains open.

Defensive Tactics

The stakes for both the bidder and the target company's management are often quiet high in a takeover attempt. Takeover battles may be waged with military intensity. Over the years, creative bidding strategies have been met by equally inventive defensive tactics.

The following is a list of the more commonly employed measures to prevent a hostile takeover attempt from being successful or to discourage unfriendly suitors from even making a bid.

- *The poison pill.* A special class of preferred stock with exorbitant dividend rights is distributed to existing shareholders. These rights are essentially valueless until a hostile bid is made, at which time they become effective. The bidder must purchase the shares from existing shareholders or continue to pay the high dividends (i.e., forcing the bidder to swallow a poison pill).
- *The sale of crown jewels.* Crown jewels are the target company's most prized assets. By selling them, the takeover target presumably becomes less attractive.
- *Golden parachute.* A golden parachute means an overly generous severance compensation package for senior target management if a hostile bidder gains control of the company.
- *Greenmail.* This technique refers to a maneuver in which an unfriendly suitor accumulates a large block (but not a controlling interest) in a target company. To prevent further accumulations of shares by the bidder, the target company management agrees to buy back the stock at a substantial premium above the existing market price.
- *The pac-man defense.* This term describes the situation in which the target makes a counterbid to acquire the stock of the suitor.
- *Shark repellant.* This term encompasses any number of defense tactics designed to make a takeover attempt unsuccessful. The most common of these is a so-called supermajority provision in the bylaws of a target company that raises the percentage of shareholder votes necessary to approve a merger or sale of the company to as high as 80 percent.
- *White knight.* A white knight is a third company that the target management persuades to make a bid for the target in hopes that it will lead to a friendlier takeover.

Most defensive tactics are designed to thwart a *hostile* bidder from succeeding or from pursuing the target company in a takeover attempt. Thus even though they may be triggered by *any* bid, antitakeover measures usually can be deoperationalized by the board of directors when a friendly suitor appears on the scene or when a hostile bidder changes the terms of its offer so that management now believes it to be in the best interests of the company.

In the mid-1980s, when the last wave of takeover activity was at its peak, companies commonly implemented so-called shareholder rights plans. These plans, however, were typically nothing more than defensive tactics that often were not even submitted to shareholders for a vote. These shareholder rights plans essentially give management the unilateral authority to choose among bidders based on what management determines to be the best deal.

In recent years, investors (particularly institutional investors) have sought to force companies to submit shareholder rights plans to a vote of the shareholders at large. In other cases shareholders that are would-be suitors themselves have initiated proxy contests to have a target company's defensive tactics abolished altogether. Figure 7–3 contains excerpts from the 1993 proxy statement of Allergan, Inc., in which an institutional shareholder has proposed that the board of directors submit its existing poison pill plan to a binding vote of public shareholders. Notice that the shareholder proposal does *not* seek to eliminate the poison pill defense, only to enable shareholders to decide if it should be retained.

STOCKHOLDER PROPOSAL

Proposal 3

Approval of the Stockholder Proposal set forth below requires the affirmative vote of the majority of the votes which all Stockholders present at the meeting are entitled to cast with respect to such proposal.

Stockholder Proposal Regarding the Shareholder Rights Plan

The State of Wisconsin Investment Board, P.O. Box 7842, Madison, Wisconsin (which owns 1,618,700 shares) has notified the Company in writing that it intends to present the following resolutions at the annual meeting.

WHEREAS, our Board has unilaterally adopted a "poison pill" shareholder rights plan which would discriminate against certain shareholders, and refuses to submit this plan to the shareholders for our approval;

WHEREAS, many shareholders, including some who find "poison pill" plans are sometimes desirable, believe that such plans so significantly affect shareholder interests that shareholders should vote on such plans;

WHEREAS, a 1986 study by the SEC's Chief Economist found that "poison pill" plans often harm stockholders by reducing the value of their shares;

WHEREAS, some courts have found that management's adoption of "poison pill" plans violates management's fiduciary duties to the shareholders and "effectively precludes a hostile takeover, and thus allows management to take the shareholders hostage. To buy [the company], you must buy out its management." Another court held that the "pill" creates an impermissible discrimination among shareholders of the same class [and] favors certain shareholders over others";

WHEREAS, during 1990 and 1991 twenty proposals similar to this one received a majority of the votes cast at major corporations; in 1992 the twenty-four proposals voted on received an average of 42% of the votes cast, two receiving over 60%.

THEREFORE, BE IT RESOLVED, that the shareholders request the Board to submit the "poison pill" plan to a binding vote of the shareholders.

Supporting Statement:

Allergan's "poison pill" provides that, when triggered by anyone (or a group) acquiring 20% of its common stock such shareholder's stock will be greatly diluted both in net asset value per share and in voting rights by, in effect, multiplying the voting and economic rights of all *other* shareholders. We believe that these discriminatory provisions, which permit the Board, in its sole discretion, to discriminate against given shareholders, with extremely severe economic consequences to those shareholders, solely because of the size of their holdings, violate fundamental principles of fairness as well as the classical principles of corporate law that all shares of the same class shall be treated identically. We believe that the ability of a self-interested management, to act unilaterally to treat shareholders unequally will inevitably undermine public confidence in the stock market.

Prior to the spinoff whereby Allergan became a public company, management placed in Allergan's Articles of Incorporation numerous provisions which have never been submitted to the public shareholders for their approval, including (i) virtually a flat prohibition against *any* takeover for two years; (ii) a classified board; and (iii) limitations on the ability of shareholders to bring matters up at the annual meeting.

Figure 7–3

We do not oppose all "poison pills." We do believe, however, that the "pill" should be resubmitted for shareholder approval every three years so that the shareholders can decide whether management's performance warrants keeping the "pill" in place for the ensuing period, or whether it should be removed in order to facilitate a change in management.

We therefore believe that Allergan's "poison pill" is sufficiently important, and so materially affects the rights of shareholders, and the potential value of their stock, that it should be submitted to a shareholder vote.

Management's Statement in Opposition:

The Board of Directors and Management recommend that the Stockholders vote **AGAINST** this proposal. Proxies solicited hereby will be voted **AGAINST** the proposal unless a vote for the proposal or abstention is specifically indicated on the proxy.

Allergan's Rights Plan is intended to protect all of the Company's stockholders, not to inhibit any potential change in management. On May 18, 1989, the Board of Directors of the Company and its then sole stockholder declared a dividend distribution of one Right for each outstanding share of Common Stock of the Company. (A summary of the Rights Plan may be obtained from the Company upon written request.) In adopting the Rights Plan, the Company's goal was (and still is) to protect the interests of the Company and all stockholders.

The Rights Plan is designed to prevent an acquirer from gaining control of the Company without offering all stockholders what the Board believes to be the full value of their investment. In particular, the Rights Plan is designed to prevent coercive or abusive takeover practices such as two-tiered, partial or "bust-up" tender offers, "squeeze-out" mergers and self-dealing transactions. Such practices do not treat all stockholders fairly and equally, and pressure stockholders into disposing their common stock at less than fair value. The Rights Plan is also designed to prevent a raider from acquiring a controlling interest in the Company through open market purchases without paying a control premium to all stockholders.

The Rights Plan will not prevent a bidder from making a tender offer for the Company, but it may result in a higher price for all the stockholders if an offer is made. The basic objective of the Rights Plan is to encourage prospective acquirers to come forward with a sound offer at the earliest possible time and to negotiate with the Board. It is well recognized that the price an acquirer is ultimately willing to pay for a company's stock can far exceed the initial offer, especially when the acquirer must negotiate with the target's board of directors.

In contrast to the 1986 study referred to by the proponent, two 1988 Georgeson & Company Inc. studies have found different results. The first 1988 study found that companies with rights plans received substantially higher premiums than companies without rights plans. The second study, which analyzed stock prices over a 21-month period, found that the total appreciation in stockholder value for companies with rights plans was 54.8%, while companies without such plans gained only 45.2%. As an example, the 1988 bid for Federated Department Stores started at $47 per share. A bidding process was made possible by the existence of a rights plan which resulted in a final price of $73.50 per share, an increase of more than 50%.

The Board believes that adoption of the Rights Plan was an essential exercise of its fiduciary obligations to the stockholders. Such exercises of a Board's authority have been consistently supported by Delaware case law. The Delaware Supreme Court has held that adoption of a rights plan is a valid exercise of a board's business judgment. In addition, the Delaware courts, as well as courts in many other jurisdictions, have recognized the appropriateness of rights plans and their value when used in a manner consistent with the fiduciary obligations of a board of directors.

With the Rights Plan in place, the Company's management has been free to concentrate on improving the Company's performance and upon increasing the return to stockholders.

The Board believes that the proper time to consider redemption of the Company's Rights Plan is when a specific offer is made to acquire the Company's stock. Redemption of the Rights Plan prior to that time would expose the Company's stockholders to the abusive takeover tactics of the 1980's, remove any incentive for a potential acquirer to approach the Board, and deprive the Board of the time to evaluate the offer and to maximize value for all stockholders of the Company either through negotiations or the development of alternatives.

It is, therefore, recommended that the stockholders vote AGAINST this proposal.

Figure 7–3 (*continued*)

The Business Judgment Rule

The extent to which corporate management may institute and retain defensive tactics against a hostile takeover is assessed within the context of the "business judgment rule." The corporation laws of all states impose a business judgment rule, which in effect is a rebuttable presumption that directors are better equipped than the courts to make business decisions. To take advantage of this rule, directors must act in good faith and with due care and not in a self-serving manner.

As it relates to antitakeover measures, the business judgment rule gives directors the authority to consider a broad range of factors in deciding what is in the target entity's best interests. Thus the tender offer *price* alone need not be determinative. In addition, management may consider the following:

- The short- and long-term interests of a broad range of constituencies, including the fates of employees, customers, and creditors
- The economy and state of the jurisdictions in which the company operates
- The quality of the consideration (e.g., the default risk associated with bonds or other credit securities to be paid to shareholders)
- Whether, in general, the interests of all involved will best be met if the target remains independent[14]

Shareholders, on the other hand, are primarily interested in receiving the highest price possible for their shares. For the most part they are not concerned with less tangible factors such as the continued welfare of employees or the future of a small town whose economy might be devastated by a plant closing after a takeover. Because of this conflict shareholders have come to question whether antitakeover measures in general have the effect of diminishing shareholder value in favor of the interests of other constituencies.

CHAPTER SUMMARY

Proxies are the votes of security holders on corporate matters. The most common matters for which management solicits proxies are (1) the election of directors and (2) the ratification of the selection of the company's accountants. When proxies are solicited, shareholders must be provided with a proxy statement accompanied by the entity's annual report. For the most part the annual shareholders' report contains the same company-specific information required in Form 10–K filed with the SEC. When directors are to be elected, the proxy statement must contain, among other information, details about executive compensation, including how it is determined and how it relates to corporate performance. Even when proxies are not solicited, the 1934 act requires shareholders to be furnished with an annual report and much the same information called for in a proxy statement.

The Williams Act, which is actually a series of provisions within the 1934 act, regulates corporate takeovers. The Williams Act protects shareholders of the takeover target and attempts to put the managements of the bidder and the target on relatively equal footing. During the 1980s a number of companies adopted various defensive measures (often called shareholder rights plans) designed to prevent unfriendly takeovers. In recent years institutional stockholders have sought to have such plans resubmitted to shareholders for a vote to determine whether they should be retained. In the view of some institutional investors, defensive tactics provide management with too much discretionary authority to choose among bidders for the company.

DISCUSSION QUESTIONS

1. The new executive compensation disclosures focus, in part, on the tie-in between the CEO's compensation and return on investment. Do you think that this emphasis on stock price is appropriate? What other measures of performance could be used?

2. A great many companies seek shareholder approval of the company's selection of auditors. Why do you think this practice is so prevalent?

3. The New York Stock Exchange requires all members of the audit committee to be independent from management. The American Stock Exchange and NASDAQ require only that a majority of directors on the audit committee be independent. Do you think that the New York Stock Exchange's rule is too harsh?

4. Some observers support the idea that every director of a public company should be independent from management. What do you think would be the purpose of such a rule? Discuss the advantages and disadvantages.

5. Do you feel that institutional investors should use their clout to influence corporate managements to make changes in their operations, or do you believe in the "support management or sell your stock" rule. Explain your answer.

ENDNOTES

1. Not all public companies solicit proxies. Thus, when the management group controls sufficient votes to assure the outcome of a matter requiring shareholder approval, there is no need for a general solicitation of proxies.

2. Most companies permit shareholders that have cast their proxies to withdraw them and vote their shares in person if they attend the annual meeting.

3. The SEC has ruled, however, that management need not circulate all such shareholder proposals. Some proposals may be omitted on the grounds that they involve the issuers' ordinary business operations. For example, the SEC has agreed with managements of several companies that proposals to ban smoking or to establish a scholarship fund involved day-to-day operations and thus did not call for a shareholder vote.

4. Larry D. Sondquist, *Understanding the Securities Laws,* 2d ed. (New York: Practicing Law Institute, 1990) p. 227.

5. The same information generally is required not only for directors and nominees but also for executive officers.

6. Reflecting the public's outrage as well against exorbitant executive pay, Congress amended the

tax laws so that executive compensation in excess of $1 million is no longer deductible for tax purposes unless it is based on performance goals set by a compensation committee consisting of independent directors and approved by a company's shareholders.

7. Although not required, some companies also disclose the amount of the audit fee for the most recent year and the aggregate fee for nonaudit (i.e., tax and consulting) services.

8. Information regarding changes in and disagreements with auditors is part of the basic information package (BIP) and thus must be disclosed in 1933 act registration statements and 1934 act Forms 10–K and 10–Q. A change in accountants is also an event that triggers the filing of a current report on Form 8–K. It is considered so important by the SEC that, disclosure in any or all of these forms notwithstanding, a change in accountants must also be reported in the proxy statement.

9. For companies whose securities are listed in the New York Stock Exchange, *all* members of the audit committee must be independent. An audit committee is not a requirement of the SEC but is a condition for listing set by the exchanges and NASDAQ themselves.

10. The 1992 changes to the proxy rules came only after considerable pressure on the SEC, particularly on matters concerning executive compensation and communications among shareholders themselves. Two of the highest and most vocal forces for proxy reform were the United Shareholders of America (USA) and the California Public Employees Retirement System (CalPERS). USA was formed to represent small individual shareholders, who are perceived to have virtually no influence with corporate managements. USA focused on public campaigns designed to embarrass companies it deemed unfriendly to shareholders. CalPERS, on the other hand, is one of the nation's largest institutional investors. CalPERS employs what it calls a long-term view of its holdings and believes that the accountability of corporate managers to shareholders is an essential element of its investment strategy. Although less visible to the public than USA, CalPERS was just as influential in getting corporate managements to become more "shareholder friendly" and in convincing the SEC that changes in the manner in which executive compensation is disclosed were necessary. Both organizations saw management as viewing shareholders as mere investors in a corporation, not as *owners*. CalPERS, of course, still exists. With the 1992 changes to the proxy rules, however, USA saw its mission as complete and thus closed its doors on December 31, 1993.

11. See Note 1.

12. Not all takeover bids are hostile. In some cases management of the target company will court a potential suitor. In other cases a tender offer to shareholders will be supported by management of the target company.

13. The Williams Act is not a separate act; it actually comprises several sections of the 1934 act.

14. A recent quintessential example of a tender offer battle involved the hotly contested and protracted attempt to take over Paramount Communications, Inc., by rival bidders QVC Network, Inc., and Viacom, Inc. Paramount and Viacom negotiated a friendly deal under which Viacom made a tender offer of $62.96 per share for Paramount's outstanding shares, payable in a combination of cash and stock. QVC, an unfriendly suitor, entered the picture and matched Viacom's price. After numerous counterbids by both parties, QVC's tender offer price reached $90.01 per share, which was nearly *$10* per share higher than Viacom's final offer. Nevertheless, Paramount's management rejected QVC's bid on the grounds that a merger with Viacom would be a better long-term fit and that QVC's offer contained too many legal uncertainties.

In response, QVC mounted a court challenge seeking to have Paramount's poison pill defense and "lock-up" arrangement with Viacom struck down. The lock-up arrangement provided that Viacom would receive a fee of $100 million from Paramount (or from QVC, if it took over Paramount) and the option to purchase 23.7 million new shares of Paramount at a price of approximately $70 per share (for which QVC would have to pay $90.01 per share to Paramount under the terms of its tender offer). The lock-up arrangement would thus have cost QVC an extra $600 million to acquire Paramount.

In a move that surprised a number of experts, the Delaware Chancery Court threw out the lock-up arrangement, saying that it effectively discouraged other bids and thus resulted in a breach of fiduciary duty by Paramount's board of directors. In addition, the court ruled that Paramount's board did not adequately consider QVC's offer. Some legal scholars believe that the Chancery Court's decision, which was upheld by the Delaware Supreme Court, reinterprets the business judgment rule as it is applied in that state. Thus it may no longer be sufficient for directors to approve a friendly deal just because they believe it has more long-term value; that belief will have to be based on hard data.

8

The SEC's Small
Business Initiatives

Small businesses represent an important part of the foundation of the U.S. economy. According to the U.S. Small Business Administration, approximately twenty million such entities (1) employ over 50 percent of the domestic labor force, (2) produce nearly half of the gross domestic product, and (3) create the majority of new jobs.[1] In addition, small businesses are often on the cutting edge in the development of new technology, patents, products, and services.

Congress and the SEC have long recognized that a critical aspect in the continued viability of small businesses is access to capital above and beyond that which can be provided by banks.[2] On one hand, smaller firms making a 1933 act offering pay a proportionately higher rate for underwriting commissions and for accounting and legal fees. Moreover, on a relative basis, continuous reporting requirements exact a greater toll of human and economic resources on small businesses than large corporations. On the other hand, however, there is ample evidence that a substantial portion of securities fraud is committed by new speculative enterprises.[3] Such, then, is the dilemma faced by Congress and the SEC: how to ease the financial and regulatory impediments for small companies without compromising investor protection.

The 1933 act empowers the SEC to exempt small offerings and limited offerings from registration. Over the years, these exempt offerings (which are referred to as Regulation A and Regulation D offerings, respectively) have been important sources of financing for enterprises in the development stage and for small, established companies alike. In addition, in 1978 the commission introduced a simplified form (Form S-18) for full *registration* under the 1933 act of securities offered in small IPOs.[4]

RECEN

)f initiatives designed specifically to aid small busi-
mpted by a combination of factors, including the

aller companies
ie inability to obtain financing, small U.S. companies
gy development would have to sell out to foreign

concessions to small businesses, congressional senti-
eet" America) would be unsympathetic to the SEC's
ease the regulatory burden for foreign companies that
the U.S. public or to have their shares traded in the

es that were finding it difficult and costly to raise capi-
c financing abroad

iat a relative handful of smaller U.S. companies had
in "going public" in England, where the regulatory sys-

of small business initiatives, which was proposed and
onsisted of the following measures:

ffering limit was raised to $5 million every twelve

closure format for offering circulars required to be fur-
ation A small offerings was instituted.
npanies to solicit "indications of interest" from prospec-
ring the costs of preparing and filing a Regulation A

mediate *resale* of securities by investors in a Regulation
nillion or less was removed. Previously such securities
ed" securities with limited short-term transferability.
ation D offerings of more than $1 million continue to be

grated disclosure system for registration under the 1933
act and for continuous reporting under the 1934 act was created. Compared with
what is called for in the traditional registration and reporting forms under the 1933
and 1934 acts, significantly less information is required in the new small business
forms.

REGULATION A OFFERINGS

Regulation A is the principal small-offering exemption, although in recent years its use has waned. By raising the ceiling to $5 million as part of the commission's small business initiatives, however, Regulation A has taken on new importance as a mechanism for raising capital without the task of registration under the 1933 act.

Because securities sold in a Regulation A offering are exempt from registration, a full-blown registration statement is not required. An *offering circular,* however, must be filed with the SEC and furnished to prospective investors. Although much information about the company and the securities being sold called for in a prospectus covering securities in *a registered* offer is also required in an offering circular, the information may be provided in considerably less detail than in S-1, S-2, or S-3 filings.

The main advantages of a Regulation A offering over a registered offering are the following:

- A Regulation A offering does not, of itself, trigger entry into the 1934 act continuous reporting system.[7]
- Financial statements in a Regulation A offering circular need *not* be audited (although audited statements that are available because they have been prepared for some other purpose must be included).
- In general, a balance sheet only as of the *latest* fiscal year's end and income statements and cash flow statements for each of the *two* most recent fiscal years must be included in a Regulation A offering. This is in contrast to registered offerings on Form S-1, S-2, or S-3, which call for balance sheets as of each of the latest *two* years and income statements and cash flow statements for each of the *three* most recent years.
- Although financial statements in a Regulation A offering must be in compliance with GAAP, they need not include the expanded disclosures called for by Regulation S-X that are required in registered offerings.
- An issuing company may make written information available to prospective purchasers to determine whether there is any investor interest in the securities being offered. In addition, an issuing company may make a scripted radio or television broadcast to the public at large to solicit indications of interest. Either or both of these steps (referred to as "testing the waters") may be taken *before* costs are incurred to prepare and file an offering circular, only to find out that prospective purchasers have little or no interest in the offering. This is in stark contrast to registered offerings, which prohibit publicity until a preliminary prospectus is filed with the commission.

Testing-the-waters documents are subject to SEC oversight. Any such document (including the actual radio or television script) must be sent to the commission on or before the date it will be used. Only factual information may be included in a testing-the-waters document, but it *must* state that:

- No money is being solicited and will not be accepted
- No sales of securities will be made and no commitment to purchase will be accepted until investors are furnished with an offering circular
- An indication of interest from a prospective investor does not constitute an obligation or commitment

An offering circular becomes "qualified" in a procedure similar to that under which a registration statement becomes effective. Likewise, SEC staff reviews a Regulation A offering circular in the same manner as a full registration statement is examined.[8] Even though Regulation A offerings are exempt from registration under the 1933 act, the antifraud provisions of the securities laws remain applicable to such offerings.

REGULATION D OFFERINGS

Although Regulation D is referred to as the limited-offering exemption, it actually embodies three different exemptions from registration under the 1933 act. The exemptions are known by their respective Regulation D rule numbers. Each exemption has its own set of requirements and restrictions, as summarized in Table 8-1.

The Concept of an Accredited Investor

Rules 505 and 506 refer to accredited investors. The following classes of investors qualify as accredited investors under Regulation D:

- Banks and thrift institutions
- Brokers and dealers in securities
- Insurance companies
- Investment companies
- Pension plans
- Individuals with a net worth of more than $1 million
- Individuals with an annual income in excess of $200,000 ($300,000 when counting spousal income) in each of the latest two years *and* who expect to reach that level again in the current year

By and large, accredited investors are institutional investors thought to have the expertise and savvy necessary to assess the risks and potential rewards of a given investment opportunity. Accredited investors—as a class—are able to fend for themselves and thus are thought not to need the full measure of protection provided to the public at large in a registered 1933 act offering. As explained in Chapter 2, it is precisely this point (i.e., the offerees' need for protection) that distinguishes a private offering from a public one. The antifraud provisions of the securities laws, however, apply to all Regulation D offerings.

TABLE 8-1 SUMMARY OF REGULATION D PROVISIONS

Type of Exemption	Maximum Aggregate Offering Price	Availability	Number and Type of Investors	Resale of Securities by Investors
Rule 504	$1 million	Available only to nonpublic entities	No restrictions	Unrestricted
Rule 505	$5 million	Available to both both public and nonpublic entities	No limit on the number of "accredited" investors; nonaccredited investors limited to	Limited transferability
Rule 506	No limit	Available to both public and nonpublic entities	No limit on the number of "accredited" investors; nonaccredited investors limited to thirty-five. The nonaccredited investors must also qualify, however, as "sophisticated" investors.	Limited transferability

The status of purchasers as accredited investors is important in Rule 505 and 506 offerings. Under both rules, offers may be made to an *unlimited* number of such investors.

The Concept of a Sophisticated Investor

A sophisticated investor is different from an accredited investor. In a Rule 506 offering, *each nonaccredited* investor (either alone or through an adviser) must be a sophisticated investor. Sophistication is defined as having sufficient knowledge and experience in financial and business matters to be capable of evaluating the merits and risks of the offering.

Unfortunately, very little formal guidance exists regarding how sophistication is determined. A professional investment adviser may be presumed to possess the requisite attributes. But what about individual investors who do not utilize the services of an adviser? How are their levels of sophistication measured? Not surprisingly, the courts have tied sophistication to income and net worth. But the SEC must have had more than those traits in mind, or the commission would merely have issued monetary guidelines similar to those set for an individual qualifying as an *accredited* investor.

Although the accumulation of substantial wealth and a substantial annual income are surely indications of investment sophistication, other characteristics play an important role as well, including:

- Prior investment experience

- Intelligence
- Membership or participation in investment groups
- Subscriptions to investment advisory letters

Disclosure Requirements

The information required to be provided in a Regulation D offering depends on (1) under which rule the offering is being made, (2) the amount of the offering, (3) to whom the securities are being offered, and (4) whether the issuer is a publicly held or a privately held company.

In a Rule 504 offering (i.e., $1 million or less), *no* disclosure document whatsoever is required, although prospective investors are likely to request *some* information. Rules 505 and 506 require abbreviated nonfinancial disclosures similar to that of a Regulation A offering.

In a Rule 505 offering or in a Rule 506 offering of $7.5 million or less by a *privately held* company, the financial statement requirements are virtually identical to what must be included in a Regulation A offering (i.e., a balance sheet only as of the latest year and income statements and cash flow statements only for the latest two years). In a Rule 506 offering of more than $7.5 million, the same financial statements that are required in a 1933 act *registration* statement (i.e., balance sheets for two years and income and cash flow statements for three years) must be presented. As with Regulation A, all financial statements must be in compliance with GAAP but need not include additional Regulation S-X disclosures.

Unlike Regulation A, which permits unaudited statements, financial statements in Rule 505 and Rule 506 offerings must be audited. To accommodate small companies, however, Regulation D provides a *hardship* exception to this requirement. If a private company is unable to obtain audits of income statements and cash flow statements without unreasonable effort or expense, only the *balance sheet* is required to be audited. As explained in Chapter 3, it is often very difficult, if not impossible, to audit financial statements of previous years retroactively. Thus as a practical matter, if audited statements are not otherwise available, offerings under Rules 505 and 506 almost certainly will include unaudited statements for prior periods.

A *publicly held* company making a Rule 505 or Rule 506 offering must present the same financial statements required in Form 10–K. This requirement is easily met by simply providing investors with the latest Form 10–K filed with the SEC. In addition, the hardship exception does not apply, because publicly held companies must have their financial statements audited to comply with the requirements of the 1934 act.

The disclosures generally called for by Rules 505 and 506 need only be furnished to nonaccredited investors. Thus no disclosure document at all is required if securities are offered solely to *accredited* investors.[9] This is based on the notion that accredited investors know what information is important and will request it from the issuing company.

Regulation D disclosure requirements and restrictions on the number and type of investors escalate as the maximum aggregate offering price increases. Thus there are no disclosures required nor are there any limitations on who may purchase securities in a Rule 504 offering. But that type of offering is limited to $1 million. Rule 505, which permits offerings of $5 million or less, imposes a limit on the number of nonaccredited investors and also requires that a disclosure document be provided to such investors. Finally, Rule 506, which has no limit on the aggregate offering price, imposes a sophistication test for nonaccredited investors and requires privately held companies to present additional financial information for offerings exceeding $7.5 million.

Limited Resale of Securities

Securities sold pursuant to Rules 505 and 506 of Regulation D are so-called restricted securities having limited transferability.[10] This means that the securities may not be *resold* without full registration under the 1933 act unless another exemption is available. The obvious reason for this resale restriction is to prevent an issuing company from selling securities in an exempt transaction to an underwriter who then immediately resells them to the public at large, thus completely circumventing the registration provisions of the 1933 act.

Notwithstanding this restriction, some relief is available through Rule 144, which permits investors that have held restricted securities for *two years* to resell their shares in limited amounts.[11] If restricted securities are held for at least three years, they may be disposed of without regard to quality.

The two-year holding period is intended to provide evidence that investors that purchase securities in a Rule 505 or Rule 506 exempt offering have not done so with a view of acting as underwriters to immediately reselling them. Thus two years is thought to be long enough to demonstrate that the original purchasers have borne the economic risks of ownership. Consistent with the purpose of an exempt offering, the limitation on amounts that may be resold after two years is based on the idea that small quantities periodically introduced into the market do not resemble a public offering in which a large number of securities hit the market all at once.

To ensure that investors are aware of the limitations on short-term transferability and that purchasers are acquiring the securities for investment purposes, a legend must be placed on each stock certificate in a Rule 505 or Rule 506 offering stating that the securities have not been registered under the 1933 act and that their transferability is restricted.[12]

THE SMALL BUSINESS INTEGRATED DISCLOSURE SYSTEM

Besides amending Regulations A and D to make them more attractive, as part of the SEC's overall program to assist smaller companies in obtaining easier and less-expensive access to the capital markets, it also established the small business integrated disclosure system. In the view of many observers, this represents the most significant action ever taken by the commission to help small companies.

Earlier efforts included the introduction of a separate form (Form S-18) for full registration under the 1933 act of IPOs up to $7.5 million. Form S-18 had somewhat less detailed disclosure requirements than the traditional S forms, but the benefits of less-burdensome disclosure did not carry over to the 1934 act continuous reporting scheme. With the establishment of the small business IDS, so-called small business issuers may now take advantage of a truly integrated system of streamlined registration and periodic reporting under both the 1933 and 1934 acts.

Overall, small business issuers are subject to the same requirements as larger companies. The principal difference is in the *extent* of the information required to be disclosed.

Definition of a Small Business Issuer

A small business issuer is defined as a company with revenues of less than $25 million *and* a public float (i.e., the aggregate market value of its outstanding stock) of less than $25 million. In addition to the tens of thousands of entities that qualify for use of the small business IDS in an initial public offering, the SEC estimates that more than *3,000* entities that are *already* public are eligible to use the new system.[13]

Dedicated Forms

The small business IDS has its own set of dedicated forms. Thus with the exception of Form 8–K for current events, the same form used by larger companies, small business issuers are able to comply with all registration and periodic reporting requirements by utilizing only small business IDS forms.

There are two small business registration forms under the 1933 act:

- Form SB-1 for the registration of securities with an aggregate offering price of no more than $10 million
- Form SB-2 for the registration of securities with no limit on the aggregate offering price

The small business forms under the 1934 act are:

- Registration Form 10–SB
- Annual report Form 10–KSB
- Quarterly report Form 10–QSB
- Current report Form 8–K (the same form used by larger companies)

Disclosure Requirements

In general, the same *types* of disclosures are required of small business issuers and larger companies. One main difference is that Regulation S-B, the small business counterpart of Regulation S-K, does not have the same specificity of detail concerning the information to be presented, thus leaving a small business issuer with more room for judgment regarding the *scope* of disclosure. Another important difference is that certain items that comprise the basic information package[14] for large companies are not required under the small business IDS, including:

- A summary of selected financial data that highlights trends in the company's financial condition
- Quarterly data about sales, gross profit, and earnings

One main advantage of the small business IDS involves financial statement requirements. Small business issuers must present audited financial statements that are in conformity with GAAP, but the statements do not have to comply with the expanded disclosure requirements of Regulation S-X.[15] In addition, a balance sheet only as of the latest year and income statements and cash flow statements only for each of the last two years are required.

Although incorporation by reference into 1933 act *small business forms* is not allowed, small business issuers that otherwise qualify are permitted to use Forms S-2 and S-3 and to incorporate information therein from 1934 act Forms 10–KSB and 10–QSB. This is an important feature of the small business IDS, as it enables smaller, seasoned companies to take full advantage of dramatically streamlined registration Forms S-2 and S-3 while maintaining their reduced disclosure levels in 1934 act reports.

A COMPARISON OF FINANCIAL STATEMENT REQUIREMENTS

As discussed in previous chapters, Congress and the SEC view financial statements as crucial to the operation of full and fair disclosure under the federal securities laws. Moreover, the SEC believes that an independent audit that attests to the accuracy of an entity's financial statements is also an essential element of both the 1933 and 1934 acts. Nevertheless, to one degree or another Regulations A and D and the small business IDS contain requirements calling for financial statements that are less in scope and cover fewer periods than those in traditional 1933 act registered offerings. In addition, Regulation A does not require financial statements to be audited, and Regulation D permits an escape from the requirement for an audit of all periods.

Table 8–2 summarizes the financial statement requirements for exempt offerings under Regulation A and Regulation D (for nonpublic companies) and for registered offerings under the small business IDS. The table also compares these requirements with those for traditional registration under the 1933 act.

TABLE 8-2 SUMMARY OF FINANCIAL STATEMENT REQUIREMENTS

	Regulation A	Regulation D Rule 504	Regulation D Rule 505	Rule 506	Small Business IDS	Traditional 1933 Act Registered Offerings
Balance sheet	Latest year	None	Latest year	Latest year	Latest year	Latest two years
Income statements and cash flow statements	Latest two years	None	Latest two years	Latest two years	Latest two years	Latest three years
Compliance with GAAP	Yes	N/A[a]	Yes	Yes	Yes	Yes
Compliance with expanded disclosure requirements of Regulation S-X	No	N/A	No	No	No	Yes
Audit required	No	N/A	Yes, but only the balance sheet must be audited	Yes, but only the balance sheet must be audited	Yes	Yes

[a]N/A = not applicable.

As it concerns financial statements, the overall scheme seems to be that the highest level of protection should be afforded in large offerings involving a large number of investors. Conversely, the lowest level of protection is provided if only a relative handful of investors is involved or if the offer is for a relatively small dollar amount.

But even within these bounds, there are inconsistencies. An offer for, say, $5 million would not require an audit if made under Regulation A. The same offer made under the small business IDS, however, would require an audit. Finally, that same $5 million offer made under the traditional 1933 act registration system would call for expanded financial statement information covering more years, which would all have to be audited. All three of these offerings would be made to the public at large without regard to the number or type of investors, yet the breadth and depth of financial information and the extent to which the information could be relied upon by investors, through an independent audit, differs for each of the offerings.

CHAPTER SUMMARY

In recent years the SEC has made it easier for smaller companies to access the capital markets. These small business initiatives consist mainly of (1) making exempt offerings more attractive and (2) streamlining the 1933 act and 1934 act registration and continuous reporting processes for smaller businesses.

The main exemptions from registration are Regulation A and Regulation D offerings, which call for much less company-specific information than required in full 1933 act registration statements. A Regulation A offering is limited to $5 million. Although securities may be issued to an unlimited number of investors, a Regulation A offering does not subject the issuing company to the continuous reporting requirements of the 1934 act. Regulation D, referred to as the limited-offering exemption, actually comprises three separate exemptions from registration. Depending which exemption an offer is made under, securities may be offered only to "accredited investors" and to "sophisticated investors." Under most Regulation D offerings, purchasers are subject to limited resales of the securities acquired.

The small business IDS, available only to companies with revenues of less than $25 million and a public float of less than $25 million, calls for less information in documents filed with the SEC than required of larger entities.

Specifically, financial statements of small business issuers must comply with GAAP but are not subject to the additional disclosure requirements of Regulation S-X. In addition, small business issuers are required to furnish financial statements for one less year than their larger counterparts.

DISCUSSION QUESTIONS

1. List the factors that an issuer might consider in choosing Regulation A over Rule 505 of Regulation D in a $5 million offering.

2. The SEC feels that auditors protect public investors. Why, then, do you think that *unaudited* financial statements are permitted in a Regulation A offering? Keep in mind that both Regulation D offerings and registered offerings under the small business IDS must contain audited statements.

3. How do you think that "sophistication" should be determined in connection with a Rule 506 offering? In particular, do you believe that income and net worth guidelines are important? What other characteristics should sophisticated investors possess?

4. Some observers believe that all companies, small or large, should be subjected to the highest level of disclosure under the federal securities laws. They feel, in essence, that small businesses deserve no special treatment. Do you agree? Explain your position.

5. Comment on the observation that the Rule 505 exemption from registration has created a paradox: A disclosure document must be provided to nonaccredited investors that presumably are the least likely to read and understand it, whereas no such documents need be furnished to accredited investors that presumably would benefit the most from the information.

ENDNOTES

1. Securities Act Release No. 6924, March 11, 1992.
2. See Chapter 2 for a discussion of the limitations of bank financing.
3. Louis Loss and Joel Seligman, *Securities Regulation* (Boston: Little, Brown, 1989), p. 1308.
4. Form S-18, which could be used for an offering of no more than $7.5 million, was rescinded in 1992 as part of the commission's broad plan for assisting small companies in gaining access to the public market.
5. In 1993 the SEC made minor modifications to the original initiatives passed in 1992.
6. See Chapter 9 for a discussion of foreign issuers of securities.
7. Regulation A exempt offerings are also available to companies that have previously offered *registered* securities to the public. Thus such companies must continue to file the periodic reports under the 1934 act. Moreover, if as a result of a Regulation A offering the number of an entity's stockholders exceeds 500 *and* the company's total assets exceeds $5 million, *registration* under the *1934* act is required. Such registration makes a company subject to the 1934 act continuous reporting requirements. (See Chapter 3.)
8. Unlike a registration statement, which is filed with the commission's office in Washington, D.C., an offering circular may be filed with the SEC's regional office nearest the issuer's principal place of business. Some observers contend that because regional SEC offices do not employ personnel with the same breadth and depth of knowledge and savvy as are employed in the Washington office, staff reviews of offering circulars are not as rigorous as reviews of registration statements.
9. Even though a disclosure statement must be furnished only to nonaccredited investors, issuers typically provide all prospective purchasers—regardless of their status—with an offering memorandum that contains financial and other information about the issuer.
10. Until 1992 securities sold in a Rule 504 offering were also restricted as to resale. As part of its package of small business initiatives, however, the SEC removed the restriction on free transferability of securities acquired in a Rule 504 exempt offering.

11. The amount that may be resold in any three-month period is generally the greater of 1 percent of the total number of shares outstanding or, if securities of the same class are traded, the average weekly reported volume during the most recent four-week calendar period.

12. In 1990 the SEC adopted Rule 144A, which permits immediate resales of restricted securities under certain circumstances to so-called qualified institutional buyers. Although Rule 144A applies equally to securities of domestic companies, its primary purpose is to assist foreign issuers. See Chapter 9.

13. Securities Act Release No. 6949 (July 30, 1992).

14. See Chapter 3 for a discussion of the basic information package.

15. See Chapter 4 for a discussion of some of these additional requirements.

9

Foreign Issuers and International Offerings

When the federal securities laws were enacted, virtually all public offerings in the United States involved domestic companies. Over the years, however, the number of foreign entities seeking access to U.S. capital has proliferated. From October 1989 through April 1993 alone, 208 foreign companies from thirty countries entered the U.S. public securities markets for the first time. During those same three and a half years foreign companies registered *$80 billion* of securities for sale to the U.S. public. As of May 1, 1993, a total of 530 foreign entities representing thirty-seven countries filed 1934 act reports with the SEC. Of that number, approximately 55 percent were Canadian companies, 12 percent were companies from the United Kingdom or Ireland, 7 percent were from Israel, and 4 percent each were from Australia and Japan.[1]

Some of the principal reasons for entering the U.S. capital markets include the following:[2]

- *Reduced cost of capital.* This is especially true for companies with large funding needs in countries with small, inelastic capital markets.
- *Increased managerial autonomy.* In countries such as Germany and Japan, where bank debt is a primary source of capital, lenders often play an important role in managing the companies they finance. By replacing bank debt with public capital, managers may be able to increase their autonomy.
- *Reduced currency exchange rate risks.* Funding expansion, debt service, and operating requirements with U.S.-raised capital helps reduce exchange rate risks.
- *Enhanced name recognition.* This could result in creating or increasing U.S. demand for a foreign entity's products.

THE INTEGRATED DISCLOSURE SYSTEM
FOR FOREIGN ISSUERS

Foreign companies issuing securities in the United States are, by and large, subject to the same rules and regulations as domestic companies. Thus such companies must register securities under the 1933 act and, to some extent, must file periodic reports with the SEC under the 1934 act.[3]

In 1982, shortly after the commission introduced IDS for domestic issuers, it adopted a separate integrated disclosure scheme for foreign companies. Like the domestic IDS, the foreign system is premised on the idea that a foreign entity already furnishing information on a continuous basis under the 1934 act should be able to use that information in a public offering.

The three principal 1933 act forms under the foreign IDS are F-1, F-2, and F-3. These forms roughly parallel Forms S-1, S-2, and S-3 in the domestic system. As with their domestic counterparts, all three F forms have identical requirements regarding information to be disclosed; the main difference among the forms is the manner in which each F form requires the information to be disseminated.

Form F-3 relies heavily on incorporation by reference of company-specific information from 1934 act reports. Form F-2 also relies on incorporation by reference but requires that 1934 act reports from which information has been incorporated be separately furnished to investors along with the prospectus. Form F-1 requires that all information must be included in the prospectus itself; incorporation by reference from 1934 act reports is not permitted.

Eligibility to use form F-2 or F-3 depends on the status of the issuer and the type of offering being made. In general, to use Form F-3 a foreign issuer must have been subject to the 1934 act continuous reporting requirements for the previous three years and must not have defaulted on debt or preferred stock. In addition, the issuer must have a worldwide public float (i.e., the market value of its common stock) of at least $300 million. An issuer that meets the float requirement is referred to as a "world-class issuer."

To be eligible to use Form F-2, a foreign company generally may be *either* a world-class issuer (i.e., it meets the $300 million float condition) that has *not* been subject to the 1934 act ongoing reporting requirements for at least the past three years or a *non*–world-class issuer (i.e., it does not have a $300 million worldwide float) that *has* been subject to the continuous disclosure requirements for the prior three years. In either case, the issuer must not have defaulted on debt or preferred stock. A non–world-class issuer that has been a 1934 act reporting company for only *one* year may also use Form F-2 provided that investment-grade debt securities are being offered.[4]

Form F-1 must be used when a foreign company is offering securities to the U.S. public for the first time or when the issuer does not otherwise qualify for streamlined registration on Form F-2 or F-3.

Continuous Reporting under the 1934 Act

Foreign companies must file annual reports with the SEC on Form 20-F, the counterpart to Form 10-K for domestic issuers. Unlike U.S. companies, which must file quarterly reports on Form 10-Q, foreign entities are required to file only semiannually on Form 6-K. This represents a significant accommodation to foreign issuers, because no other country in the world requires periodic reporting more frequently than every six months. Thus, if foreign issuers had to file quarterly reports in the United States, they would be forced to prepare financial statements and other disclosures more often than they would in their home jurisdictions.

As another accommodation, the semiannual information filed with the SEC on Form 6-K need be no more extensive than what the issuer is required to furnish to shareholders or to the stock exchange in the company's home jurisdiction.

In addition to being the semiannual reporting form, Form 6-K also functions as the foreign equivalent of current reporting Form 8-K for U.S. companies. For the most part, the events that trigger filing of Form 8-K also require filing of Form 6-K, again limited by the overriding constraint that no information need be furnished to the SEC that is not required in the issuer's home country.

U.S. GAAP and Regulation S-X

Even though the SEC has made some concessions, a number of practical problems face foreign issuers seeking to raise funds from the U.S. public. The major impediment, however, relates to the differences in accounting and disclosure standards between the United States and other countries. Efforts to harmonize accounting and financial reporting rules across countries continue, but the pace of progress is slow and significant differences remain.

Although financial statements of foreign companies may be prepared in accordance with home country principles, the SEC requires that such financial statements be in the same basic form and contain the same informational content as financial statements prepared in accordance with U.S. GAAP and Regulation S-X. In addition, foreign financial statements must be accompanied by a discussion of the differences from U.S. GAAP and by separate *reconciliations* of net income and stockholders' equity computed under home country standards with corresponding amounts computed under U.S. GAAP.[5] In annual reports on Form 20-F the additional disclosures called for by Regulation S-X are not required, but those disclosures *must* be made in financial statements appearing in a 1933 act offering on Form F-1, F-2, or F-3.[6] Thus for all intents and purposes, these requirements have the effect of forcing a foreign issuer to comply with U.S. GAAP and Regulation S-X even though the formal basis of preparation for its financial statements is its home country standards.

Figure 9–1 is an example of the manner in which reconciliations to U.S. GAAP are typically presented. It is taken from a note to the financial statements in the F-1 registration statement of Consorcio G Grupo Dina, S.A. de C.V., a Mexican company that manu-

(19) Reconciliation of Mexican GAAP to U.S. GAAP:

(Thousands of Mexican pesos and thousands of U.S. dollars, except for share and per share data)

	Year Ended December 31,			
	1990	**1991**	**1992**	**1992**
Net Income:				
Net income applicable to majority interest under Mexican GAAP	NPs.113,105	NPs.299,916	NPs.255,895	$ 81,994
Approximate U.S. GAAP adjustments:				
Deferred income tax	(2,546)	(9,200)	(21,361)	(6,844)
Deferred employee profit sharing	(20,685)	(15,113)	(26,772)	(8,578)
Pension plan costs	(4,392)	(2,803)	(7,182)	(2,301)
Gain on zero coupon bond	—	(9,937)	9,937	3,184
Compensation expense for stock sales plan	—	—	(542)	(173)
Subsequent expenses applied to negative goodwill	(11,364)	—	—	—
Effects of inflation accounting on U.S. GAAP adjustments	15,855	9,717	13,427	4,300
Effects on minority interest of U.S. GAAP adjustments	287	2,880	4,602	1,475
	(22,845)	(24,456)	(27,891)	(8,937)
Approximate net income under U.S. GAAP	NPs. 90,260	NPs.275,460	NPs.228,004	$ 73,057
Weighted average common shares outstanding	44,895,240	88,082,620	169,833,640	169,833,640
Approximate net income per share under U.S. GAAP	NPS. 2.01	NPs. 3.13	NPs. 1.34	$ 0.43

Under U.S. GAAP, the utilization of tax loss carryforwards for all income statement periods shown, would not be presented as extraordinary items. Tax loss carryforwards are presented as a component of the tax provision under U.S. GAAP. For 1992, the tax effect of the available tax loss carryforwards (NPs.46,643) was offset against the deferred tax expense.

The adjustment for deferred taxes under U.S. GAAP results mainly from the difference between the book and tax value of property, plant and equipment, the difference between cost of sales and purchases, labor and overhead, reserves and the technology development trust.

Figure 9–1   Reconciliation to U.S. GAAP

factures medium and heavy-duty trucks. Not shown in Figure 9–1 are the discussions of the differences between Mexican GAAP and U.S. GAAP and the additional information required by Regulation S-X.

For most foreign companies, converting to U.S. accounting standards is prohibitively costly, both in terms of time and money. Even for a major company in a country with its own developed accounting and disclosure rules, the cost of conversion can run

	December 31,		
	1991	**1992**	**1992**
Majority Stockholders' Equity:			
Stockholder's equity under Mexican GAAP	NPs.381,953	NPs.512,329	$164,161
Approximate U.S. GAAP adjustments:			
Deferred income tax	(2,861)	(22,931)	(7,348)
Deferred employee profit sharing	(66,808)	(85,219)	(27,306)
Pension plan accumulated costs	(9,870)	(13,278)	(4,254)
Gain on zero-coupon bond	(9,937)	—	—
Receivable from trust for stock sales plan	—	(20,706)	(6,635)
Effects on minority interest of U.S. GAAP adjustments	287	3,167	1,015
	(89,189)	(138,967)	(44,528)
Approximate stockholder's equity under U.S. GAAP	NPs.292,764	NPs.373,362	$119,633

Figure 9–1 Reconciliation to U.S. GAAP (*continued*)

into the millions of dollars and thousands of hours. For companies in countries with lesser-developed accounting systems, the costs are even higher.[7]

Although the SEC has eased a number of other requirements for the benefit of foreign companies, its position regarding compliance with U.S. GAAP and Regulation S-X is unwavering.[8] A number of well thought out arguments on both sides of this highly charged issue can be summarized as follows:

ARGUMENTS AGAINST THE SEC'S POSITION

- The commission's stubbornness will keep foreign companies from entering the U.S. capital markets, thus casting the U.S. stock exchanges and the over-the-counter market in the role of "regional" rather than global marketplaces.

- U.S. citizens can and do purchase foreign stocks. They do so, however, in foreign exchanges at a greater cost than if those foreign securities could be bought in the United States. By making it easier for foreign companies to sell securities in the United States, U.S. citizens would get the benefit of *some* SEC oversight and thus would have more protection than they now have.

- As the most elaborate accounting and disclosure schemes in the world, U.S. GAAP and Regulation S-X simply do not make the U.S. market any more efficient than markets not governed by these rules.

- SEC rules requiring foreign firms to reconcile to U.S. GAAP may actually be counterproductive in that they may reduce investor understanding of the cultural and economic differences among countries. A mechanical reconciliation may even suggest a comparability that does not exist.

- The SEC should generally remain rigid in its stance concerning accounting and disclosure, but exceptions should be made for the 200 or so largest foreign companies. For these entities, the commission should accept home country financial statements. This suggestion is based on the premise that the fates and fortunes of such companies are widely followed by security analysts around the world who have already sorted through accounting differences from country to country.

ARGUMENTS FOR THE SEC'S POSITION

- If U.S. GAAP and Regulation S-X, which together are acknowledged as the most advanced system in the world, do indeed help protect U.S. investors, to require anything less from foreign entities would imply that U.S. investors need more protection from U.S. companies than they do from foreign issuers.
- The SEC believes that the U.S. accounting system is not just the most advanced but that it is also the best in terms of recognition, measurement, and disclosure. To accept any other system would inevitably lead to a flight from quality.

The debate continues, although more and more informed observers and commentators seem to be lining up on the side of compromise. In the meantime, the SEC appears to be adamant, with no indication whatsoever that it will relax the accounting and reporting burden for foreign issuers.

Interim Financial Statements in 1933 Act Offerings

Identical to their U.S. counterparts, foreign companies must generally present the following audited *annual* financial statements in 1933 act registration statements:

- Balance sheets as of the end of each of the two most recent fiscal years
- Income statements and cash flow statements for each of the three most recent fiscal years

Interim statements, which may be unaudited, were until quite recently also required when annual statements would be older than six months on the effective date of the registration statement. This requirement was similar to the rule for domestic issuers whose latest financial statements may not be older than 134 days on the effective date.[9]

The practical implication of the six-month rule, however, was to create another obstacle for foreign issuers by requiring them, under certain circumstances, to provide interim financial information more frequently than what was called for in their home jurisdictions.

In many industrialized nations, the due date for annual financial statements is six months after the end of the fiscal year and the due date for semiannual statements is four months following the close of the semiannual period. Thus, assuming that year-end and semiannual statements of a foreign issuer were not available until their respective home due dates (i.e., June 30 and October 31, respectively, for a company on a calendar year), the period in which a registration statement could not become effective (because the latest financial statements would be older than six months) might extend to a full ten months. This was obviously an unacceptably long blackout.

To alleviate this burden, the SEC recently amended the rules relating to the age of financial statements of foreign issuers. Under the new requirements, unaudited interim statements must be included in 1933 act filings only when needed to bring the most recent financial statements to a date not later than *ten* months from the effective date of the registration statement. Many observers view the new rules as a significant accommodation to foreign companies.

AUDITS OF FOREIGN ENTITIES

The commission's position regarding audits of foreign issuers is as clear and unequivocal as it is about U.S. GAAP. Audits of foreign entities must be conducted substantially in accordance with U.S. generally accepted auditing standards (including standards regarding independence) by an accounting firm knowledgeable about U.S. GAAP and Regulation S-X. A foreign auditor, in all likelihood, will be required to engage, as a consultant, a U.S. accounting firm (or the foreign office of a U.S. firm) that is currently practicing before the SEC and with whose work the commission is familiar. Moreover, in countries without well-developed auditing standards, the SEC will demand a so-called joint audit performed by the foreign firm under the supervision and direction of a U.S. accounting firm. In a joint audit, the auditor's report is signed by both the local auditor and the U.S. accounting firm.

PRIVATE PLACEMENTS

For many foreign entities, compliance with U.S. GAAP requirements and Regulation S-X, the need for interim statements more frequently than semiannually to effect a public offering and adherence to other rules make registration under the 1933 act impractical or even impossible. For those companies that remain intent on entering the U.S. capital markets, the private placement of securities (i.e., through a transaction such as a Regulation D offering that is exempt from registration under the 1933 act) is the only practical alternative. Until recently, though, the severe restrictions imposed on *resales* of securities acquired in an exempt offering, thus resulting in limited liquidity for original purchasers, made foreign private placements relatively unattractive to U.S. investors.[10]

In 1990, following initiatives by the private securities bar, the SEC adopted Rule 144A, which dramatically relaxed the restrictions on immediate resales of privately placed securities. Although Rule 144A applies to domestic companies as well, its adoption was primarily intended to attract foreign entities to the U.S. private-placement market by establishing a more liquid and efficient institutional resale system for unregistered securities.

Unlike related Rule 144, which permits original investors of privately placed securities to resell them only in small increments over a three-year period, Rule 144A imposes no limitations on when such securities may be resold or in what quantities. Rule 144A does, however, restrict resales to so-called qualified institutional buyers (QIBs). In general, banks, thrift institutions, insurance companies, and other financial institutions that own and invest on a discretionary basis at least $100 million of securities are eligible as QIBs. Banks and thrift associations, however, must meet an additional net worth test of $25 million. Broker-dealers also may be QIBs if they own and invest on a discretionary basis at least $10 million of securities.

Rule 144A also imposes a nonfungibility test such that privately placed securities (including American depositary receipts; see Note 3) of the same *class* as securities listed on a U.S. stock exchange or those traded in the national over-the-counter system are not eligible for resale under the rule.

From the foreign issuer's standpoint, a major benefit of Rule 144A is the relatively low disclosure threshold compared with what is required in a 1933 act registration statement. All that is called for is a brief description of the entity's business and the products and services it offers and balance sheets and income statements for the preceding three years. Financial statements need not be audited if audits cannot be "reasonably" obtained, and the financial statements must be only as current as required in the foreign company's home jurisdiction. Finally, financial statements may be prepared on the basis of home country accounting standards *without* a discussion of the variances from or reconciliation to U.S. GAAP.

As with other offerings that are exempt from registration, elaborate disclosures are not required in a Rule 144A private placement based on the "fend-for-themselves" theory. That is, QIBs (like accredited investors and sophisticated investors in Regulation D offerings) are thought to have enough savvy so that they do not need the protection afforded by registration and enough clout to obtain additional information from the issuer.

As an integral part of the commission's attempt to entice more foreign issuers to utilize private placements by adopting Rule 144A, the SEC concurrently approved the establishment of a separate market system for secondary trading of Rule 144A securities. The system, run by the National Association of Securities Dealers, is called private offerings, resales, and trading through automated linkages (PORTAL).

Even though data regarding the number and dollar amount of Rule 144A offerings are not yet available, activity among foreign issuers has been relatively brisk since Rule 144A and PORTAL were introduced.

INTERNATIONAL OFFERINGS BY U.S. ISSUERS

Given the growth in international trade and commerce since the 1970s, a number of U.S. companies have found that penetrating foreign capital markets can be advantageous for many of the same reasons that foreign entities find the U.S. capital market attractive.

A different regulatory problem arises when U.S. issuers offer securities abroad. Under a literal reading of the 1933 act, international offerings by U.S. entities require full registration in the United States. In 1964, however, the SEC took the position that an offering sold in a manner reasonably designed to preclude distribution in the United States did not require 1933 act registration.[11] Twenty-five years of case-by-case interpretations of whether a given international offering did or did not require registration followed.

In 1990 the SEC finally took a definitive stance with the adoption of Regulation S as part of the commission's three-pronged effort (along with the adoption of Rule 144A and the establishment of PORTAL) to facilitate U.S. offerings by foreign issuers and international offerings by U.S. companies. Under Regulation S, two general conditions must be met for an international offering to be deemed to have taken place outside the United States and thus not be subject to the registration requirements of the 1933 act:

- The sale must be made in a so-called offshore transaction in which no offer is made to investors in the United States.
- No direct selling efforts may be made in the United States.

Regulation S also contains certain other requirements depending on the likelihood that securities offered abroad will flow back and ultimately come to rest in the United States and on the extent to which information about the issuer is available to U.S. investors.

As with all other offerings that are exempt from registration, securities sold abroad under Regulation S remain subject to the antifraud provisions of the securities laws.

GLOBAL OFFERINGS

A global offering differs from an international offering. An international offering is made in one or more foreign jurisdictions but does not include an offering of securities in the issuer's home jurisdiction. A global offering combines an international offering with an offering in the company's home country.

Global offerings must, of course, comply with the securities laws of each country affected. For U.S. and foreign issuers alike, this means that registration under the 1933 act will be necessary unless the U.S. tranche is structured as a private placement.

CANADIAN OFFERINGS IN THE UNITED STATES

Until recently, the SEC considered Canadian companies to be the substantial equivalent of U.S. issuers. Although at first blush, this would appear to be favorable treatment, the practicalities were otherwise. For example, Canadian issuers were required to file full U.S. *domestic* disclosure documents (e.g., on Forms S-1 and 10-K). Thus, unlike other foreign companies, Canadian entities were unable to take advantage of any of the commission's concessions. In July 1991 the SEC began treating Canadian companies like other foreign entities, which, among other benefits, gave them access to the foreign integrated disclosure system.

Also in July 1991 the SEC and its counterparts in Canada[12] introduced the multijurisdictional disclosure system (MJDS), which is intended to facilitate U.S./Canadian cross-border securities offerings. Under MJDS, so-called substantial issuers may conduct public offerings in both jurisdictions on the basis of *home* country rules and may satisfy their continuous reporting obligations in both jurisdictions through the use of home country disclosures.

For the most part, substantial Canadian issuers (i.e., those having a three-year continuous reporting history in Canada and meeting certain public float size tests) may offer securities in the United States through the use of the *same* prospectus they file with Canadian authorities. Generally, SEC staff will *not* review MJDS registration statements; instead they will rely on review procedures applied in Canada. Thus a simultaneous U.S./Canadian offering may proceed in the United States immediately after the registration statement has been cleared in Canada.

Under MJDS, substantial U.S. issuers are afforded similar treatment for offerings made in Canada.

The Reasons behind MJDS

Given the commission's position regarding the superiority of the U.S. system, MJDS represents a significant step by the SEC in terms of its recognition of a foreign jurisdiction's securities laws. The SEC chose Canada as a partner for MJDS because of the similarity between the U.S. and Canadian regulatory regimes and because of the substantial presence of Canadian companies in the U.S. capital markets. Although the details differ, the regulatory systems in the two countries share the common purpose of providing investors with adequate and timely information.[13]

The Nagging Problem of U.S. GAAP

MJDS is based on the use by eligible Canadian and U.S. issuers of their respective home country's disclosure documents. By and large, that is true, except as it applies to financial statements. When the reciprocal scheme was negotiated, the SEC insisted that if other than investment-grade debt securities were being offered, Canadian issuers would have to provide reconciliations to U.S. GAAP. The reconciliation requirement, however, was to be dropped on July, 1, 1993, two years after MJDS was established, absent any SEC action to retain it.

Most observers felt that the commission's insistence on a reconciliation to U.S. GAAP undercut the spirit in which MJDS was established. After all, they contended, Canadian accounting standards more closely resemble U.S. rules than do those of any other country in the world.[14] Moreover, observers wondered why the major obstacle to U.S. registration by foreign issuers should not be lifted in a comprehensive system of reciprocity and mutual recognition. In any event, just about every informed source believed that after two years the SEC would simply let the reconciliation requirement lapse.

The SEC did not. Citing significant differences between the two sets of accounting standards that materially affect reported financial condition and operating results, the SEC acted at the eleventh hour to retain the requirement for a reconciliation to U.S. GAAP indefinitely.

The significance of the SEC's decision extends well beyond the U.S./Canadian multijurisdictional system. Indeed, it signals that whatever other accommodations the commission might make for foreign issuers, accounting and financial reporting concessions are out of the question.

RIGHTS OFFERINGS BY FOREIGN ISSUERS

When raising additional equity capital, many foreign companies choose (or are required by law) to offer existing shareholders the rights to purchase the additional shares, often at a substantial discount.[15] The additional shares, like any other public offering in the United States, must, of course, be fully registered under the 1933 act.

Preparing a registration statement, even on streamlined Form F-3 (including a reconciliation to U.S. GAAP), is often considered too burdensome for many foreign issuers. Under the laws of some foreign jurisdictions (including the United Kingdom), not all shareholders must be treated equally. Accordingly, in some instances, relying either on local law or practice, U.S. shareholders of foreign companies have simply been excluded from participating in rights offerings. In such a case, the rights otherwise allocable to U.S. shareholders are sold in the open market with the proceeds remitted to the U.S. shareholders. Even though they receive cash, U.S. shareholders are usually disadvantaged by exclusion; if the offering is at a substantial discount from market, the interests of U.S. shareholders will be diluted. The cash received is often not equal to the lost opportunity to purchase additional shares at a favorable price.

Recognizing this inequity, the SEC has proposed to facilitate cross-border rights offerings by permitting foreign issuers to file only the same disclosure documents required in their home countries, *without* reconciliations to U.S. GAAP. Under MJDS, Canadian companies making rights offerings to existing U.S. shareholders are already able to do so by filing home jurisdiction documents, without U.S. GAAP reconciliations.

CHAPTER SUMMARY

For the most part, foreign issuers of securities in the United States are subject to the same requirements as domestic companies. Foreign issuers must register shares under the 1933 act. Foreign companies are required to file annual report forms with the SEC under the 1934 act, but unlike their domestic counterparts' requirement to file quarterly reports, foreign entities need only file with the commission semiannually. The major practical problem facing foreign issuers is the requirement that financial statements contained in SEC filings must either be prepared on the basis of U.S. GAAP or, if based on home country GAAP, reconciled to U.S. GAAP. The SEC also requires that audits of the financial statements of foreign issuers be conducted in accordance with U.S. GAAS. Recognizing that compliance with U.S. GAAP and GAAS may cause many foreign companies to avoid the U.S. securities markets, the SEC recently eased the rules for private-sector placements of securities of foreign issuers with so-called qualified institutional buyers.

To facilitate international offerings by U.S. companies, Regulation S provides for an exemption from registration under the 1933 act for securities that are offered solely to investors outside the United States. In a major move to accommodate substantial Canadian issuers, the SEC and the Canadian securities regulators recently adopted the U.S./Canadian multijurisdictional disclosure system, whereby eligible U.S. and Canadian public companies are allowed to offer securities in both countries simultaneously on the basis of their home country rules.

DISCUSSION QUESTIONS

1. In addition to those discussed in the text, name some other reasons why a foreign company would want to enter the U.S. capital market.

2. Some observers and commentators have suggested that the periodic reporting requirement for U.S. firms to file quarterly be changed to semiannually. This would not only put the United States in line with other countries, they contend, but it would refocus the American corporation toward decisions for the longer term. Do you feel that this is a valid suggestion? Explain your answer.

3. Under what circumstances, if any, do you feel that the SEC should relent from its position of requiring foreign companies to reconcile to U.S. GAAP?

4. Some have argued that any concessions made to foreign companies (e.g., semiannual instead of quarterly reporting) undermine the securities regulation system in the United States. What is good enough for U.S. companies is good enough for foreign companies, they assert. Do you agree? Explain your answer.

ENDNOTES

1. *Survey of Financial Statement Reconciliations by Foreign Registrants* (Washington, D.C.: U.S. Securities and Exchange Commission, 1993), p. 1.

2. These same reasons may apply to other foreign capital markets as well.

3. Many foreign companies choose to register American depositary receipts (ADRs) instead of the securities themselves. ADRs are certificates evidencing American depositary shares (ADSs), which in turn represent the underlying foreign securities that are deposited with a U.S. bank. ADSs are attractive to U.S. investors because unlike the foreign securities themselves, ADSs settle and are traded on the same basis as U.S. securities. Thus dividends or interest in the deposited securities are payable in U.S. dollars. Many people use the terms ADR (the certificate) and ADS (the security) interchangeably.

4. See Chapter 3 (and note 13 thereto) for a discussion of investment-grade debt.

5. Although rarely used, foreign issuers always have the option of adopting U.S. GAAP as the basis of presentation for their financial statements.

6. Even though instructions to annual report Form 20-F do not require compliance with Regulation S-X per se, as a practical matter many foreign issuers are forced to comply if they plan to incorporate by reference the information therefrom into a 1933 act public offering. This

is because all three 1933 act forms require financial statements that contain the expanded disclosures of Regulation S-X.

7. The author is aware of a situation involving a substantial South American company that estimated its cost of accumulating the necessary U.S. GAAP and Regulation S-X information to be approximately $18 million over twenty-eight months.

8. In 1993, Daimler-Benz Group became the first German company to have its securities listed on the New York Stock Exchange. After years of discussion with SEC officials, Daimler-Benz was not able to get the commission to budge. In the end, the company adopted U.S. GAAP as the basis of preparation for its financial statements. This was seen as an important victory for the SEC. The unique significance of the Daimler-Benz situation is that German accounting principles permit the use of so-called hidden reserves to be increased or drawn upon, as the case may be, to smooth earnings from period to period. Under U.S. GAAP, Daimler-Benz reported significant losses in each of the latest two years; under German accounting rules, it had reported modest profits for the same period.

9. See Chapter 4 for an explanation of the 134-day rule.

10. See Chapter 8 for an explanation of the limited transferability of restricted securities in exempt Regulation D offerings and for a discussion of the piecemeal resales permitted by Rule 144.

11. 1933 Act Release No. 4708 (July 9, 1964).

12. Unlike the United States, Canada does not have a national securities regulatory agency. MJDS was negotiated between the SEC and the various Canadian *provincial* securities administrators.

13. The establishment of MJDS took more than six years and originally was to include the United Kingdom in a three-party reciprocal arrangement. The United Kingdom was dropped because, among other reasons, its securities laws were undergoing substantial change at the time, and the U.K. system was thought to be philosophically too divergent from those of the United States and Canada. It is expected, however, that a separate MJDS between the United States and the United Kingdom will eventually be negotiated.

14. Research suggests that the stringency of a country's securities regulatory scheme in general is highly correlated with its accounting and disclosure standards. A recent survey (Gary C. Biddle and Shahrokh M. Saudagaran, "Foreign Stock Listings: Benefits, Costs, and the Accounting Policy Dilemma," *Accounting Horizons*, September 1991, p. 74) revealed the following overall ranking of the reporting and regulatory regimes of the top eight jurisdictions (from most to least stringent): (1) United States, (2) Canada, (3) United Kingdom, (4) Netherlands, (5) France, (6) Japan, (7) Germany, and (8) Switzerland.

15. The United States has no law requiring that existing shareholders be given the opportunity to purchase more shares before those shares are offered to the public at large. Some corporations do, however, have such a provision in their charters. Over the years, rights offerings by U.S. companies as a financing technique have diminished considerably .

SECURITIES AND EXCHANGE COMMISSION
Washington, D.C. 20549
Form 10-K

[X]   **ANNUAL REPORT PURSUANT TO SECTION 13 or 15(d) OF
THE SECURITIES EXCHANGE ACT OF 1934 [FEE REQUIRED]**

For the fiscal year ended December 31, 1992

OR

[ ]   **TRANSITION REPORT PURSUANT TO SECTION 13 or 15(d)
OF THE SECURITIES EXCHANGE ACT OF 1934 [NO FEE REQUIRED]**

Commission File Number 1-1430

REYNOLDS METALS COMPANY
A Delaware Corporation
(IRS Employer Identification No. 54-0355135)
6601 West Broad Street, P. O. Box 27003, Richmond, Virginia 23261-7003
Telephone: (804) 281-2000

Securities registered pursuant to Section 12(b) of the Act:

Title of Each Class	Name of Each Exchange on Which Registered
Common Stock, no par value	New York Stock Exchange
Preferred Stock Purchase Rights	New York Stock Exchange

Securities registered pursuant to Section 12(g) of the Act: None

Indicate by check mark whether the Registrant (1) has filed all reports required to be filed by Section 13 or 15(d) of the Securities Exchange Act of 1934 during the preceding 12 months, and (2) has been subject to such filing requirements for the past 90 days. Yes √ No ___

Indicate by check mark if disclosure of delinquent filers pursuant to Item 405 of Regulation S-K is not contained herein, and will not be contained, to the best of the Registrant's knowledge, in definitive proxy or information statements incorporated by reference in Part III of this Form 10-K or any amendment to this Form 10-K. [√]

As of February 15, 1993:

(a)   the aggregate market value of the voting stock held by nonaffiliates* of the Registrant was approximately $2.6 billion.

(b)   the Registrant had 59,780,521 shares of Common Stock outstanding and entitled to vote.

DOCUMENTS INCORPORATED BY REFERENCE

Portions of the Proxy Statement for the Annual Meeting of Stockholders to be held on April 21, 1993 - Part III

---

* For this purpose, "nonaffiliates" are deemed to be persons other than directors, officers and persons owning beneficially more than five percent of the voting stock.

NOTE

This copy includes only EXHIBIT 22 of those listed on pages 48-52.

In accordance with the Securities and Exchange Commission's requirements, we will furnish copies of the remaining exhibits listed below upon payment of a fee of 10 cents per page. Please remit the proper amount with your request to:

> Secretary
> Reynolds Metals Company
> P.O. Box 27003
> Richmond, Virginia 23261-7003

Exhibits have the following number of pages:

EXHIBIT 3.1	27	EXHIBIT 10.7	3
EXHIBIT 3.2	19	EXHIBIT 10.8	2
EXHIBIT 4.1	27	EXHIBIT 10.9	7
EXHIBIT 4.2	18	EXHIBIT 10.10	6
EXHIBIT 4.3	165	EXHIBIT 10.11	10
EXHIBIT 4.4	6	EXHIBIT 10.12	9
EXHIBIT 4.5	138	EXHIBIT 10.13	1
EXHIBIT 4.6	18	EXHIBIT 10.14	7
EXHIBIT 4.7	32	EXHIBIT 10.15	7
EXHIBIT 4.8	24	EXHIBIT 10.16	12
EXHIBIT 4.9	5	EXHIBIT 10.17	13
EXHIBIT 4.10	74	EXHIBIT 10.18	1
EXHIBIT 4.11	2	EXHIBIT 10.19	2
EXHIBIT 4.12	2	EXHIBIT 10.20	1
EXHIBIT 4.13	2	EXHIBIT 10.21	1
EXHIBIT 4.14	2	EXHIBIT 10.22	1
EXHIBIT 4.15	10	EXHIBIT 10.23	4
EXHIBIT 4.16	14	EXHIBIT 10.24	3
EXHIBIT 4.17	9	EXHIBIT 10.25	3
EXHIBIT 10.1	21	EXHIBIT 10.26	3
EXHIBIT 10.2	16	EXHIBIT 10.27	3
EXHIBIT 10.3	19	EXHIBIT 10.28	2
EXHIBIT 10.4	6	EXHIBIT 24	1
EXHIBIT 10.5	3	EXHIBIT 25	21
EXHIBIT 10.6	3	EXHIBIT 28	6

TABLE OF CONTENTS

PART I

PART I

Item 1. BUSINESS

Reynolds Metals Company (the "Registrant") was incorporated in 1928 under the laws of the State of Delaware. As used herein, "Reynolds" and "Company" each means the Registrant and its consolidated subsidiaries unless otherwise indicated.

GENERAL

Reynolds serves global markets as a supplier and recycler of aluminum and other products, with its core business being as an integrated producer of a wide variety of value-added aluminum products. Reynolds produces alumina, carbon products and primary and reclaimed aluminum, principally to supply the needs of its fabricating operations. These fabricating operations produce aluminum sheet, plate, can, foil and extruded products (including heat exchanger tubing, driveshafts, bumpers and windows), flexible packaging and wheels, among other items. Reynolds also produces a broad range of plastic products, including film, bags, containers and lids, for consumer products, foodservice and packaging uses. The Company markets an extensive line of consumer products under the Reynolds brand name, including the well-known Reynolds Wrap aluminum foil. Reynolds' largest market is packaging and containers, which includes consumer products. Reynolds is also a gold producer, owning one gold mining operation and having interests in two others.

To describe more fully the nature of its operations, Reynolds has separated its vertically integrated operations into two areas -- (1) Production and Processing and (2) Finished Products and Other Sales.

Production and Processing includes the refining of bauxite into alumina, calcination of petroleum coke and production of prebaked carbon anodes, all of which are vertically integrated with aluminum production and processing plants. These plants produce and sell primary and reclaimed aluminum and a wide range of semifinished aluminum mill products, including flat rolled products, extruded and drawn products and other aluminum products. Examples of flat rolled products include aluminum can stock and machined plate. Examples of extruded and drawn products include architectural and building products. Production and Processing also includes the sale of gold and other nonaluminum products, technology, and various licensing, engineering and other services related to the production and processing of aluminum.

Finished Products and Other Sales includes the manufacture and distribution of various finished aluminum products, such as cans, containers, flexible packaging products, foodservice and household foils (including Reynolds Wrap), laminated and printed foil and aluminum building products. Finished Products and Other Sales also includes the sale of plastic bags and food wraps (for example, Reynolds Plastic Wrap, Reynolds Crystal Color Plastic Wrap, Reynolds Sure-Seal Zipper Plastic Bags, Colorific zipper sandwich bags and Qwik Seal reclosable food storage bags), plastic lidding and container products, plastic film packaging, Reynolds Microwave Wrap cooking paper, Reynolds Freezer Paper, Reynolds Baker's Choice baking cups, Reynolds Cut-Rite wax paper and wax paper sandwich bags, composite and nonaluminum building products, and printing cylinders and machinery.

In September, 1992, Reynolds concluded the sale of its North American electrical cable operations to BICC Cables Corporation ("BICC") and BICC affiliates, with the proceeds of the sale being reinvested in Reynolds' core businesses. Included in the sale were Reynolds' four cable plants located in Malvern, Arkansas, Marshall, Texas, Longview, Washington and La Malbaie, Quebec, and its cable technology center in Marshall, Texas. Reynolds has agreed to provide aluminum redraw rod to the cable plants from its Becancour, Quebec, rod mill under a long-term supply agreement with BICC.

-1-

In January, 1993, Reynolds agreed to sell its Benton Harbor, Michigan aluminum reclamation plant to ALRECO Acquisition Corp., a subsidiary of FFS Inc.   The transaction, which is subject to certain conditions, is scheduled for completion in March, 1993.   Proceeds of the sale will be reinvested in Reynolds' core businesses. The plant, which has an annual rated capacity of 54,000 metric tons, supplies secondary aluminum to the automotive die cast industry.

Information on shipments and net sales by classes of similar products is shown in Table 1.

TABLE 1

Shipments and Net Sales

(Metric tons in thousands, dollars in millions)

	1992		1991		1990	
	Tons	Amounts	Tons	Amounts	Tons	Amounts
Production and processing						
Primary aluminum	275.2	$ 364.4	307.8	$ 426.2	233.2	$ 404.4
Flat rolled	455.6	1,187.4	430.7	1,225.2	434.7	1,330.1
Extruded and drawn	189.2	683.4	189.2	746.8	197.4	844.4
Other aluminum	174.7	398.4	173.3	409.1	185.0	472.5
Other nonaluminum		278.6		331.1		368.4
Gold		98.2		103.7		89.6
	1,094.7	$ 3,010.4	1,101.0	$3,242.1	1,050.3	$3,509.4
Finished products and other sales						
Packaging and containers:						
Aluminum	268.3	1,357.2	272.1	$1,399.6	269.8	$1,378.8
Nonaluminum		522.6		456.6		455.0
Other aluminum	111.1	339.9	96.2	311.9	100.0	350.1
Other nonaluminum		362.5		319.9		329.1
	379.4	2,582.2	368.3	2,488.0	369.8	2,513.0
Net sales	1,474.1	$5,592.6	1,469.3	$5,730.1	1,420.1	$6,022.4
Revenues per pound						
Primary aluminum		$0.60		$0.63		$0.79
Fabricated aluminum products		$1.61		$1.72		$1.79

Financial information relating to Reynolds' operations and identifiable assets by major operating and geographic areas is presented in Note I to the consolidated financial statements in Item 8 of this report.

Reynolds' products are generally sold to producers and distributors of industrial and consumer products in various markets. Information on sales of products by principal geographic and business markets is shown in Tables 2 and 3.

TABLE 2

Principal Geographic Markets

	Approximate Percentage of Sales		
	1992	1991	1990
United States	75%	75%	77%
Canada	5	5	4
Other (Principally Europe)	20	20	19
Total	100%	100%	100%

TABLE 3

Principal Business Markets

	Approximate Percentage of Sales		
	1992	1991	1990
Packaging and Containers	45%	44%	43%
Distributors and Fabricators	15	15	16
Architectural, Building and Construction	12	12	13
Transportation, Aircraft and Automotive	11	9	11
Electrical*	5	5	6
Other	12	15	11
Total	100%	100%	100%

*Reynolds sold its North American electrical cable operations in September, 1992. See "General."

COMPETITION

Reynolds' principal competitors in the sale in North America of products derived from primary aluminum are ten other domestic companies, a Canadian company and other foreign companies. Reynolds and many other companies produce reclaimed aluminum.

In the sale of semifinished and finished products, Reynolds competes with (i) other producers of primary and reclaimed aluminum, which are also engaged in fabrication, (ii) other fabricators of aluminum and other products and (iii) other producers of plastic products. Reynolds' principal competitors in Europe are seven major multinational producers and a number of smaller European producers of aluminum semifabricated products. Aluminum and related products compete with various products, including those made of iron, steel, copper, zinc, tin, titanium, lead, glass, wood, plastic, magnesium and paper. Plastic products compete with products made of glass, aluminum, steel, paper, wood and ceramics, among others. Competition is based upon price, quality and service.

RAW MATERIALS AND PRECIOUS METALS

Bauxite, Alumina and Related Materials

Bauxite, the principal raw material used in the production of aluminum, is refined into alumina, which is then reduced by an electrolytic process into primary aluminum.

Reynolds' bauxite requirements and a portion of its alumina requirements are met from sources outside the United States.

Reynolds has long-term arrangements to obtain bauxite from sources in Australia, Brazil, Guinea, Guyana, Indonesia and Jamaica. Reynolds also obtains bauxite in the open market.

Reynolds refines bauxite into alumina at its Sherwin plant near Corpus Christi, Texas. Reynolds also acquires alumina from two joint ventures in which it has interests, one located in Western Australia, known as the Worsley Joint Venture ("Worsley"), and the other located in Stade, Germany, known as Aluminium Oxid Stade ("Stade"). See Table 4 on page 9 and the discussion of Worsley under "Australia."

Production and purchases of bauxite and production of alumina are adjusted from time to time in response to changes in demand for primary aluminum and other factors.

Australia

Reynolds has a 50% ownership interest in Worsley, which has a rated capacity of 1,600,000 metric tons of alumina per year (expandable to 2,400,000 metric tons per year). Worsley has proven bauxite reserves sufficient to operate the alumina plant at its rated capacity (taking into account future expansions to increase rated capacity to up to 2,400,000 metric tons per year) for at least the next 50 years. The joint venture has no specified termination date.

Reynolds has a long-term purchase arrangement under which it may purchase from a third party an aggregate of approximately 19,000,000 dry metric tons of Australian bauxite for the period 1993 through 2021.

Reynolds has long-term purchase agreements under which it has agreed to purchase from two other third parties an aggregate of 600,000 dry, and 400,000 wet, metric tons, respectively, of Australian bauxite for the period 1993 through 1994.

Brazil

Reynolds and various other companies are participants in the Trombetas bauxite mining project in Brazil. Reynolds has a 5% equity interest in the project and has agreed to purchase an aggregate of approximately 2,800,000 dry metric tons of Brazilian bauxite from the project for the period 1993 through 1999.

Reynolds is also maintaining an interest in other, undeveloped bauxite deposits in Brazil.

Guinea

Reynolds owns a 6% interest in Halco (Mining), Inc. ("Halco"). Halco owns 51% and the Guinean government owns 49% of Compagnie des Bauxites de Guinee ("CBG"), which has the exclusive right through 2038 to develop and mine bauxite in a 10,000 square-mile area in northwestern Guinea. Reynolds has a bauxite purchase contract with CBG which will provide Reynolds with an aggregate of approximately 1,800,000 dry metric tons of Guinean bauxite for the period 1993 through 1995.

Guyana

Reynolds and the Guyanese government each own a 50% interest in a bauxite mining project in the Berbice region of Guyana. Reynolds has a bauxite purchase contract under which it has agreed to purchase 400,000 dry metric tons of Guyanese bauxite from the project in 1993.

Indonesia

Reynolds has a long-term purchase arrangement under which it has agreed to purchase from a third party an aggregate of 1,200,000 dry metric tons of Indonesian bauxite for the period 1993 through 1995.

Jamaica

Reynolds has a long-term purchase arrangement under which it has agreed to purchase from a third party an aggregate of 3,000,000 dry metric tons of Jamaican bauxite for the period 1993 through 1995.

Reynolds' present sources of bauxite and alumina are more than adequate to meet the forecasted requirements of its primary aluminum production operations for the foreseeable future. To utilize excess alumina capacity, Reynolds enters into third-party arrangements providing for the tolling and sale of alumina. Reynolds intends to enter into arrangements to sell bauxite in excess of its needs to third parties.

Other materials used in making aluminum are either purchased from others or supplied from Reynolds' carbon products plants in Baton Rouge and Lake Charles, Louisiana.

Precious Metals

Reynolds is a 50% participant in the Mt. Gibson gold project, a 40% participant in the Boddington gold project, and the owner of the Marvel Loch gold property, all located in Western Australia. Mt. Gibson commenced production in late 1986; Boddington commenced production in mid-1987; and Reynolds acquired Marvel Loch in 1991.

In 1992, Mt. Gibson produced for Reynolds' account 31,900 ounces of gold. Mt. Gibson has a mining and processing capacity of up to 1.1 million metric tons of ore annually using standard carbon-in-leach technology. Beginning in 1993, Mt. Gibson will have the capacity to process an additional 2.0 million metric tons of ore annually using heap leach techniques.

In 1992, Boddington produced for Reynolds' account 138,300 ounces of gold. Boddington has a mining and processing capacity of up to 7.2 million metric tons of ore per year. Beginning in 1993, Boddington will have the capacity to process up to 100,000 additional metric tons of ore annually from a new underground mine. Boddington currently ranks as the largest gold operation in Australia.

The Marvel Loch gold property, the principal asset of Reynolds Yilgarn Gold Operations Limited ("RYGOL"), has a processing capacity of up to 1.0 million metric tons of ore annually. In 1992, RYGOL produced 101,200 ounces of gold.

Each of the Australian sites is being prospected for possible additional reserves. Reynolds is also searching for gold at other sites in Australia and in North America.

ALUMINUM PRODUCTION

Reynolds owns and operates three primary aluminum production plants in the United States and one located at Baie Comeau, Quebec, Canada. Reynolds is also entitled to a share of the primary aluminum produced at three joint ventures in which it participates, one located in Quebec, Canada, known as the Becancour joint venture ("Becancour"), one located in Hamburg, Germany, known as Hamburger Aluminium-Werk GmbH ("Hamburg"), and the third in Ghana, Africa, known as Volta Aluminium Company Limited ("Ghana"). See Table 5 on page 9 and note (h) thereto for information on these primary aluminum production plants. Reynolds also buys primary aluminum on the open market.

Reynolds has a 25% equity interest in Becancour and is entitled to a proportionate share of production. The plant currently consists of three fully operational potlines, each with a capacity of 120,000 metric tons of aluminum per year.

Production at the primary aluminum plants listed in Table 5 can vary due to a number of factors, including changes in worldwide supply and demand. As a result of the oversupply of aluminum on world markets, Reynolds temporarily closed its primary aluminum plant at Troutdale, Oregon in 1991. At December 31, 1992, all plants listed in Table 5, other than Troutdale (which remains idle), were operating at full capacity. See Table 6 on page 10.

Reynolds has an 8% equity interest in C.V.G. Aluminio del Caroni, S.A., which produces primary aluminum in Venezuela.

Reynolds has agreed to acquire a 10% equity interest in the Aluminum Smelter Company of Nigeria (ALSCON), with the Nigerian government and private interests holding the remaining equity. As part of the arrangement, Reynolds will purchase at market-related prices 140,000 metric tons of primary aluminum annually from a 180,000 metric ton smelter being constructed by ALSCON in Nigeria.

Reynolds currently produces reclaimed aluminum from aluminum scrap at Bellwood, Virginia; Sheffield, Alabama; and Benton Harbor, Michigan. See Table 6 on page 10. Scrap for these facilities is obtained through Reynolds' nationwide recycling network and other scrap purchases and from Reynolds' manufacturing operations. In 1992, Reynolds obtained approximately 344,000 metric tons of recycled aluminum from its recycling network and other scrap purchases. Also in 1992, Reynolds completed installation of a recycling and casting plant in Venafro, Italy. Reynolds has agreed to sell its Benton Harbor, Michigan facility. See "General."

FABRICATING OPERATIONS

Reynolds' semifinished and finished aluminum products and nonaluminum products are produced at numerous domestic and foreign plants wholly or partly owned by Reynolds. These plants are included in Table 7 on pages 11-13. The annual capacity of these plants depends upon the variety and type of products manufactured.

In line with Reynolds' strategy to emphasize its downstream fabricating operations, Reynolds has over the past three years (1) continued to upgrade and modernize its extrusion, sheet, plate, foil, can and plastics manufacturing facilities, particularly facilities for production of such high value-added products as can stock and aerospace components, (2) developed new types of, and applications for, aluminum cans, (3) increased its investment in manufacturing equipment and facilities for composite, vinyl and plastic building products, (4) acquired in 1990 a 75% interest in an aluminum wheel plant in Ontario, Canada, and completed an expansion of the plant in 1992, (5) completed an expansion in 1992 of a joint venture facility to produce aluminum cans in Brazil, (6) acquired in 1990 the balance (50%) of the interest in an aluminum can facility in Austria and completed in 1991 an expansion of the facility, (7) doubled in 1990 its foil rolling capacity in Spain, (8) expanded in 1990 its automobile aluminum bumper plant in the Netherlands, (9) completed in 1991 a new aluminum casting facility at its Alloys Plant in Alabama, (10) completed in 1991 an expansion of its Bellwood extrusion plant in Virginia, (11) completed in 1992 an expansion at its McCook sheet and plate plant in Illinois, increasing machined aluminum plate capacity by 50%, (12) entered into an agreement with Mitsubishi Materials Corporation, Mitsubishi Aluminum Co., Ltd. and Mitsubishi Corporation, and an agreement with Sumitomo Light Metal Industries, Ltd., to pursue joint research and development work on new technologies and processes in the production of aluminum extrusion and sheet applications, respectively, for the worldwide automotive industry, both in 1992, (13) announced in 1992 plans to build in Indiana a $26 million fabricating plant to produce aluminum automotive extruded components, with startup scheduled for late 1993, and (14) announced in 1992 the new Spin Flow can necking process (perfected by Reynolds in conjunction with Ball Corporation) for forming the neck of aluminum cans at high speeds.

In line with Reynolds' objective to expand its packaging and consumer products business, Reynolds has over the past three years (1) completed an expansion at Presto Products Company doubling the Company's plastic reclosable food storage bag production capacity, and opened a new Mt. Vernon Plastics Corporation plastics thermoforming plant which produces a variety of plastic products, both in 1990, (2) introduced new products, including Reynolds Qwik Seal reclosable sandwich bags and Reynolds Microwave Wrap non-stick cooking paper, both in 1990, and Regard stretch pallet overwrap film (manufactured by Presto Products Company), Reynolds Sure-Seal Colorific zipper sandwich bags, and Reynolds Micro-Redi microwavable containers, all in 1992, and (3) reintroduced in 1991 Reynolds Cut-Rite wax paper sandwich bags.

ENERGY

Reynolds consumes substantial amounts of energy in refining bauxite into alumina and in reducing alumina to aluminum.

Alumina is produced by a process requiring high temperatures at various stages. These temperatures are achieved by burning natural gas or coal at the alumina plants. Natural gas and coal are purchased under long- and short-term contracts. See Table 4 on page 9.

Primary aluminum is produced from alumina by an electrolytic process requiring large amounts of electric power. Electricity required for Reynolds' primary aluminum production plants is purchased under long-term contracts. See Table 5 on page 9.

Reynolds expects to meet its energy requirements for primary aluminum production for the foreseeable future under long-term contracts. Under these contracts, however, Reynolds may experience shortages of interruptible power from time to time at its Washington, Oregon, New York, Becancour and Ghana reduction plants. Production at Ghana is dependent on hydroelectric power and has from time to time been curtailed by drought.

ENVIRONMENTAL COMPLIANCE

For many years, Reynolds has expended substantial effort and funds on environmental controls in response to regulatory requirements and to ensure that discharges from Reynolds' facilities do not cause any significant degradation of the environment. The area of environmental controls continues to be in a state of scientific, technological and regulatory evolution. For example, the effect of the Clean Air Act Amendments of 1990 on Reynolds' operations will depend on how the Act is interpreted and implemented pursuant to regulations that are currently being developed. Consequently, it is not possible for Reynolds to predict accurately the total expenditures necessary to meet all future environmental requirements. Reynolds expects, however, to add or modify environmental control facilities at a number of its worldwide locations to meet existing and certain anticipated regulatory requirements.

Capital expenditures for equipment designed for environmental control purposes were approximately $58 million in 1990, $44 million in 1991 and $63 million in 1992. The portion of such amounts expended in the United States was $19 million in 1990, $28 million in 1991 and $57 million in 1992. Expenditures in 1992 included $32 million for construction of a facility in Arkansas to convert spent potliner from Reynolds' and other producers' aluminum smelting operations into an environmentally safe material with potential for recycling. Reynolds estimates that capital expenditures for environmental control facilities will be approximately $50 million in 1993 (including $20 million to complete construction of the spent potliner facility begun in 1992) and $20 million in 1994. Future capital expenditures for environmental control facilities cannot be predicted with accuracy for the reasons cited above; however, it may be expected that environmental control standards will become increasingly stringent and that the expenditures necessary to comply with them could increase substantially.

Reynolds has been identified as a potentially responsible party and is involved in remedial investigations and remedial actions under the Comprehensive Environmental Response, Compensation and Liability Act (Superfund) and similar state laws regarding the past disposal of wastes at sites in the United States. Under such statutes, responsible parties can be required to fund remedial action regardless of fault, legality of the original disposal or ownership of the disposal site. In addition, Reynolds is investigating possible environmental contamination, which may also require remedial action, at certain of its present and former United States manufacturing facilities, including contamination by polychlorinated biphenyls (PCBs) at its Massena, New York primary aluminum production plant which will require remediation.

The estimated capital expenditures referred to above do not include costs arising from such remedial actions. Estimating the costs of remedial actions is subject to a number of uncertainties, including the following: the developing nature of administrative standards promulgated under Superfund and other environmental laws; the unavailability of information regarding the condition of potential sites; the lack of standards and information for use in the apportionment of remedial responsibilities; the numerous choices and costs associated with diverse technologies that may be used in remedial actions at such sites; the availability of insurance coverage; the ability to recover indemnification or contribution from third parties; and the time periods over which eventual remediation may occur.

See the discussion on page 19 under "Costs and Expenses" in Item 7 of this report regarding the Company's anticipated costs of environmental compliance.

RESEARCH AND DEVELOPMENT

Reynolds engages in a continuous program of basic and applied research and development. This program deals with new and improved materials, products, processes and related environmental compliance technologies. It includes the development and expansion of products and markets which benefit from aluminum's light weight, strength, resistance to corrosion, ease of fabrication, high heat and electrical conductivity, recyclability and other properties. Materials involving aluminum, plastics, ceramics and various polymers and their processing are also included in the scope of Reynolds' research and development activity. Expenditures for Reynolds-sponsored research and development activities were approximately $37 million in 1990, $37 million in 1991 and $38 million in 1992.

Reynolds owns certain patents relating to its products and processes based predominantly upon its in-house research and development activities. The patents owned by Reynolds, or under which it is licensed, generally concern particular products or manufacturing techniques. Reynolds' business is not, however, materially dependent on patents.

EMPLOYEES

At December 31, 1992, Reynolds had approximately 29,300 employees. In the second quarter of 1992, Reynolds and the United Steelworkers of America and the Aluminium, Brick and Glass Workers International Union agreed to a one-year extension of labor contracts which will expire in May, 1993. In the fourth quarter of 1992, Reynolds approved an early retirement window for eligible salaried employees. Information pertaining to the labor contracts and early retirement window is contained in Item 7 of this report under the caption "Costs and Expenses."

TABLE 4
Alumina Plants and Energy Supply

Plants	Rated Capacity(a) at December 31, 1992 Metric Tons	Energy Purchased(b)	Principal Energy Contract Expiration Date
Corpus Christi, Texas	1,700,000(c)	Natural Gas	1993 (d)
Worsley, Australia	800,000(e)	Coal	2002
Stade, Germany	350,000(e)	Natural Gas	1996

TABLE 5
Primary Aluminum Production Plants and Energy Supply

Plant	Rated Capacity(a) at December 31, 1992 Metric Tons	Energy Purchased(b)	Principal Energy Contract Expiration Date
Baie Comeau, Canada	400,000	Electricity	2011 and 2014
Longview, Washington	204,000	Electricity	2001
Massena, New York	123,000	Electricity	2013(f)
Troutdale, Oregon	121,000(g)	Electricity	2001
Becancour, Canada	90,000(h)	Electricity	2014
Hamburg, Germany	33,000(h)	Electricity	1995
Ghana, Africa	20,000(h)	Electricity	1997(i)

TABLE 6
Aluminum Capacity and Production

(Metric Tons)

Year	Primary Aluminum(j) Rated Capacity(a),(g)	Production(g)	Reclaimed Aluminum(k) Rated Capacity(a)	Production
1990	840,000	852,000	502,000	404,000
1991	991,000	948,000	510,000	414,000
1992	991,000	880,000	510,000	445,000

NOTES TO TABLES 4, 5, and 6.

(a)   Ratings are estimates at the end of the period based on designed capacity and normal operating efficiencies and do not necessarily represent maximum possible production.

(b)   See "Energy."

(c)   In order to balance its alumina supply system, Reynolds has reduced production at its Sherwin alumina plant near Corpus Christi, Texas in connection with the curtailment of operations at its Troutdale primary aluminum plant. See "Aluminum Production." At December 31, 1992, the Sherwin plant was operating at 77% of capacity.

(d)   At current production levels, approximately 85% of the plant's natural gas requirements is purchased under long-term contracts (having terms of up to three years) and the remainder is purchased under short-term contracts. As production increases, additional natural gas requirements will be purchased under short-term contracts. The base term of the long-term contracts referred to above will conclude in the latter part of 1993, but the contracts will extend from month to month unless terminated by one of the parties. New contracts will be negotiated to replace such long-term contracts.

(e)   Reynolds is entitled to 50% of the production of Worsley and of Stade. Capacity figures reflect Reynolds' share.

(f)   The power contract terminates in 2013, subject to earlier termination by the supplier in 2003 if its federal license for a hydroelectric project is not renewed.

(g)   Reynolds curtailed 70,500 metric tons of production at its Troutdale primary aluminum plant in the third quarter of 1991 and the remainder of the plant's capacity in the fourth quarter of 1991. The Troutdale plant remains idle. See "Aluminum Production."

(h)   Reynolds is entitled to 25% of the production of Becancour, 33-1/3% of the production of Hamburg, and 10% of the production of Ghana. Capacity figures reflect Reynolds' share.

(i)   The power contract provides for a 20-year extension at the option of the smelter owners.

(j)   Production is from Reynolds' primary aluminum production operations listed in Table 5.

(k)   Production is from Reynolds' Bellwood, Virginia; Sheffield, Alabama; and Benton Harbor, Michigan reclamation facilities. Reynolds has agreed to sell its Benton Harbor, Michigan facility. See "General."

Item 2. PROPERTIES

For information on the location and general nature of Reynolds' principal domestic and foreign properties, see **Item 1, BUSINESS**. Table 7 lists as of February 15, 1993 Reynolds' wholly-owned domestic and foreign operations and shows the domestic and foreign locations of operations in which Reynolds has interests.

TABLE 7

Wholly-Owned Domestic and Foreign Operations

Manufacturing, Mining and Distribution

Alumina:
Corpus Christi, Texas
Malakoff, Texas

Recycling:
Recycling Plants and
 Centers (U.S.)(700)

Calcined Coke:
Baton Rouge, Louisiana
Lake Charles, Louisiana

Reclamation:
Sheffield, Alabama (2)
Benton Harbor, Michigan
Bellwood, Virginia

Carbon Anodes:
Lake Charles, Louisiana

Mill Products:
Sheffield, Alabama
McCook, Illinois
Bellwood, Virginia
Cap-de-la-Madeleine,
 Quebec, Canada
Hamburg, Germany
Latina, Italy

Primary Aluminum
Massena, New York
Troutdale, Oregon
Longview, Washington
Baie Comeau, Quebec, Canada

Extruded Products:
Torrance, California
Louisville, Kentucky
El Campo, Texas
Ashland, Virginia
Bellwood, Virginia
Richmond Hill, Ontario, Canada
Ste. Therese, Quebec, Canada
Nachrodt, Germany
Harderwijk, Netherlands
Lelystad, Netherlands
Maracay, Venezuela

Aluminum Cans:
San Francisco, California
Torrance, California
Tampa, Florida
Honolulu, Hawaii
Kansas City, Missouri
Middletown, New York
Salisbury, North Carolina
Houston, Texas
Seattle, Washington
Rocklin, California (ends)
Bristol, Virginia (ends)
Enzesfeld, Austria
Guayama, Puerto Rico

Powder and Paste:
Louisville, Kentucky

Electrical Rod:
Becancour, Quebec, Canada

Foil Feed Stock:
Hot Springs, Arkansas

Packaging and Consumer Products:
Waterbury, Connecticut
Louisville, Kentucky
Mt. Vernon, Kentucky
Sparks, Nevada
Downingtown, Pennsylvania
Lewiston, Utah
Bellwood, Virginia
Grottoes, Virginia
Richmond, Virginia
South Boston, Virginia
Appleton, Wisconsin (2)
Little Chute, Wisconsin
Weyauwega, Wisconsin
Rexdale, Ontario, Canada
Cap-de-la-Madeleine,
  Quebec, Canada
Montreal, Quebec, Canada
Latina, Italy

Wheels:
Ferrara, Italy

Gold:
Marvel Loch,
  Western Australia, Australia

Research and Development

Richmond, Virginia:
Can Development Center
Corporate Research
  and Development
  Central Laboratories
Packaging Technology

Building and Construction Products:
Eastman, Georgia
Bourbon, Indiana
Ashville, Ohio
Lynchburg, Virginia
Weston, Ontario, Canada
Montreal, Quebec, Canada
Merxheim, France
Nachrodt, Germany
Dublin, Ireland
Harderwijk, Netherlands
Lisburn, Northern Ireland
Service Centers (U.S.)(44)

Printing Cylinders:
Longmont, Colorado
Atlanta, Georgia
Clarksville, Indiana
Louisville, Kentucky
Newport, Kentucky
Battle Creek, Michigan
St. Louis, Missouri
Phoenix, New York
Wilmington, North Carolina
Exton, Pennsylvania
Franklin, Tennessee
Richmond, Virginia

Can Machinery and Systems:
Richmond, Virginia

Reynolds Aluminum Supply Company:
Service Centers (U.S.)(22)
Processing Centers (U.S.)(2)

Corpus Christi, Texas:
Alumina Technology

Sheffield, Alabama:
Manufacturing Technology
  Laboratory

**Other Domestic and Foreign Operations
In Which Reynolds Has Interests**

Australia:
Bauxite and alumina, gold (2)

Ghana:
Primary aluminum

Belgium:
Building products and extrusions

Guinea:
Bauxite

Brazil:
Bauxite, aluminum cans
  and ends, recycling

Guyana:
Bauxite

Italy:
Machinery and equipment,
  reclamation

Canada:
Primary aluminum, electric
  power generation, aluminum
  wheels, precious metals
  exploration

Philippines:
Mill products, extrusions, foil

Colombia:
Mill products, extrusions,
  foil

Spain:
Mill products, extrusions, foil,
  wire and cable, packaging
  and consumer products, printing
  cylinders

Egypt:
Extrusions

Venezuela:
Primary aluminum, mill products,
  foil, aluminum cans and ends,
  recycling, aluminum wheels

Germany:
Alumina, primary aluminum

Certain of Reynolds' properties are subject to liens of mortgages under project financings or are held under installment purchase arrangements, financing leases or operating leases, none of which is expected to limit Reynolds' use of such properties.

The titles to Reynolds' various properties were not examined specifically for this report.

Reynolds has agreed to sell its wholly-owned Benton Harbor, Michigan reclamation facility referred to above. See the discussion under Item 1 of this report under the caption "General."

Item 3. LEGAL PROCEEDINGS

On January 11, 1993, the Registrant received from the California Earth Corps ("CEC") a 60-day notice of intent to sue under the "Proposition 65" provision of the California Health and Safety Code. The notice alleges that the Registrant's Torrance Can Plant failed to provide a required warning of the public's exposure to certain chemicals listed pursuant to California law. Under California law, if state authorities do not take action within 60 days with respect to the violations alleged in the notice, CEC may take action against the Registrant and receive a bounty if the action is successful. The potential action could seek penalties of up to $2,500 per day of violation. The Registrant has responded to the notice, denying the alleged violations.

As previously reported in the Registrant's Report on Form 10-Q for the Quarter ended June 30, 1992, on July 29, 1992, the U.S. Environmental Protection Agency (the "Agency") filed an administrative complaint against the Registrant alleging paperwork violations and failure to determine whether certain materials in storage constituted hazardous wastes under the federal Resource Conservation and Recovery Act and state hazardous waste regulations at the Registrant's Longview, Washington primary aluminum production plant. The Agency sought $296,000 in civil penalties. Based on the Registrant's response to the complaint, the Agency dropped certain claims and amended others. The Agency now seeks penalties of $110,875. The Registrant disputes the remaining allegations and its position is that the amount of penalties sought is excessive in view of the alleged violations being primarily of a paperwork nature.

Various other suits and claims are pending against Reynolds. In the opinion of Reynolds' management, after consultation with counsel, disposition of these suits and claims and the actions referred to in the preceding paragraphs will not involve sums having a material adverse effect upon Reynolds' consolidated financial position.

Item 4. SUBMISSION OF MATTERS TO A VOTE OF SECURITY HOLDERS

No matters were submitted to a vote of the Registrant's security holders during the fourth quarter of 1992.

Item 4A. EXECUTIVE OFFICERS OF THE REGISTRANT

The executive officers of the Registrant are as follows:

Name	Age	Positions Held During Past Five Years
Richard G. Holder	61	Chairman of the Board and Chief Executive Officer since May 1992. President and Chief Operating Officer 1988-1992. Executive Vice President and Chief Operating Officer 1986-1988. Director since 1984.
Yale M. Brandt	62	Vice Chairman since May 1992. Executive Vice President, Fabricated Industrial Products 1990-1992. Executive Vice President, Fabricating Operations 1988-1990. Senior Vice President, Fabricating Operations 1986-1988. Director since 1988.
Henry S. Savedge, Jr.	59	Executive Vice President and Chief Financial Officer since May 1992. Vice President, Finance 1990-1992. Vice President, Planning and Analysis 1987-1990. Director since September 1992.
Randolph N. Reynolds	51	Executive Vice President, International since December 1990. Vice President 1985-1990. President, Reynolds International, Inc., a subsidiary of the Company, since November 1980, and Chief Executive Officer of that subsidiary since November 1981. Director since 1984.
Donald T. Cowles	45	Executive Vice President, Human Resources and External Affairs since February 1993. Vice President, General Counsel and Secretary 1989-1993. Secretary and Assistant General Counsel 1985-1989.

Harry V. Helton*	58	To retire effective March 1, 1993. Executive Vice President, Metals and Raw Materials since December 1990. Vice President, Raw Materials and Primary Metals Division 1988-1990.
Jeremiah J. Sheehan*	54	Executive Vice President, Consumer and Packaging Products since December 1990. Vice President, Can Division 1988-1990.
J. Wilt Wagner*	51	Executive Vice President, Fabricated Industrial Products since May 1992. Vice President, Mill Products Division 1990-1992. Mill Products Division General Manager 1989-1990. Mill Products Division Operations Manager 1988-1989. Manager of the Company's Listerhill Alloys Plant 1983-1988.
Joseph F. Awad	63	To retire effective March 1, 1993. Vice President, Public Relations since April 1989. Corporate Director of Public Relations 1968-1989.
David C. Bilsing	59	To retire effective March 1, 1993. Vice President, Controller since April 1988. Controller 1979-1988.
Rodney E. Hanneman	56	Vice President, Quality Assurance and Technology Operations since March 1985.
Douglas M. Jerrold	42	Vice President, Tax Affairs since April 1990. Corporate Director of Tax Affairs 1987-1990.
D. Michael Jones	39	Vice President, General Counsel and Secretary since February 1993. Associate General Counsel and Assistant Secretary 1990-1993. Senior Attorney and Assistant Secretary 1987-1990.
John M. Lowrie	52	Vice President, Consumer Products Division since October 1988. General Manager, Consumer Products Division October 1988. Vice President, Marketing and Food Services, Durkee French Foods 1987-1988.
John R. McGill	57	Vice President, Human Resources (formerly Personnel) since 1982.
John M. Noonan	59	Vice President, Construction Products and Properties Divisions since January 1984.
William G. Reynolds, Jr.	53	Vice President, Government Relations and Public Affairs since 1980.
Julian H. Taylor	49	Vice President, Treasurer since April 1988. Treasurer 1981-1988.

---

* Effective upon Mr. Helton's retirement, Mr. Sheehan will serve as Executive Vice President, Fabricated Products and Mr. Wagner will serve as Executive Vice President, Raw Materials, Metals and Industrial Products.

C. Stephen Thomas	53	Vice President, Mill Products Division since May 1992. Vice President, Can Division 1990-1992. Vice President, Operations, Can Division July-December 1990. Vice President, Extrusion Division 1987-1990.
Nicholas D. Triano	61	Vice President, Materials Management since April 1989. Corporate Director, Materials Management 1987-1989.
Allen M. Earehart	50	To succeed David C. Bilsing as Controller, effective March 1, 1993. Director, Corporate Accounting since October 1982.

PART II

Item 5. MARKET FOR REGISTRANT'S COMMON EQUITY AND RELATED STOCKHOLDER MATTERS

The Registrant's Common Stock is principally traded on the New York Stock Exchange. At February 15, 1993, there were 11,177 holders of record of the Registrant's Common Stock.

The high and low sales prices for shares of the Registrant's Common Stock as reported on the New York Stock Exchange Composite Transactions and the dividends declared per share during the periods indicated are set forth below:

	High	Low	Dividends
1992			
First Quarter	$59-3/8	$48-7/8	$.45
Second Quarter	64-3/8	54	.45
Third Quarter	60-1/2	48-5/8	.45
Fourth Quarter	56-5/8	47	.45
1991			
First Quarter	$65-3/8	$52	$.45
Second Quarter	64-7/8	53-3/4	.45
Third Quarter	63-3/4	56-1/8	.45
Fourth Quarter	57-7/8	46	.45

On February 19, 1993, the Board of Directors declared a dividend of $0.45 per share of Common Stock, payable April 1, 1993 to stockholders of record on March 5, 1993.

Item 6. SELECTED FINANCIAL DATA

Consolidated Income Statements (In millions, except per share amounts)

	1992	1991	1990	1989	1988
Net sales	$5,592.6	$5,730.1	$6,022.4	$6,143.1	$5,567.1
Equity, interest and other income	27.7	54.4	53.3	68.0	51.5
Gain on sale of investment	36.1	-	-	-	-
	5,656.4	5,784.5	6,075.7	6,211.1	5,618.6
Cost of products sold	4,761.9	4,760.2	4,823.4	4,775.9	4,292.0
Selling, administrative and general expenses	368.7	378.0	370.1	364.1	339.0
Depreciation and amortization	284.0	265.1	214.2	199.8	183.6
Interest expense	166.8	160.9	96.1	113.0	145.3
Provision for estimated environmental costs	164.0	-	150.0	-	-
Operational restructuring and asset revaluation costs	106.4	-	-	-	-
	5,851.8	5,564.2	5,653.8	5,452.8	4,959.9
Income (loss) before income taxes and cumulative effects of accounting changes	(195.4)	220.3	421.9	758.3	658.7
Taxes on income (credit)	(86.2)	66.2	125.3	225.6	176.7
Income (loss) before cumulative effects of accounting changes	(109.2)	154.1	296.6	532.7	482.0
Cumulative effects of accounting changes (1)	(639.6)	-	-	-	-
Net income (loss)	$(748.8)	$154.1	$296.6	$532.7	$482.0
Amounts per common share					
Primary earnings	($12.56)	$2.60	$5.01	$9.20	$9.01
Cash dividends declared	$1.80	$1.80	$1.80	$1.70	$.90
Other items:					
Total assets	$6,897.0	$6,685.3	$6,527.1	$5,555.6	$5,031.7
Long-term debt, excluding convertible subordinated debentures	$1,797.7	$1,854.3	$1,741.5	$1,115.2	$1,080.1

(1) See Item 8. Financial Statements and Supplementary Data - Note A.

Item 7. MANAGEMENT'S DISCUSSION AND ANALYSIS OF FINANCIAL CONDITION AND RESULTS OF OPERATIONS

Item 7 should be read in conjunction with the consolidated financial statements and notes thereto, and with the other sections of this report.

<u>RESULTS OF OPERATIONS</u>

<u>Shipments</u>

The domestic market for primary aluminum strengthened in 1992 as foreign markets were weakening. The Company's domestic shipments improved approximately 27%, mostly offsetting a decline of more than 40% to foreign markets. Shipments to foreign markets had reached high levels in 1991 reflecting the strength of foreign economies as compared to the U.S.

Shipments of fabricated aluminum products improved approximately 3% in 1992 despite the sale in the third quarter of the Company's aluminum wire and cable operations. Most markets for fabricated aluminum products were adversely affected by the weak economy in 1991 except the consumer and container markets which remained relatively stable. With the domestic economy improving slightly in 1992, higher shipments were realized to the automotive, construction and distributor markets, particularly for sheet and building products. Shipments to the consumer market improved slightly in 1992 but shipments to the container market, particularly can sheet, were lower due to a cooler than normal summer which lessened demand for beer and soft drinks. Shipments by foreign fabricating operations improved slightly despite weakening foreign economies.

<u>Revenues</u>

Depressed prices for aluminum products continue to dramatically affect the aluminum industry and the Company. This has been the most significant factor in the decline of net sales and margins for the past three years. These lower prices have resulted from a worldwide oversupply of aluminum caused by high exports from the Commonwealth of Independent States, start-up of substantial new capacity and economic weakness.

Excluding the cumulative effects of accounting changes and special charges in 1992, the Company's operations remained profitable despite the difficult pricing situation. The Company was able to achieve these results through continued emphasis on cost reduction and performance improvement programs as well as continuing benefits from value-added fabricated aluminum products businesses. These businesses accounted for approximately 70% of net sales over the past three years.

Sales of nonaluminum products continue to be strong, contributing approximately 20% to net sales over the past three years. These products primarily consist of plastics serving the consumer, packaging and construction markets, gold and certain raw materials used in the production of primary aluminum.

In 1992 the Company completed the sales of its 84% interest in Eskimo Pie Corporation, realizing a pretax gain of $36.1 million, and its aluminum wire and cable operations for approximately book value. These dispositions will not have a material impact on future operating results. Proceeds are being used to expand the Company's core businesses serving the consumer, can, flexible packaging and transportation markets around the world.

Costs and Expenses

Certain cost items, such as energy and outside purchases of aluminum scrap and other aluminum products, are related to the price of primary aluminum and have fallen accordingly in 1992 and 1991. Productivity improvements and cost reductions, resulting partly from the Company's capital investment program, have also favorably impacted costs and have more than offset the effects of inflation and increases in depreciation expense. Costs have been adversely affected by rising health care costs and, in 1992, the effects of the early adoption of Financial Accounting Standard (FAS) No. 106 - Employers' Accounting for Postretirement Benefits Other Than Pensions (see Note A to the consolidated financial statements).

In the second quarter of 1992 the Company and its major unions agreed to a one-year extension of labor contracts which will expire in May 1993. The extension agreement, which covers approximately 7,000 hourly employees, provided a cash signing bonus of $1,000 for each hourly employee and an increase in pension benefits. The Company and the unions continue to discuss and analyze major issues, including rising health care costs.

The Company has spent, and will spend, substantial capital and operating amounts relating to ongoing compliance with environmental laws, including regulations to be implemented under the Clean Air Act Amendments of 1990. In 1992 and 1990, the Company recorded charges of $164 million and $150 million, respectively, to cover anticipated environmental remediation costs. These amounts reflect management's best estimates of the Company's ultimate liability for remediation costs, taking into consideration available documentation, studies and cost estimates associated with each site, the extent of the Company's involvement, joint and several liability provisions of applicable laws and the ability to obtain contributions from other potentially responsible parties toward remediation costs. Due to the uncertainties associated with insurance coverage for environmental remediation, insurance recoveries are not considered in estimating the Company's share of anticipated remediation costs. The Company's policy is to accrue remediation costs when it is probable that such efforts will be required and the related costs can be reasonably estimated. As a result of factors such as the continuing evolution of environmental laws and regulatory requirements, the availability and application of technology, the identification of presently unknown remediation sites and the allocation of costs among potentially responsible parties, estimated costs for future environmental compliance and remediation are necessarily imprecise.

On a quarterly basis, the Company evaluates the status of all significant existing or potential environmental issues, develops or revises estimates of costs to satisfy known remediation requirements and adjusts its accruals accordingly. Based upon information presently available, such future costs are not expected to have a material adverse effect on the Company's competitive or financial position. However, it is not possible to predict the amount or timing of future costs of environmental remediation requirements which may subsequently be determined. Such costs could be material to future quarterly or annual results of operations.

The Company recorded charges of $106 million in 1992 for operational restructuring and asset revaluation costs. The charges provided amounts for the disposal of certain uneconomic assets, organizational restructuring and an early retirement option for qualifying salaried employees. These actions are part of the Company's intensive performance improvement process which also includes other cost reduction and improvement programs and stronger emphasis on the Company's value-added businesses. This companywide effort is intended to achieve pretax performance improvements at an annual rate of $250 million by the end of 1993.

The majority of the Company's U.S. inventories and some foreign inventories are carried at LIFO costs which results in the cost of products sold approximating current costs, thereby moderating the effects of inflation on the Company's operating results. For information concerning the effect of LIFO accounting on the Company's results see Note A to the consolidated financial statements.

The increase in interest expense in 1991 was due to higher amounts of debt outstanding and lower amounts of interest capitalized.

Operating Outlook

Due to the continuing worldwide oversupply of aluminum that has severely depressed prices, 1993 is expected to be another difficult and challenging year for the aluminum industry. The Company is particularly concerned about the severity of these conditions in the historically weak first quarter when it expects to incur a loss. The Company is continuing in its efforts to meet this challenge by implementation of the intensive performance improvement process which began in 1992. Gradual improvement should occur as the year progresses and benefits of this process take hold.

Taxes on Income

In 1992 the Company elected early adoption of FAS No. 109 - Accounting for Income Taxes, which resulted in a cumulative effect charge of $29.6 million as of January 1, 1992. The Company has recorded deferred tax assets totaling $745 million as of December 31, 1992 which are subject to evaluation regarding the ultimate realization of such assets. The Company has evaluated the future realization of its deferred tax assets after giving consideration to the availability of carryback opportunities, the reversals of existing taxable temporary differences and, to a lesser extent, certain tax planning strategies and expectations of continued earnings. The realization of a portion of the deferred tax assets resulting from the adoption of FAS No. 106 is dependent upon future levels of taxable income consistent with amounts experienced in recent years. Based upon its evaluation of these matters, the Company has concluded that these deferred tax assets will be realized and it is not aware of events or uncertainties which would significantly affect its conclusions regarding realization. The Company has deferred tax assets relating to certain foreign entities of approximately $40 million against which a full valuation allowance has been recorded. The Company is in the process of evaluating alternatives which may result in the ultimate realization of a portion of these assets. On a quarterly basis, the Company will reassess the future realization of deferred tax assets and, if necessary, adjust its valuation allowance accordingly.

For additional information on the various types of deferred tax items, reconciliation of the effective tax rates and other information concerning taxes, see Note H to the consolidated financial statements.

Mineral Resources and Production

As a vertically integrated manufacturer of primary aluminum and fabricated aluminum products, the Company requires bauxite, an aluminum bearing ore, and alumina for its operations. The Company's present sources of bauxite and alumina (including joint ventures and long-term supply contracts) are more than adequate to meet the forecasted requirements of its primary aluminum operations for the foreseeable future.

The Company's internal sources of primary aluminum include production at wholly-owned facilities and its share of production through participation in three joint ventures. These facilities produced approximately 880,000 metric tons in 1992, 948,000 metric tons in 1991 and 852,000 metric tons in 1990. In 1990 these facilities operated at full capacity. In 1991, due to the oversupply of aluminum on world markets, the Company temporarily closed its facility at Troutdale, Oregon which has a rated capacity of 121,000 metric tons per year. The remainder of the Company's primary aluminum facilities operated at full capacity in 1991 and 1992.

The Company also produces reclaimed aluminum at five domestic facilities (445,000 metric tons in 1992, 414,000 metric tons in 1991 and 404,000 metric tons in 1990). Reclaimed aluminum is produced from recyclable aluminum scrap which is purchased through an extensive national network of collection points and is generated from the Company's fabricating operations.

Gold Operations

The Company has a 40% interest in the Boddington gold mine and a 50% interest in the Mt. Gibson gold mine, both located in Western Australia. In 1991 the Company acquired additional gold assets, principally the Marvel Loch gold property located in Western Australia. The Company's share of the mining and processing capacities at these facilities is approximately four million metric tons of ore per year. The Company's share of gold produced at these facilities was approximately 271,000 ounces in 1992, 263,000 ounces in 1991 and 212,000 ounces in 1990.

LIQUIDITY AND CAPITAL RESOURCES

Working Capital

Working capital totalled $572 million at December 31, 1992 compared to $764 million at December 31, 1991 and $842 million at December 31, 1990. The ratio of current assets to current liabilities was 1.5/1 at December 31, 1992 compared to 1.8/1 at December 31, 1991 and 1.9/1 at December 31, 1990. The decline in working capital was due primarily to an increase in the current maturities of long-term obligations and accruals relating to the adoption of FAS 106.

Working capital would increase if inventories were valued on the FIFO (first-in, first-out) method, which more closely relates to realizable value than the LIFO (last-in, first-out) method. See Note A to the consolidated financial statements for the effects of LIFO accounting on inventories.

Operating Activities

Cash generated from operations in 1992 provided amounts for investing activities and financing activities. Cash generated from operations in 1991 and 1990 was supplemented with borrowings to meet the needs of investing activities.

Investing Activities

Substantial investments have been made to strengthen the Company's raw materials base. Expansions at the Company's lowest cost primary aluminum facilities in Quebec, Canada were completed in 1991. Annual capacity at the Company's wholly-owned facility at Baie Comeau was increased by 120,000 metric tons to 400,000 metric tons. Annual capacity at the Company's 25% owned facility at Becancour was increased by 120,000 metric tons to 360,000 metric tons. To support the primary aluminum expansions, modernizations and expansions have been completed at bauxite, alumina and carbon anode operations. Modernizations and expansions have also been completed at the Company's aluminum recycling operations including the completion of an Italian facility in 1992. In addition, a new facility is being constructed in Arkansas that will process spent potliner from primary aluminum operations into environmentally acceptable residues.

Substantial investments have also been made and are continuing to strengthen the Company's value-added aluminum fabricating operations that serve the packaging, consumer, transportation and construction markets. Modernizations and expansions have been completed at sheet, plate, can, foil and extrusion facilities. Most significant is a major modernization program at the Company's aluminum sheet facility in Alabama which includes the construction of a state-of-the-art cast house that was completed in 1991. In addition the Company completed construction of a Canadian redraw rod facility in 1992, is a 35% participant in a Brazilian can facility that was constructed in 1990 and expanded in 1992 and is a minority participant in a joint venture to construct an aluminum foil mill in Russia.

In nonaluminum operations, investments have been made to expand capacity at plastic film, container and bag facilities and at gold operations in Western Australia.

Acquisitions in the past three years include a 75% interest in an aluminum wheel production facility in Canada and the remaining 50% interest in an Austrian can facility in 1990 and a gold operation in Western Australia in 1991. The Canadian wheel facility was expanded in 1992 and the Austrian can facility was expanded in 1991.

The proceeds from the sales of assets in 1992 relate primarily to sales of the Company's investment in Eskimo Pie Corporation and its aluminum wire and cable operations.

<u>Financing Activities</u>

In 1990 the Company increased its shelf registration to $1 billion, increased the authorized amount of its commercial paper program to $350 million and borrowed $150 million under a bank credit agreement (which was voluntarily prepaid in 1992). Debt securities issued under the shelf registration in 1990 consisted of $200 million of floating rate notes (which were voluntarily prepaid in 1991) and $288 million of medium term notes at an average rate of 9.5% and maturing in 1991 to 2005. The proceeds were used for financing needs arising from the Company's capital investment program.

In 1991 the Company increased the shelf registration to $1.65 billion. Debt securities issued under the shelf registration in 1991 consisted of $100 million of 9% debentures due 2003 and $406 million of medium term notes at an average rate of 9.1% and maturing in 1997 to 2006. These proceeds and a net increase in short-term borrowings of approximately $120 million were used for the Company's capital investment program and to make a voluntary prepayment of $200 million on the Company's floating rate notes and for other net reductions in long-term obligations of $187 million.

In 1992 the Company issued $97 million of medium term notes under the shelf registration, $43 million of tax-exempt bonds and had a net increase in short-term borrowings of approximately $200 million, of which $173 million has been reclassified to long-term. The medium term notes were issued at an average rate of 8.3% and mature in 1999 to 2007. The tax-exempt bonds were issued at a variable rate and mature in 2022. The proceeds were used for voluntary prepayments on higher cost debt, scheduled debt payments and other financing activities. A portion of the proceeds from the tax-exempt bonds is being temporarily invested pending expenditures on the spent potliner facility in Arkansas.

<u>Financial Outlook</u>

Capital investments in 1993 are presently expected to be in a range of $300 to $325 million. The Arkansas spent potliner facility, funded primarily with tax-exempt debt, is expected to be completed in 1993. With a stronger raw materials base, the Company is continuing to concentrate on value-added aluminum fabricating businesses. Major projects include a new automotive extrusions facility in Indiana, continuing improvements at the Alabama sheet facility, expansion and modernization of domestic can body and end facilities and equipment upgrades at European extrusion operations that serve automotive, construction and other markets. These expenditures are expected to be funded primarily with cash generated by operations.

At December 31, 1992 $300 million of the Company's $1.65 billion shelf registration remained available for the issuance of debt securities. In early 1993, the Company issued $50 million of medium term notes under the shelf registration. In the first half of 1993, the Company intends to issue $285 million of debt securities under a new shelf registration and to borrow $150 million under a five-year bank credit agreement. The proceeds from these borrowings will be used to voluntarily prepay $150 million of the term loan agreement and approximately $335 million of short-term obligations. These actions are being taken to lower the Company's overall borrowing costs, extend debt maturities and to take advantage of certain foreign tax benefits, of which $4.8 million were realized in the fourth quarter of 1992. Other financing activities in 1993 are expected to generally consist of advantageous refinancing opportunities.

Item 8. FINANCIAL STATEMENTS AND SUPPLEMENTARY DATA

STATEMENT OF CONSOLIDATED INCOME AND RETAINED EARNINGS

Reynolds Metals Company

Years ended December 31, 1992, 1991 and 1990

(In millions, except per share amounts)	1992	1991	1990
REVENUES			
Net sales	$5,592.6	$5,730.1	$6,022.4
Equity, interest and other income	27.7	54.4	53.3
Gain on sale of investment	36.1	-	-
	5,656.4	5,784.5	6,075.7
COSTS AND EXPENSES			
Cost of products sold	4,761.9	4,760.2	4,823.4
Selling, administrative and general expenses	368.7	378.0	370.1
Provision for depreciation and amortization	284.0	265.1	214.2
Interest - principally on long-term obligations	166.8	160.9	96.1
Provision for estimated environmental costs	164.0	-	150.0
Operational restructuring and asset revaluation costs	106.4	-	-
	5,851.8	5,564.2	5,653.8
EARNINGS			
Income (loss) before income taxes and cumulative effects of accounting changes	(195.4)	220.3	421.9
Taxes on income (credit)	(86.2)	66.2	125.3
Income (loss) before cumulative effects of accounting changes	(109.2)	154.1	296.6
Cumulative effects of accounting changes (Note A)	(639.6)	-	-
NET INCOME (LOSS)	(748.8)	154.1	296.6
RETAINED EARNINGS			
Balance at beginning of year	2,203.9	2,156.6	1,966.5
	1,455.1	2,310.7	2,263.1
Cash dividends	107.3	106.8	106.5
Retained earnings at end of year	$1,347.8	$2,203.9	$2,156.6
EARNINGS PER COMMON SHARE			
Average shares outstanding	59.6	59.3	59.1
Income (loss) before cumulative effects of accounting changes	$(1.83)	$2.60	$5.01
Cumulative effects of accounting changes	(10.73)	-	-
Net income (loss)	$(12.56)	$2.60	$5.01
CASH DIVIDENDS PER COMMON SHARE	$1.80	$1.80	$1.80

See notes to consolidated financial statements

CONSOLIDATED BALANCE SHEET

Reynolds Metals Company

December 31, 1992, 1991 and 1990

(In millions)	1992	1991	1990
ASSETS			
Current assets			
Cash and short-term investments	$80.4	$67.0	$89.5
Receivables			
Customers, less allowances of $16.2 (1991 - $24.2, 1990 - $21.4)	673.8	712.6	797.1
Other	123.8	107.1	56.7
Total receivables	797.6	819.7	853.8
Inventories	818.1	834.0	821.9
Prepaid expenses	60.7	59.3	50.4
Total current assets	1,756.8	1,780.0	1,815.6
Unincorporated joint ventures and associated companies	849.8	832.6	803.4
Property, plant and equipment - net	3,210.2	3,254.1	3,139.8
Deferred taxes (Note H)	246.8	-	-
Other assets	833.4	818.6	768.3
Total Assets	$6,897.0	$6,685.3	$6,527.1
LIABILITIES AND STOCKHOLDERS' EQUITY			
Current liabilities			
Accounts payable, accrued and other liabilities	$824.3	$774.4	$867.7
Indebtedness	361.0	242.0	106.2
Total current liabilities	1,185.3	1,016.4	973.9
Long-term debt	1,797.7	1,854.3	1,741.5
Postretirement benefits (Note G)	1,196.5	132.2	146.5
Environmental and restructuring	346.0	160.2	154.8
Deferred taxes (Note H)	165.9	404.8	424.2
Other liabilities	145.6	157.3	157.8
Stockholders' equity			
Common stock	750.2	742.0	734.2
Retained earnings	1,347.8	2,203.9	2,156.6
Cumulative currency translation adjustments	(1.7)	14.2	37.6
Pension liability adjustment (Note G)	(36.3)	-	-
Total stockholders' equity	2,060.0	2,960.1	2,928.4
Contingent liabilities and commitments (Note J)			
Total Liabilities and Stockholders' Equity	$6,897.0	$6,685.3	$6,527.1

See notes to consolidated financial statements

CONSOLIDATED STATEMENT OF CASH FLOWS

Reynolds Metals Company

Years ended December 31, 1992, 1991 and 1990

(In millions)	1992	1991	1990
OPERATING ACTIVITIES			
Net income (loss)	$(748.8)	$154.1	$296.6
Adjustments to reconcile to net cash provided by operating activities:			
Cumulative effects of accounting changes	639.6	-	-
Depreciation and amortization	284.0	265.1	214.2
Estimated environmental, operational restructuring and asset revaluation costs	268.2	-	150.0
Deferred taxes	(119.1)	(19.1)	15.2
Other	64.4	65.3	39.0
Changes in operating assets and liabilities net of effects from acquisitions and dispositions:			
Accounts payable, accrued and other liabilities	(2.5)	(49.9)	(113.1)
Receivables	31.9	7.1	82.9
Inventories	(34.6)	(26.7)	1.3
Deferred charges and other	(81.9)	(60.4)	(69.4)
Net cash provided by operating activities	301.2	335.5	616.7
INVESTING ACTIVITIES			
Purchases of property, plant and equipment	(302.2)	(397.5)	(936.3)
Proceeds from sales of assets	95.6	-	5.8
Acquisitions	-	(15.8)	(54.6)
Investments in and advances to unincorporated joint ventures, associated and related companies	(22.6)	(95.1)	(116.3)
Other	(22.4)	4.6	30.3
Net cash used in investing activities	(251.6)	(503.8)	(1,071.1)
FINANCING ACTIVITIES			
Proceeds from long-term obligations	316.3	517.4	698.6
Reduction of long-term debt and other financing liabilities	(276.8)	(387.0)	(105.5)
Net increase (decrease) in short-term borrowings	31.6	122.2	(13.2)
Cash dividends paid	(107.3)	(106.8)	(106.5)
Net cash provided by (used in) financing activities	(36.2)	145.8	473.4
NET INCREASE (DECREASE) IN CASH AND SHORT-TERM INVESTMENTS	13.4	(22.5)	19.0
CASH AND SHORT-TERM INVESTMENTS AT BEGINNING OF YEAR	67.0	89.5	70.5
CASH AND SHORT-TERM INVESTMENTS AT END OF YEAR	$80.4	$67.0	$89.5

See notes to consolidated financial statements

NOTES TO CONSOLIDATED FINANCIAL STATEMENTS

REYNOLDS METALS COMPANY

(In millions, except share amounts. Certain amounts have been reclassified to conform to the 1992 presentation.)

NOTE A - SIGNIFICANT ACCOUNTING POLICIES

Principles of consolidation
The accounts of Reynolds Metals Company and majority-owned subsidiaries are included in the consolidated financial statements after elimination of intercompany transactions and profits and losses. Investments in associated (20% to 50% owned) companies are carried at cost, adjusted for the Company's equity in their undistributed net income. Unincorporated joint ventures are production facilities which have no marketing or sales activities and are accounted for on an investment cost basis adjusted for the Company's share of the non-cash production charges of the operation.

Inventories
Inventories are stated at the lower of cost or market. Cost of inventories of $307.6 million in 1992, $320.2 million in 1991 and $280.5 million in 1990 is determined by the last-in, first-out (LIFO) method. Remaining inventories of $510.5 million in 1992, $513.8 million in 1991 and $541.4 million in 1990 are determined by the average or first-in, first-out (FIFO) methods. If the FIFO method was applied to LIFO inventories, the amount for inventories would increase by $447.0 million at December 31, 1992, $476.4 million at December 31, 1991 and $532.5 million at December 31, 1990. As a result of LIFO, costs decreased by $21.8 million in 1992, $55.7 million in 1991 and $5.9 million in 1990. Costs decreased $7.1 million in 1990 resulting from liquidation of certain LIFO inventories carried at lower costs prevailing in prior years as compared with current costs.

Since certain inventories of the Company may be sold at various stages of processing, no practical distinction can be made between finished products, in-process products and other materials, and therefore inventories are presented as a single classification.

Depreciation and amortization
Depreciation of plant and equipment is provided by the straight-line method over their estimated useful lives. Improvements to leased properties are amortized generally on the basis of the shorter of the terms of the respective leases or the estimated useful lives of the related facilities.

Investment tax credits
Investment tax credits are accounted for by the flow-through method (Note H).

Statement of cash flows
For purposes of the Statement of Cash Flows, the Company considers all highly liquid short-term investments purchased with a maturity of three months or less to be cash equivalents.

NOTE A - SIGNIFICANT ACCOUNTING POLICIES - continued

Financial Instruments

The Company utilizes forward, futures and option contracts and swap agreements related to certain of its business activities. Gains and losses on these contracts are recognized or accrued as a component of the related transactions. The Company is exposed to certain losses in the event of non-performance by the other parties to these agreements, but the Company does not anticipate non-performance by the counterparties.

The Company manages a portion of its exposures to fluctuations in aluminum prices, raw material prices and production costs with short and long-term strategies after giving consideration to market conditions, contractual agreements and other factors affecting the Company's risk profile. At the end of 1992, to hedge costs on a long-term basis, the Company had $320 million of aluminum contracts (1991 - $200 million, 1990 - $139 million) that fix a portion of the variable costs of certain fixed-price aluminum sales commitments which run from 1993 to 1999 and $100 million of natural gas contracts (1991 - $75 million) that fix the variable price of natural gas supply agreements which run from 1993 to 1994. The Company also had $281 million of foreign currency contracts (1991 - $116 million, 1990 - $127 million) which hedge certain aluminum sales and raw material acquisitions in foreign markets. In addition, to hedge aluminum prices on a short-term basis at the end of 1991, the Company had $194 million of aluminum contracts.

The Company manages its exposure to interest rate fluctuations after giving consideration to market conditions and levels of variable-rate and fixed-rate debt outstanding. At the end of 1992 the Company had $225 million (1991 - $590 million, 1990 - $500 million) of agreements which fix the interest rate on certain variable-rate debt through 1994. The Company also had $300 million of long-term agreements (maturing in 1995) which convert fixed-rate debt to variable-rate debt (increased by $300 million in early 1993 which mature in 1996).

At the end of 1992, the fair value of the financial instruments discussed above was approximately the same as contractual value. The carrying amount of short-term investments and long-term debt approximates fair value. The fair value of financial instruments was estimated based upon quoted prices for comparable contracts and discounted cash flow analyses.

Changes in accounting policy

In the fourth quarter of 1992, the Company elected early adoption of Financial Accounting Standards (FAS) No. 106 - Employers' Accounting for Postretirement Benefits Other Than Pensions (Note G) and No. 109 - Accounting for Income Taxes (Note H). FAS 106 generally requires the accrual of the expected cost of postretirement benefits (health care and life insurance) by the date that employees attain full eligibility for benefits to be received. Previously, the expense for these benefits was recognized when costs were incurred or claims were received. FAS 109 generally requires a change from the deferred to the liability method of computing deferred income taxes. Prior interim periods of 1992 have been restated to reflect these accounting changes. Charges of $610.0 million (FAS 106, net of taxes of $365.0 million) and $29.6 million (FAS 109) were recognized in the restated first quarter of 1992 for the cumulative effects of these accounting changes. The adoption of FAS 109 enabled full recognition of the deferred tax benefits associated with the adoption of FAS 106. In addition, the adoption of FAS 106 resulted in a decrease in income before the cumulative effects of accounting changes for 1992 of $32.5 million ($52.0 million before tax) or $.54 per share, while the effect of adoption of FAS 109 on income before the cumulative effects of accounting changes for the year was not significant.

NOTE B - UNINCORPORATED JOINT VENTURES AND ASSOCIATED COMPANIES

The Company has interests in unincorporated joint ventures which produce alumina and gold (Note A). It also has interests in foreign based associated companies which provide the Company with bauxite, alumina, primary aluminum and hydroelectric power. At December 31 the Company's investment in these activities consisted of the following:

	1992	1991	1990
Unincorporated Joint Ventures			
Current assets	$28.9	$30.2	$24.8
Current liabilities	(12.7)	(22.7)	(24.3)
Property, plant and equipment and other assets	602.3	622.7	623.4
Net investment	$618.5	$630.2	$623.9
Associated Companies			
Investments	$225.8	$189.4	$171.2
Advances	5.5	13.0	8.3
Net investment	$231.3	$202.4	$179.5

The Company has committed to pay its proportionate share of annual production charges (including debt service) relating to its interests in certain of these entities. These arrangements include minimum commitments of approximately $50 million annually through 1997 and additional amounts thereafter which together, at present value, aggregate $241 million at December 31, 1992, after excluding interest of $70 million and variable operating costs of the facilities. During 1992 the Company purchased approximately $200 million (1991 - $230 million, 1990 - $170 million) of raw materials under these arrangements.

NOTE C - PROPERTY, PLANT AND EQUIPMENT - AT COST

Components of property, plant and equipment are as follows:

	1992	1991	1990
Land, land improvements and mineral properties	$287.8	$297.3	$239.6
Buildings and leasehold improvements	988.3	987.3	753.4
Machinery and equipment	4,417.3	4,301.3	3,566.8
Construction in progress	183.3	199.3	950.8
Funds designated for capital expenditures	25.6	3.7	8.1
	5,902.3	5,788.9	5,518.7
Less: Allowances for depreciation and amortization	2,692.1	2,534.8	2,378.9
Net property, plant and equipment	$3,210.2	$3,254.1	$3,139.8

NOTE D - CURRENT LIABILITIES

	1992	1991	1990
Trade payables	$370.6	$352.5	$401.9
Accrued compensation and related amounts	223.5	173.0	209.4
Payables to associated companies	46.4	49.1	44.6
Other liabilities	183.8	199.8	211.8
Accounts payable, accrued and other liabilities	824.3	774.4	867.7
Notes payable to banks	191.2	169.9	50.7
Long-term obligations (Note E)	169.8	72.1	55.5
Indebtedness	361.0	242.0	106.2
Total current liabilities	$1,185.3	$1,016.4	$973.9

NOTE E - FINANCING ARRANGEMENTS

Debt

Long-term debt outstanding at December 31:

	1992	1991	1990
Shelf registration issues:			
Medium term notes	$933.5	$846.5	$447.0
9% debentures	100.0	100.0	-
9-3/8% debentures	99.8	99.8	99.8
Floating rate notes	-	-	200.0
Other issues:			
Term loan agreement	274.2	306.6	328.2
Industrial and environmental control revenue bonds	220.9	224.7	228.6
Mortgages and other notes payable	141.1	176.7	215.8
Bank credit agreement	-	150.0	150.0
Commercial paper	25.0	22.1	127.6
Short-term borrowings, reclassified	173.0	-	-
	1,967.5	1,926.4	1,797.0
Amounts due within one year	169.8	72.1	55.5
Long-term debt	$1,797.7	$1,854.3	$1,741.5

Maturities of long-term debt are $120.2 million in 1994, $96.3 million in 1995, $98.9 million in 1996, $44.7 million in 1997 and $1,437.6 million from 1998 to 2022. Interest paid amounted to $169.6 million, $157.2 million and $90.4 million during 1992, 1991 and 1990, respectively, net of interest capitalized of $13.6 million, $19.4 million and $44.0 million.

The Company has on file a shelf registration to issue up to $1.65 billion of debt securities. The medium term notes, 9% debentures due 2003 and 9-3/8% debentures due 1999 were issued under the shelf registration. The medium term notes bear interest at an average rate of 9.2% and have maturities ranging from 1993 to 2007. The floating rate notes were also issued under the shelf registration but were voluntarily prepaid in 1991. At December 31, 1992, $300 million of debt securities remained unissued under the Company's shelf registration.

The term loan agreement bears interest at a variable rate (4.1% at December 31, 1992) and requires principal repayments through 1996.

Industrial and environmental control revenue bonds consists principally of variable rate debt averaging approximately 3% at December 31, 1992. These bonds require principal repayment periodically or in a lump sum through 2022. $206.8 million of these bonds are supported by bank letters of credit. Early in 1993 an additional $8.2 million of variable rate bonds due 2022 were issued.

NOTE E - FINANCING ARRANGEMENTS - continued

Debt - continued

Mortgages and other notes payable consists of fixed rate debt at an average rate of 9.3% and requires principal repayment through 2009.

At December 31, 1992, $25.0 million of commercial paper was outstanding at an average rate of 3.9%. The commercial paper and certain other short-term borrowings are classified as long-term debt since it is the Company's intent (supported by $200 million in revolving credit facilities) to refinance the debt on a long-term basis. The Company has an additional $290 million in revolving credit facilities, of which $250 million expire in 1995.

In the fourth quarter of 1992, the Company borrowed $230 million under a short-term credit facility. The proceeds were used to voluntarily prepay the $150 million bank credit agreement and $80 million of short- term borrowings. In early 1993, the Company issued $50 million of medium term notes under the shelf registration (at an average rate of 7.8% and maturing in 2004 to 2013). In the first half of 1993, the Company intends to issue $285 million of debt securities under a new shelf registration and to borrow $150 million under a five-year bank credit agreement. The proceeds from these borrowings will be used to voluntarily prepay $150 million of the term loan agreement and to repay $230 million borrowed under the short-term credit facility in the fourth quarter of 1992 and other short-term obligations.

Certain of the Company's financing arrangements contain restrictions which, among other things, require maintenance of certain financial ratios.

NOTE F - STOCKHOLDERS' EQUITY

Common stock

	Shares	Amount
Authorized, without par value	200,000,000	
Outstanding:		
At beginning of 1990	59,329,614	$726.1
Shares issued pursuant to employee benefit plans:		
1990	164,525	8.1
1991	112,821	7.8
1992	153,259	8.2
At end of 1992	59,760,219	$750.2

Stock option plan

The Company has a non-qualified stock option plan under which stock options may be granted to key employees of the Company at a price generally equal to the fair market value at the date of grant. Transactions involving the plan are summarized as follows:

	1992	1991	1990
Outstanding January 1	2,609,856	2,063,506	1,715,081
Granted	620,700	622,600	605,750
Cancelled	(26,550)	(4,750)	(15,000)
Exercised	(65,150)	(71,500)	(242,325)
Outstanding at December 31	3,138,856	2,609,856	2,063,506
Exercisable at December 31	2,531,056	1,987,256	1,467,756
Options available for grant	2,655,850	3,250,000	620,350
Weighted average prices:			
Exercised	$36.50	$41.00	$36.25
Outstanding at December 31	52.75	51.25	49.25
Exercisable at December 31	51.50	49.50	47.00

NOTE F - STOCKHOLDERS' EQUITY - continued

Preferred stock

The Company has 21,000,000 shares of preferred stock authorized of which 2,000,000 shares have been designated Series A Junior Participating Preferred. At December 31, 1992, none of the Company's preferred stock was issued or outstanding.

Shareholder rights plan

Each share of the Company's common stock has one right attached. The rights trade with the common stock and are exercisable only if a person or group buys 20% or more of the Company's common stock, or announces a tender offer for 30% or more of the outstanding common stock. When exercisable, each right will entitle a holder to buy one-hundredth of one share of the Company's Series A Junior Participating Preferred Stock at an exercise price of $125.

If at any time after the rights become exercisable, the Company is acquired in a merger or other business combination or if 50% of its assets or earning power is sold or transferred, each right would enable its holder to buy common stock of the acquiring company at a 50% discount. In addition, if a person or group acquires 30% or more of common stock or if certain other events occur, each right would enable its holder to buy common stock of the Company at a 50% discount. The rights, which do not have voting privileges, expire in 1997, but may be redeemed by action of the Board prior to that time, under certain circumstances, for $0.05 per right. Until the rights become exercisable, they have no dilutive effect on earnings per share.

Although these rights should not interfere with a business combination approved by the Board of Directors, they will cause substantial dilution to a person or group that attempts to acquire the Company without conditioning the offer on redemption of the rights or acquiring a substantial number of the rights.

Cumulative currency translation adjustments

	1992	1991	1990
At beginning of year	$14.2	$37.6	$(8.5)
Currency translation adjustments	(15.0)	(24.2)	49.0
Income taxes	(.9)	.8	(2.9)
At end of year	$(1.7)	$14.2	$37.6

NOTE G - POSTRETIREMENT BENEFITS

Pensions

The Company has several noncontributory defined benefit pension plans covering substantially all employees. Plans covering salaried employees provide pension benefits that are based on a formula which considers length of service and earnings during years of service. Plans covering hourly employees generally provide a specific amount of benefits for each year of service. The Company's funding policies meet or exceed all regulatory requirements.

Net pension costs were as follows:

	1992	1991	1990
Service cost	$27.1	$24.1	$23.8
Interest cost	107.7	100.1	94.7
Actual (return) loss on plan assets	(43.5)	(181.3)	4.3
Net amortization and deferrals	(27.1)	117.6	(62.1)
Other	12.8	9.9	5.5
Total	$77.0	$70.4	$66.2

Assumptions utilized in accounting for the Company's principal pension plans are as follows:

	1992	1991	1990
Weighted average discount rate	8.5%	8.75%	9.5%
Approximate weighted average rate of increase in compensation levels (salaried plan only)	4.5%	5.0%	5.0%
Expected long-term rate of return on assets	9.25%	9.0%	9.0%

NOTE G - POSTRETIREMENT BENEFITS - continued

The following table sets forth information on the Company's principal pension plans at December 31:

	1992	1991		1990	
	Accumulated benefit obligation exceeds assets	Assets exceed accumulated benefit obligation	Accumulated benefit obligation exceeds assets	Assets exceed accumulated benefit obligation	Accumulated benefit obligation exceeds assets
Actuarial present value of pension benefit obligation:					
Vested	$1,109.3	$443.7	$574.2	$389.4	$490.8
Nonvested	130.5	59.5	28.8	47.3	27.0
Accumulated	$1,239.8	$503.2	$603.0	$436.7	$517.8
Projected	$1,346.9	$518.1	$709.0	$453.0	$619.8
Plan assets at fair value	1,110.8	549.9	527.8	472.7	431.2
Plan assets (in excess of) less than pension benefit obligation	236.1	(31.8)	181.2	(19.7)	188.6
Items not yet recognized:					
Unrecognized net gain (loss)	(151.4)	4.0	(91.0)	(16.3)	(76.6)
Unrecognized prior service cost, etc.	(102.8)	(40.3)	(53.9)	(43.0)	(60.9)
Recognition of minimum liability	163.0	-	60.7	-	70.0
Net pension (asset) liability	$144.9	$(68.1)	$97.0	$(79.0)	$121.1

In addition to recording the minimum liability, the Company has recorded an offsetting intangible asset which represents unrecognized prior service cost and unrecognized net obligation at transition of under-funded plans. At the end of 1992, the Company recorded an equity adjustment of $36.3 million (net of deferred income taxes of $18.8 million) for the excess of the minimum liability over the amount recorded for the intangible asset.

At December 31, 1992, approximately 48% of the plans' assets were invested in corporate equity securities, 35% in corporate bonds, 10% in government debt securities and cash equivalents and 7% in real estate property.

NOTE G - POSTRETIREMENT BENEFITS - continued

Other postretirement benefits
In addition to providing pension benefits, the Company provides health care and life insurance benefits to most domestic retired employees. Substantially all of the Company's domestic employees may become eligible for these benefits if they reach retirement age while working for the Company. In 1992 the Company announced that the plan for salaried employees would be changed to provide for additional cost-sharing features with future retirees such as the elimination of certain reimbursements and requiring retiree contributions based upon age and service criteria and at certain specified cost levels. These changes are expected to reduce the cost of providing these benefits by approximately 20%. The Company's policy is to fund the cost of these benefits when actual expenses are incurred.

The Company's accumulated postretirement benefit obligation is comprised of the following:

	1992	
	December 31	January 1
Retirees	$589.1	$580.4
Active employees fully eligible	117.7	132.0
Active employees not fully eligible	249.3	262.6
Unamortized plan change benefits	102.0	-
Unrecognized net loss	(31.1)	-
	$1,027.0	$975.0

Net periodic postretirement benefit cost for 1992 (1991 - $40 million and 1990 - $35 million) included the following components:

Service cost	$16.6
Interest cost	84.7
	$101.3

The weighted-average annual assumed rate of increase in the per capita cost of covered benefits (i.e., health care cost trend rate) is 12.5% for 1993 (13% in 1992) and is assumed to decrease gradually to 6% for 2002 and remain at that level thereafter. The health care cost trend rate assumption has a significant effect on the amounts reported. For example, each one percentage point change in the assumed health care cost trend rate would change the accumulated postretirement benefit obligation as of December 31, 1992, by approximately $123 million and the aggregate of the service and interest cost components of net periodic postretirement benefit cost for 1992 by approximately $14 million.

The weighted-average discount rate used in determining the accumulated postretirement benefit obligation was 8.5% at December 31, 1992 and 8.75% at January 1, 1992.

NOTE H - TAXES ON INCOME

Effective January 1, 1992, the Company changed its method of accounting for income taxes from the deferred method to the liability method as required by FAS No. 109 - Accounting for Income Taxes (see Note A). As permitted under the new rules, prior years' financial statements have not been restated.

At December 31, 1992, the Company had various U. S. and Canadian income tax carryforward benefits of $69 million that expire at various times through 2007 and $62 million that can be carried forward indefinitely.

Deferred income taxes reflect the net tax effects of temporary differences between the carrying amounts of assets and liabilities for financial reporting purposes and the amounts used for income tax purposes. At December 31, 1992, the Company had $745 million of deferred tax assets and $664 million of deferred tax liabilities which have been netted with respect to tax jurisdictions for presentation purposes. The significant components of these amounts as shown on the balance sheet are as follows:

	Asset	Liability
Retiree health benefits	$384.5	-
Environmental, restructuring and other costs	144.8	-
Tax carryforward benefits	68.7	$62.4
Employee benefits	12.8	-
Other	45.7	(12.6)
Tax over book depreciation	(409.7)	(215.7)
Noncurrent deferred tax assets and liabilities	$246.8	$(165.9)

The Company has deferred tax assets relating to certain foreign entities of approximately $40 million against which a full valuation reserve has been recorded. The Company is in the process of evaluating alternatives which may result in the ultimate realization of a portion of these assets.

NOTE H - TAXES ON INCOME - continued

Significant components of the provision for income taxes are as follows:

	Liability Method	Deferred Method	
	1992	1991	1990
Current:			
Federal	$10.8	$29.7	$85.8
Foreign	19.8	23.2	34.1
State	2.4	5.5	12.4
Total current	33.0	58.4	132.3
Deferred:			
Federal	(89.0)	8.8	(19.0)
Foreign	(16.9)	(10.2)	18.9
State	(17.7)	4.7	(8.4)
Total deferred	(123.6)	3.3	(8.5)
Equity	4.4	4.5	1.5
Total provision	$(86.2)	$66.2	$125.3

The major components of the deferred tax provision under the deferred method are as follows:

	1991	1990
Depreciation and amortization	$37.5	$33.9
Investment tax credits	(8.9)	9.7
Employee benefits	1.4	1.4
Facility closing and environmental costs	15.8	(49.7)
Tax loss and AMT credits	(47.5)	-
Other	5.0	(3.8)
	$3.3	$(8.5)

Other includes deferred taxes and credits for customer allowances, estimated liabilities and various other timing differences.

The Company has not provided taxes on the undistributed earnings ($730 million) of foreign subsidiaries as it is the intent of the Company to use such earnings to finance foreign expansion, reduce foreign debt and support foreign operating requirements.

NOTE H - TAXES ON INCOME - continued

The Company's effective income tax rate varied from the United States statutory rate as follows:

	Liability Method	Deferred Method	
	1992	1991	1990
United States rate	(34) %	34 %	34 %
Income taxed at other than U.S. rate	(3)	(2)	(1)
Domestic and foreign depletion allowances	(2)	(3)	(2)
State income taxes and other	(5)	1	(1)
Effective rate	(44) %	30 %	30 %

Income taxes paid were $17.1 million, $89.9 million and $138.8 million in 1992, 1991 and 1990, respectively.

NOTE I - COMPANY OPERATIONS

The Company is a vertically integrated enterprise operating predominantly in the aluminum industry in both domestic and foreign areas. The Company, in order to more fully describe the nature of its operations and to supplement the foregoing, has separated its vertically integrated operations into two groups referred to as production and processing, and finished products and other sales. Summarized financial information relating to the Company's operations and investments is as follows:

NOTE I – COMPANY OPERATIONS – continued

	Domestic			Canada		
Geographic data	1992	1991	1990	1992	1991	1990
Products and services sold						
Customers	$4,212.6	$4,272.1	$4,647.9	$276.8	$282.1	$232.3
Transfers between areas	276.4	301.4	296.2	425.5	395.5	388.3
Total products and services sold	$4,489.0	$4,573.5	$4,944.1	$702.3	$677.6	$620.6
Operating profit (loss)	$76.4	$264.5	$377.5	$27.7	($38.5)	$31.9
Equity in income of companies						
not consolidated					11.5	9.6
Interest and other income	44.7	18.2	19.8	1.2	1.1	1.3
Interest expense	(130.6)	(122.3)	(83.7)	(19.4)	(23.0)	
Income (loss) before income taxes and						
cumulative effects of accounting changes	($9.5)	$160.4	$313.6	$9.5	($48.9)	$42.8
Identifiable assets	$3,969.7	$3,757.0	$3,765.1	$1,250.5	$1,305.1	$1,268.7
Investments in and advances to						
companies and unincorporated						
joint ventures not consolidated				63.5	74.4	77.4
Total assets	$3,969.7	$3,757.0	$3,765.1	$1,314.0	$1,379.5	$1,346.1

	Production and processing		
Operating data	1992	1991	1990
Products and services sold			
Customers	$3,010.4	$3,242.1	$3,509.4
Internal transfers	770.6	783.8	845.2
Total products and services sold	$3,781.0	$4,025.9	$4,354.6
Operating profit (loss)	($45.3)	$103.4	$461.3
Equity in income of companies			
not consolidated	8.1	18.5	10.3
Interest and other income			
Interest expense			
Income (loss) before income taxes and			
cumulative effects of accounting changes			
Operating profit (loss) includes amounts for:			
Depreciation and amortization	$212.2	$201.6	$160.7
Identifiable assets	$4,117.3	$4,151.5	$4,107.0
Investments in and advances to			
companies and unincorporated			
joint ventures not consolidated	849.8	832.6	803.4
Corporate assets			
Total assets			
Capital expenditures	$238.6	$325.8	$822.4

Other foreign			Eliminations, etc.			Consolidated		
1992	1991	1990	1992	1991	1990	1992	1991	1990
$1,103.2	$1,175.9	$1,142.2				$5,592.6	$5,730.1	$6,022.4
178.8	195.8	211.7	($880.7)	($892.7)	($896.2)			
$1,282.0	$1,371.7	$1,353.9	($880.7)	($892.7)	($896.2)	$5,592.6	$5,730.1	$6,022.4
$74.9	$80.1	$208.5	($271.4)	$20.7	($153.2)	($92.4)	$326.8	$464.7
8.1	7.0	0.7				8.1	18.5	10.3
13.8	17.7	21.9	(4.0)	(1.1)		55.7	35.9	43.0
(20.8)	(16.7)	(16.2)	4.0	1.1	3.8	(166.8)	(160.9)	(96.1)
$76.0	$88.1	$214.9	($271.4)	$20.7	($149.4)	($195.4)	$220.3	$421.9
$941.4	$914.8	$921.8	($114.4)	($124.2)	($231.9)	$6,047.2	$5,852.7	$5,723.7
786.3	758.2	726.0				849.8	832.6	803.4
$1,727.7	$1,673.0	$1,647.8	($114.4)	($124.2)	($231.9)	$6,897.0	$6,685.3	$6,527.1

Finished products and other sales			Eliminations, etc.			Consolidated		
1992	1991	1990	1992	1991	1990	1992	1991	1990
$2,582.2	$2,488.0	$2,513.0				$5,592.6	$5,730.1	$6,022.4
3.8	4.0	7.4	($774.4)	($787.8)	($852.6)			
$2,586.0	$2,492.0	$2,520.4	($774.4)	($787.8)	($852.6)	$5,592.6	$5,730.1	$6,022.4
$214.1	$215.9	$169.9	($261.2)	$7.5	($166.5)	($92.4)	$326.8	$464.7
						8.1	18.5	10.3
						55.7	35.9	43.0
						(166.8)	(160.9)	(96.1)
						($195.4)	$220.3	$421.9
$71.8	$63.5	$53.5				$284.0	$265.1	$214.2
$1,156.3	$1,213.7	$1,166.3	($14.4)	($33.1)	($73.2)	$5,259.2	$5,332.1	$5,200.1
						849.8	832.6	803.4
						788.0	520.6	523.6
						$6,897.0	$6,685.3	$6,527.1
$63.6	$71.7	$113.9				$302.2	$397.5	$936.3

NOTE I - COMPANY OPERATIONS - continued

Approximately 24% of products transferred between operating areas and all transfers from other foreign areas are reflected at cost related prices. Other transfers between operating areas and transfers between Canada and domestic areas are reflected at market related prices.

Operating profit is after allocation of selling, administrative and general expenses. It does not reflect interest expense or other items of income or expense considered to be general corporate in nature. Corporate assets consist principally of cash, investments and other assets.

Research and development expenditures were $37.7 million in 1992, $37.4 million in 1991 and $37.0 million in 1990.

NOTE J - CONTINGENT LIABILITIES AND COMMITMENTS

Various suits and claims are pending against the Company. In the opinion of the Company's management, after consultation with counsel, disposition of the suits and claims will not involve sums having a material adverse effect upon the consolidated financial position of the Company.

The Company leases certain items of property, plant and equipment under long-term operating leases. Lease expense was approximately $48 million per year for the years 1990 to 1992. Lease commitments at December 31, 1992 were approximately $69 million. Leases covering major items contain renewal and/or purchase options which may be exercised by the Company.

The Company is involved in various worldwide environmental improvement activities resulting from past operations, including designation as a potentially responsible party, with others, at various EPA designated superfund sites. The Company has recorded amounts which, in management's best estimate, will be sufficient to satisfy anticipated costs of known remediation requirements. As a result of factors such as the continuing evolution of environmental laws and regulatory requirements, the availability and application of technology, the identification of presently unknown remediation sites and the allocation of costs among potentially responsible parties, estimated costs for future environmental compliance and remediation are necessarily imprecise. Based upon information presently available, such future costs are not expected to have a material adverse effect on the Company's competitive or financial position. However, it is not possible to predict the amount or timing of future costs of environmental remediation requirements which may subsequently be determined. Such costs could be material to results of operations in a future period.

NOTE K - CANADIAN REYNOLDS METALS COMPANY, LIMITED

Financial statements and financial statement schedules for Canadian Reynolds Metals Company, Limited have been omitted because the securities it intends to register under the Securities Act of 1933 (thus subjecting it to reporting requirements under Section 13 or 15(d) of the Securities Exchange Act of 1934) will be fully and unconditionally guaranteed by Reynolds Metals Company. Financial information relating to Canadian Reynolds Metals Company, Limited is presented herein pursuant to Staff Accounting Bulletin 53 as an addition to the footnotes to the financial statements of Reynolds Metals Company. Summarized financial information is as follows:

	December 31		
	1992	1991	1990
Current assets	$139.2	$151.8	$140.8
Noncurrent assets	1,094.5	1,132.6	1,106.7
Current liabilities	(245.8)	(243.9)	(151.3)
Noncurrent liabilities	(385.9)	(454.3)	(466.9)

	Year Ended December 31		
	1992	1991	1990
Sales to:			
Customers	$276.8	$282.1	$232.3
Parent Company	425.5	395.5	388.3
Total revenues	702.3	677.6	620.6
Income (loss) before income taxes	7.1	(60.1)	52.3
Net income (loss)	$28.6	$(43.7)	$40.6

Quarterly Results of Operations (Unaudited)
(In millions, except per share data)

Quarter	1992				1991			
	1st (Restated)	2nd (Restated)	3rd (Restated)	4th	1st	2nd	3rd	4th
Net Sales	$1,284.2	$1,489.8	$1,472.9	$1,345.7	$1,362.9	$1,512.4	$1,425.5	$1,429.3
Taxes on income (credit)	4.6	7.9	(1.3)	(97.4)	13.5	30.1	20.5	2.1
Income (loss) before cumulative effects of accounting changes	5.2	25.0	12.7	(152.1)	27.5	61.4	41.5	23.7
Cumulative effects of accounting changes	(639.6)							
Net income (loss)	$(634.4)	$25.0	$12.7	$(152.1)	$27.5	$61.4	$41.5	$23.7
Earnings per common share								
Income (loss) before cumulative effects of accounting changes	$0.09	$0.42	$0.21	$(2.55)	$0.46	$1.04	$0.70	$0.40
Net income (loss)	$(10.64)	$0.42	$0.21	$(2.55)	$0.46	$1.04	$0.70	$0.40

The first three quarters of 1992 were restated due to the adoption of new accounting standards in the fourth quarter of 1992 (Note A), reducing income (loss) before cumulative effects of accounting changes by approximately $8 million ($.13 per share) in each quarter. Included in income (loss) before cumulative effects of accounting changes for 1992 are charges for estimated environmental and restructuring costs of $21.4 million and $155.0 million in the first quarter and fourth quarter, respectively, and a gain on the sale of an investment of $22.6 million in the first quarter.

REPORT OF ERNST & YOUNG, INDEPENDENT AUDITORS

Stockholders and Board of Directors
Reynolds Metals Company

We have audited the accompanying consolidated balance sheets of Reynolds Metals Company as of December 31, 1992, 1991 and 1990, and the related statements of consolidated income and retained earnings and consolidated statements of cash flows for the years then ended. Our audits also included the financial statement schedules listed in the Index at Item 14(a). These financial statements and schedules are the responsibility of the Company's management. Our responsibility is to express an opinion on these financial statements and schedules based on our audits.

We conducted our audits in accordance with generally accepted auditing standards. Those standards require that we plan and perform the audit to obtain reasonable assurance about whether the financial statements are free of material misstatement. An audit includes examining, on a test basis, evidence supporting the amounts and disclosures in the financial statements. An audit also includes assessing the accounting principles used and significant estimates made by management, as well as evaluating the overall financial statement presentation. We believe that our audits provide a reasonable basis for our opinion.

In our opinion, the consolidated financial statements referred to above present fairly, in all material respects, the consolidated financial position of Reynolds Metals Company at December 31, 1992, 1991 and 1990, and the consolidated results of its operations and its cash flows for the years then ended, in conformity with generally accepted accounting principles. Also, in our opinion, the related financial statement schedules, when considered in relation to the basic financial statements taken as a whole, present fairly in all material respects the information set forth therein.

As discussed in Note A to the consolidated financial statements, the Company changed its method of accounting for postretirement benefits other than pensions and for income taxes in 1992.

/s/ ERNST & YOUNG

Richmond, Virginia
February 19, 1993

Item 9. CHANGES IN AND DISAGREEMENTS WITH ACCOUNTANTS ON ACCOUNTING AND FINANCIAL DISCLOSURE

None.

PART III

Item 10. DIRECTORS AND EXECUTIVE OFFICERS OF THE REGISTRANT

For information concerning the directors and nominees for directorship, see the information under the caption "Election of Directors" in the Registrant's Proxy Statement for the Annual Meeting of Stockholders to be held on April 21, 1993, which information is incorporated herein by reference.

Information concerning executive officers of the Registrant is shown in Part I - Item 4A of this report.

Item 11. EXECUTIVE COMPENSATION

For information required by this item, see the information under the captions "Election of Directors - Board Compensation and Benefits," "Election of Directors - Other Compensation" and "Executive Compensation" in the Registrant's Proxy Statement for the Annual Meeting of Stockholders to be held on April 21, 1993, which information is incorporated herein by reference.

Item 12. SECURITY OWNERSHIP OF CERTAIN BENEFICIAL OWNERS AND MANAGEMENT

For information required by this item, see the information under the caption "Beneficial Ownership of Securities" in the Registrant's Proxy Statement for the Annual Meeting of Stockholders to be held on April 21, 1993, which information is incorporated herein by reference.

Item 13. CERTAIN RELATIONSHIPS AND RELATED TRANSACTIONS

For information required by this item, see the information under the captions "Election of Directors - Other Compensation" and "Executive Compensation - Pension Plan Table" in the Registrant's Proxy Statement for the Annual Meeting of Stockholders to be held on April 21, 1993, which information is incorporated herein by reference.

PART IV

Item 14. EXHIBITS, FINANCIAL STATEMENT SCHEDULES, AND REPORTS ON FORM 8-K

(a)   The consolidated financial statements, financial statement schedules and exhibits listed below are filed as a part of this report.

(1)   Consolidated Financial Statements: <u>Page</u>

Statement of consolidated income and retained earnings -
Years ended December 31, 1992, 1991 and 1990.   23

Consolidated balance sheet - December 31, 1992, 1991 and 1990.   24

Consolidated statement of cash flows - Years ended December 31, 1992,
1991 and 1990.   25

Notes to consolidated financial statements.   26

Report of Ernst & Young, Independent Auditors.   45

(2)   Financial Statement Schedules   S-1

<u>Schedule No.</u>

V.   Property, plant and equipment
        1992
        1991
        1990

VI.   Accumulated depreciation, depletion and amortization
        of property, plant and equipment
        1992
        1991
        1990

IX.   Short-term borrowings
        1992, 1991, 1990

X.   Supplementary income statement information
        1992, 1991, 1990

All other schedules for which provision is made in the applicable accounting regulations of the Securities and Exchange Commission have been omitted because they are not required, are inapplicable or the required information has otherwise been given.

Individual financial statements of Reynolds Metals Company have been omitted because the restricted net assets (as defined in Accounting Series Release 302) of all subsidiaries included in the consolidated financial statements filed, in the aggregate, do not exceed 25% of the consolidated net assets shown in the consolidated balance sheet as of December 31, 1992.

Financial statements of all associated companies (20% to 50% owned) have been omitted because no associated company is individually significant. Summarized financial

-47-

information of all associated companies has been omitted because associated companies in the aggregate are not significant.

(3)   Exhibits - These Exhibits are filed under separate cover, except Exhibit 22 and Exhibits incorporated by reference.

*   EXHIBIT 3.1   -   Restated Certificate of Incorporation, as amended to the date hereof. (File No. 1-1430, Form 10-Q Report for the Quarter Ended June 30, 1992, EXHIBIT 4(a))

*   EXHIBIT 3.2   -   By-Laws, as amended to the date hereof. (File No. 1-1430, Form 10-Q Report for the Quarter Ended March 31, 1992, EXHIBIT 4(b))

EXHIBIT 4.1   -   Restated Certificate of Incorporation. See EXHIBIT 3.1.

EXHIBIT 4.2   -   By-Laws. See EXHIBIT 3.2.

*   EXHIBIT 4.3   -   Indenture dated as of April 1, 1989 (the "Indenture") between Reynolds Metals Company and The Bank of New York, as Trustee, relating to Debt Securities. (File No. 1-1430, Form 10-Q Report for the Quarter Ended March 31, 1989, EXHIBIT 4(c))

*   EXHIBIT 4.4   -   Amendment No. 1 dated as of November 1, 1991 to the Indenture. (File No. 1-1430, 1991 Form 10-K Report, EXHIBIT 4.4)

*   EXHIBIT 4.5   - $1,100,000,000 Credit Agreement (the "Credit Agreement") dated as of November 24, 1987 among Reynolds Metals Company, Canadian Reynolds Metals Company, Limited - Societe Canadienne de Metaux Reynolds, Limitee, the several banks parties thereto, Manufacturers Hanover Bank (Delaware), The Bank of Nova Scotia, Manufacturers Hanover Trust Company, and Manufacturers Hanover Agent Bank Services Corporation. (Registration Statement No. 33-20498 on Form S-8, dated March 7, 1988, EXHIBIT 4.4)

*   EXHIBIT 4.6   -   Amendment No. 1 dated as of July 1, 1988 to the Credit Agreement. (File No. 1-1430, Form 10-Q Report for the Quarter Ended June 30, 1988, EXHIBIT 4(e))

*   EXHIBIT 4.7   -   Amendment No. 2 dated as of February 8, 1989 to the Credit Agreement. (File No. 1-1430, 1988 Form 10-K Report, EXHIBIT 4.6)

*   EXHIBIT 4.8   -   Amendment No. 3 dated as of August 4, 1989 to the Credit Agreement.   (File No. 1-1430, Form 10-Q Report for the Quarter Ended June 30, 1989, EXHIBIT 4(g))

*   EXHIBIT 4.9   -   Amendment No. 4 dated as of November 1, 1990 to the Credit Agreement. (Registration Statement No. 33-38020 on Form S-3, dated November 30, 1990, EXHIBIT 4.12)

---

* Incorporated by reference.

*   EXHIBIT 4.10   -   Rights Agreement dated as of November 23, 1987 (the "Rights Agreement") between Reynolds Metals Company and The Chase Manhattan Bank, N.A. (File No. 1-1430, Registration Statement on Form 8-A dated November 23, 1987, pertaining to Preferred Stock Purchase Rights, EXHIBIT 1)

*   EXHIBIT 4.11   -   Amendment No. 1 dated as of December 19, 1991 to the Rights Agreement. (File No. 1-1430, 1991 Form 10-K Report, EXHIBIT 4.11)

*   EXHIBIT 4.12   -   Form of 9-3/8% Debenture due June 15, 1999. (File No. 1-1430, Form 8-K Report dated June 6, 1989, EXHIBIT 4)

*   EXHIBIT 4.13   -   Form of Fixed Rate Medium-Term Note. (Registration Statement No. 33-30882 on Form S-3, dated August 31, 1989, EXHIBIT 4.3)

*   EXHIBIT 4.14   -   Form of Floating Rate Medium-Term Note. (Registration Statement No. 33-30882 on Form S-3, dated August 31, 1989, EXHIBIT 4.4)

*   EXHIBIT 4.15   -   Form of Book-Entry Fixed Rate Medium-Term Note. (File No. 1-1430, 1991 Form 10-K Report, EXHIBIT 4.15)

*   EXHIBIT 4.16   -   Form of Book-Entry Floating Rate Medium-Term Note. (File No. 1-1430, 1991 Form 10-K Report, EXHIBIT 4.16)

*   EXHIBIT 4.17   -   Form of 9% Debenture due August 15, 2003. (File No. 1-1430, Form 8-K Report dated August 16, 1991, Exhibit 4(a))

    EXHIBIT 9   -   None

♦*   EXHIBIT 10.1   -   Reynolds Metals Company 1982 Nonqualified Stock Option Plan, as amended through May 17, 1985. (File No. 1-1430, 1985 Form 10-K Report, EXHIBIT 10.2)

♦*   EXHIBIT 10.2   -   Reynolds Metals Company 1987 Nonqualified Stock Option Plan. (Registration Statement No. 33-13822 on Form S-8, dated April 28, 1987, EXHIBIT 28.1)

♦*   EXHIBIT 10.3   -   Reynolds Metals Company 1992 Nonqualified Stock Option Plan. (Registration Statement No. 33-44400 on Form S-8, dated December 9, 1991, EXHIBIT 28.1)

♦*   EXHIBIT 10.4   -   Reynolds Metals Company Performance Incentive Plan, as amended and restated effective January 1, 1985. (File No. 1-1430, 1985 Form 10-K Report, EXHIBIT 10.3)

♦*   EXHIBIT 10.5   -   Consulting Agreement dated April 16, 1986 between Reynolds Metals Company and David P. Reynolds. (File No. 1-1430, Form 10-Q Report for the Quarter Ended March 31, 1986, EXHIBIT 19)

---

* Incorporated by reference.

♦ Management contract or compensatory plan or arrangement required to be filed as an exhibit pursuant to Item 601 of Regulation S-K.

♦* EXHIBIT 10.6 - Form of Deferred Compensation Agreement dated February 17, 1984 between Reynolds Metals Company and David P. Reynolds. (File No. 1-1430, 1983 Form 10-K Report, EXHIBIT 10.9)

♦* EXHIBIT 10.7 - Deferred Compensation Agreement dated May 16, 1986 between Reynolds Metals Company and David P. Reynolds. (File No. 1-1430, Form 10-Q Report for the Quarter Ended June 30, 1986, EXHIBIT 19)

♦* EXHIBIT 10.8 - Agreement dated December 9, 1987 between Reynolds Metals Company and Jeremiah J. Sheehan. (File No. 1-1430, 1987 Form 10-K Report, EXHIBIT 10.9)

♦* EXHIBIT 10.9 - Supplemental Death Benefit Plan for Officers. (File No. 1-1430, 1986 Form 10-K Report, EXHIBIT 10.8)

♦* EXHIBIT 10.10 - Financial Counseling Assistance Plan for Officers. (File No. 1-1430, 1987 Form 10-K Report, EXHIBIT 10.11)

♦* EXHIBIT 10.11 - Management Incentive Deferral Plan. (File No. 1-1430, 1987 Form 10-K Report, EXHIBIT 10.12)

♦* EXHIBIT 10.12 - Deferred Compensation Plan for Outside Directors. (File No. 1-1430, 1986 Form 10-K Report, EXHIBIT 10.9)

♦* EXHIBIT 10.13 - Amendment to Deferred Compensation Plan for Outside Directors effective December 1, 1987. (File No. 1-1430, 1987 Form 10-K Report, EXHIBIT 10.14)

♦* EXHIBIT 10.14 - Retirement Plan for Outside Directors. (File No. 1-1430, 1986 Form 10-K Report, EXHIBIT 10.10)

♦* EXHIBIT 10.15 - Death Benefit Plan for Outside Directors. (File No. 1-1430, 1986 Form 10-K Report, EXHIBIT 10.11)

♦* EXHIBIT 10.16 - Form of Indemnification Agreement for Directors and Officers. (File No. 1-1430, Form 8-K Report dated April 29, 1987, EXHIBIT 28.3)

♦* EXHIBIT 10.17 - Form of Executive Severance Agreement between Reynolds Metals Company and key executive personnel, including each of the individuals listed in Item 4A hereof (other than D. Michael Jones and Allen M. Earehart). (File No. 1-1430, 1987 Form 10-K Report, EXHIBIT 10.18)

♦* EXHIBIT 10.18 - Renewal dated February 21, 1992 of Consulting Agreement dated April 16, 1986 between Reynolds Metals Company and David P. Reynolds. (File No. 1-1430, 1991 Form 10-K Report, EXHIBIT 10.19)

♦* EXHIBIT 10.19 - Amendment to Reynolds Metals Company 1987 Nonqualified Stock Option Plan effective May 20, 1988. (File No. 1-1430, Form 10-Q Report for the Quarter Ended June 30, 1988, EXHIBIT 19(a))

---

* Incorporated by reference.
♦ Management contract or compensatory plan or arrangement required to be filed as an exhibit pursuant to Item 601 of Regulation S-K.

◆* EXHIBIT 10.20 - Amendment to Reynolds Metals Company 1987 Nonqualified Stock Option Plan effective October 21, 1988. (File No. 1-1430, Form 10-Q Report for the Quarter Ended September 30, 1988, EXHIBIT 19(a))

◆* EXHIBIT 10.21 - Amendment to Reynolds Metals Company 1987 Nonqualified Stock Option Plan effective January 1, 1987. (File No. 1-1430, 1988 Form 10-K Report, EXHIBIT 10.22)

◆* EXHIBIT 10.22 - Amendment to Reynolds Metals Company Performance Incentive Plan effective January 1, 1989. (File No. 1-1430, Form 10-Q Report for the Quarter Ended June 30, 1989, EXHIBIT 19)

◆* EXHIBIT 10.23 - Form of Stock Option and Stock Appreciation Right Agreement, as approved February 16, 1990 by the Compensation Committee of the Company's Board of Directors. (File No. 1-1430, 1989 Form 10-K Report, EXHIBIT 10.24)

◆* EXHIBIT 10.24 - Amendment to Reynolds Metals Company 1982 Nonqualified Stock Option Plan effective January 18, 1991. (File No. 1-1430, 1990 Form 10-K Report, EXHIBIT 10.25)

◆* EXHIBIT 10.25 - Amendment to Reynolds Metals Company 1987 Nonqualified Stock Option Plan effective January 18, 1991. (File No. 1-1430, 1990 Form 10-K Report, EXHIBIT 10.26)

◆* EXHIBIT 10.26 - Letter Agreement dated January 18, 1991 between Reynolds Metals Company and William O. Bourke. (File No. 1-1430, 1990 Form 10-K Report, EXHIBIT 10.29)

◆* EXHIBIT 10.27 - Form of Stock Option Agreement, as approved April 22, 1992 by the Compensation Committee of the Company's Board of Directors. (File No. 1-1430, Form 10-Q Report for the Quarter Ended March 31, 1992, EXHIBIT 28(a))

◆* EXHIBIT 10.28 - Consulting Agreement dated May 1, 1992 between Reynolds Metals Company and William O. Bourke. (File No. 1-1430, Form 10-Q Report for the Quarter Ended March 31, 1992, EXHIBIT 28(b))

EXHIBIT 11 - Omitted; see Item 8 for computation of earnings per share

EXHIBIT 12 - None

EXHIBIT 13 - Not applicable

EXHIBIT 16 - Not applicable

EXHIBIT 18 - None

EXHIBIT 19 - None

---

* Incorporated by reference.

◆ Management contract or compensatory plan or arrangement required to be filed as an exhibit pursuant to Item 601 of Regulation S-K.

EXHIBIT 22   -   List of Subsidiaries of Reynolds Metals Company

EXHIBIT 23   -   None

EXHIBIT 24   -   Consent of Independent Auditors

EXHIBIT 25   -   Powers of Attorney

EXHIBIT 28.1   -   Description of Common Stock

EXHIBIT 29   -   Not applicable

Pursuant to Item 601 of Regulation S-K, certain instruments with respect to long-term debt of the Company are omitted because such debt does not exceed 10 percent of the total assets of the Company and its subsidiaries on a consolidated basis. The Company agrees to furnish a copy of any such instrument to the Commission upon request.

(b)   Reports on Form 8-K

During the fourth quarter of 1992, the Registrant filed with the Commission a Current Report on Form 8-K dated December 3, 1992 reporting under Item 5 that the Registrant had announced that it would take total after-tax charges of approximately $827 million in connection with the adoption of Financial Accounting Standard ("FAS") 106 and FAS 109 and for additional environmental and restructuring costs. To date during the first quarter of 1993, the Registrant has filed with the Commission a Current Report on Form 8-K dated January 18, 1993 reporting under Item 5 the Registrant's results for the quarter and year ended December 31, 1992.

SIGNATURES

Pursuant to the requirements of Section 13 or 15(d) of the Securities Exchange Act of 1934, the Registrant has duly caused this report to be signed on its behalf by the undersigned, thereunto duly authorized.

REYNOLDS METALS COMPANY

By /s/Richard G. Holder
    Richard G. Holder, Chairman of
    the Board and Chief Executive
    Officer

Date February 19, 1993

Pursuant to the requirements of the Securities Exchange Act of 1934, this report has been signed below by the following persons on behalf of the Registrant and in the capacities and on the dates indicated.

By /s/Henry S. Savedge, Jr
    Henry S. Savedge, Jr., Director,
    Executive Vice President and
    Chief Financial Officer

Date February 19, 1993

By /s/Richard G. Holder
    Richard G. Holder, Director,
    Chairman of the Board and Chief
    Executive Officer

Date February 19, 1993

By *William O. Bourke
    William O. Bourke, Director

Date February 19, 1993

By /s/Yale M. Brandt
    Yale M. Brandt, Director

Date February 19, 1993

By *Thomas A. Graves, Jr.
    Thomas A. Graves, Jr., Director

Date February 19, 1993

By *Gerald Greenwald
    Gerald Greenwald, Director

Date February 19, 1993

By *John R. Hall
    John R. Hall, Director

Date February 19, 1993

By *Robert L. Hintz
    Robert L. Hintz, Director

Date February 19, 1993

By *David P. Reynolds   By /s/Randolph N. Reynolds
    David P. Reynolds, Director   Randolph N. Reynolds, Director

Date February 19, 1993   Date February 19, 1993

By *Charles A. Sanders   By *Ralph S. Thomas
    Charles A. Sanders, M.D., Director   Ralph S. Thomas, Director

Date February 19, 1993   Date February 19, 1993

By *Robert J. Vlasic   By *Joe B. Wyatt
    Robert J. Vlasic, Director   Joe B. Wyatt, Director

Date February 19, 1993   Date February 19, 1993

By /s/David C. Bilsing   *By /s/D. Michael Jones
    David C. Bilsing, Vice   D. Michael Jones, Attorney-in-Fact
    President, Controller

Date   February 19, 1993   Date February 19, 1993

FINANCIAL STATEMENT SCHEDULES

AND OTHER FINANCIAL INFORMATION

YEAR ENDED DECEMBER 31, 1992

REYNOLDS METALS COMPANY

RICHMOND, VIRGINIA

REYNOLDS METALS COMPANY AND CONSOLIDATED SUBSIDIARIES

SCHEDULE V - PROPERTY, PLANT AND EQUIPMENT (NOTE A)

Year Ended December 31, 1992

(In millions)

COL. A	COL. B	COL. C	COL. D	COL. E	COL. F
CLASSIFICATION	Balance at Beginning of Period	Additions at Cost	Retirements	Other Changes - Add (Deduct) - Describe	Balance at End of Period
Land, land improvements and mineral properties					$287.8
Buildings and leasehold improvements					988.3
Machinery and equipment					4,417.3
Construction in progress					183.3
Funds designated for capital expenditures					25.6
					$5,902.3

(A) The information required by Columns B, C, D and E has been omitted as neither the total additions ($302.2) nor the total retirements ($185.3) during the year amounted to more than 10% of the December 31, 1992 balance. Information concerning significant additions and retirements is provided under the caption "Investing Activities" in Item 7, Management's Discussion and Analysis of Financial Condition and Results of Operations.

REYNOLDS METALS COMPANY AND CONSOLIDATED SUBSIDIARIES

SCHEDULE V - PROPERTY, PLANT AND EQUIPMENT (NOTE A)

Year Ended December 31, 1991

(In millions)

COL. A	COL. B	COL. C	COL. D	COL. E	COL. F
CLASSIFICATION	Balance at Beginning of Period	Additions at Cost	Retirements	Other Changes - Add (Deduct) - Describe	Balance at End of Period
Land, land improvements and mineral properties					$297.2
Buildings and leasehold improvements					987.3
Machinery and equipment					4,301.3
Construction in progress					199.4
Funds designated for capital expenditures					3.7
					$5,788.9

(A) The information required by Columns B, C, D and E has been omitted as neither the total additions ($397.5) nor the total retirements ($99.4) during the year amounted to more than 10% of the December 31, 1991 balance. Other Changes includes $13.5 related to acquisitions, ($37.0) related to foreign currency translation and ($4.4) related to funds for plant expansion. Information concerning significant additions is provided under the caption "Investing Activities" in Item 7, Management's Discussion and Analysis of Financial Condition and Results of Operations.

REYNOLDS METALS COMPANY AND CONSOLIDATED SUBSIDIARIES

SCHEDULE V - PROPERTY, PLANT AND EQUIPMENT

Year Ended December 31, 1990

(In millions)

COL. A	COL. B	COL. C	COL. D	COL. E	COL. F
CLASSIFICATION	Balance at Beginning of Period	Additions at Cost (Note A)	Retirements	Other Changes - Add (Deduct) - Describe (Note B)	Balance at End of Period
Land, land improvements and mineral properties	$225.1	$13.6	($3.2)	$4.1	$239.6
Buildings and leasehold improvements	682.0	58.0	(5.7)	19.1	753.4
Machinery and equipment	3,140.4	364.0	(64.3)	126.7	3,566.8
Construction in progress	433.0	500.7		17.1	950.8
Funds designated for capital expenditures	38.4			(30.3)	8.1
	$4,518.9	$936.3	($73.2)	$136.7	$5,518.7

(A) Information concerning significant additions is provided under the caption "Investing Activities" in Item 7, Management's Discussion and Analysis of Financial Condition and Results of Operations.

(B) Other Changes includes $94.6 relating to acquisitions and $73.1 relating to foreign currency translation adjustments.

S-4

REYNOLDS METALS COMPANY AND CONSOLIDATED SUBSIDIARIES

SCHEDULE VI - ACCUMULATED DEPRECIATION, DEPLETION AND AMORTIZATION
OF PROPERTY, PLANT AND EQUIPMENT

Year Ended December 31, 1992

(In millions)

COL. A	COL. B	COL. C	COL. D	COL. E	COL. F
DESCRIPTION	Balance at Beginning of Period	Additions Charged to Costs and Expenses (Note A)	Retirements	Other Changes - Add (Deduct) - Describe	Balance at End of Period
Land, land improvements and mineral properties	$110.2	$7.4	($1.4)	$(9.4)	$106.8
Buildings and leasehold improvements	328.8	27.4	(9.7)	(3.4)	343.1
Machinery and equipment	2,065.9	249.2	(112.3)	9.2	2,212.0
Uneconomic operations	29.9			0.3	30.2
	$2,534.8	$284.0	$(123.4)	$(3.3)	$2,692.1

(A) Depreciation is provided by the straight-line method over the estimated useful lives of the assets. The assets have lives that vary, resulting in numerous annual rates for each classification.

S-5

193

REYNOLDS METALS COMPANY AND CONSOLIDATED SUBSIDIARIES

SCHEDULE VI - ACCUMULATED DEPRECIATION, DEPLETION AND AMORTIZATION
OF PROPERTY, PLANT AND EQUIPMENT

Year Ended December 31, 1991

(In millions)

COL. A	COL. B	COL. C	COL. D	COL. E	COL. F
DESCRIPTION	Balance at Beginning of Period	Additions Charged to Costs and Expenses (Note A)	Retirements	Other Changes - Add (Deduct) - Describe	Balance at End of Period
Land, land improvements and mineral properties	$104.6	$8.0	($2.1)	$(0.3)	$110.2
Buildings and leasehold improvements	304.0	27.7	(1.0)	(1.9)	328.8
Machinery and equipment	1,920.1	229.4	(68.3)	(15.3)	2,065.9
Uneconomic operations	50.2			(20.3)	29.9
	$2,378.9	$265.1	($71.4)	($37.8)	$2,534.8

(A) Depreciation is provided by the straight-line method over the estimated useful lives of the assets. The assets have lives that vary, resulting in numerous annual rates for each classification.

S-6

REYNOLDS METALS COMPANY AND CONSOLIDATED SUBSIDIARIES

SCHEDULE VI - ACCUMULATED DEPRECIATION, DEPLETION AND AMORTIZATION
OF PROPERTY, PLANT AND EQUIPMENT

Year Ended December 31, 1990

(In millions)

COL. A	COL. B	COL. C	COL. D	COL. E	COL. F
DESCRIPTION	Balance at Beginning of Period	Additions Charged to Costs and Expenses (Note A)	Retirements	Other Changes - Add (Deduct) - Describe	Balance at End of Period
Land, land improvements and mineral properties	$95.8	$7.0	($0.6)	$2.4	$104.6
Buildings and leasehold improvements	279.0	20.2	(4.1)	8.9	304.0
Machinery and equipment	1,740.5	187.0	(54.6)	47.2	1,920.1
Uneconomic operations	60.0			(9.8)	50.2
	$2,175.3	$214.2	($59.3)	$48.7	$2,378.9

(A) Depreciation is provided by the straight-line method over the estimated useful lives of the assets. The assets have lives that vary, resulting in numerous annual rates for each classification.

S-7

195

REYNOLDS METALS COMPANY AND CONSOLIDATED SUBSIDIARIES

SCHEDULE IX - SHORT-TERM BORROWINGS

Years Ended December 31

(In millions)

CATEGORY OF AGGREGATE SHORT-TERM BORROWINGS (A) COL. A	Balance at End of Period COL. B	Weighted Average Interest Rate COL. C	Maximum Amount Outstanding During the Period COL. D	Average Amount Outstanding During the Period (B) COL. E	Weighted Average Interest Rate During the Period (C) COL. F
1992					
Payable to banks	$191.2	8.6%	$222.6	$190.1	9.2%
Commercial paper	0.0	N/A	76.6	37.1	3.9%
	$191.2				
1991					
Payable to banks	$169.9	7.4%	$169.9	$130.2	9.6%
1990					
Payable to banks	$50.7	11.6%	$79.2	$57.9	12.3%
Commercial paper	0.0	N/A	58.8	5.4	8.4%
	$50.7				

(A) Short-term borrowings from banks represent borrowings under arrangements which have no termination date but are reviewed annually for renewal. Payable to banks and commercial paper excludes amounts classified as noncurrent.

(B) Average of month-end balances.

(C) Interest incurred divided by weighted average amount outstanding during the period.

S-8

REYNOLDS METALS COMPANY AND CONSOLIDATED SUBSIDIARIES

SCHEDULE X - SUPPLEMENTARY INCOME STATEMENT INFORMATION

Years Ended December 31

(In millions)

COL. A	COL. B		
ITEM	Charged to Costs and Expenses		
	1992	1991	1990
Maintenance and repairs	$410.0	$403.5	$372.2
Taxes, other than payroll and income	$67.1	$61.2	$50.2

S-9

197

PARENTS AND SUBSIDIARIES   EXHIBIT 22

(A)   Reynolds Metals Company has no parents.

(B)   Set forth below is a list of certain of the subsidiaries and associated companies of Reynolds Metals Company:

	Place of Incorporation Or Organization
* Aluminio Reynolds de Venezuela, S. A.	Venezuela
Aluminium Oxid Stade Gesellschaft mit beschrankter Haftung	Germany
* Austria Dosen Gesellschaft mbh & Co. KG	Austria
* Canadian Reynolds Metals Company, Limited - Societe Canadienne de Metaux Reynolds, Limitee	Quebec
* El Campo Aluminum Company	Delaware
Hamburger Aluminium-Werk Gesellschaft mit beschrankter Haftung	Germany
* Industria Navarra del Aluminio, S. A.	Spain
* Latas de Aluminio Reynolds, Inc.	Delaware
Latas de Aluminio, S. A.	Brazil
* Manicouagan Power Company - La Compagnie Hydroelectrique Manicouagan	Quebec
* Mt. Vernon Plastics Corporation	Delaware
Pechiney Reynolds Quebec, Inc.	Nebraska
* Presidential Development Corporation	New York
* RB Sales Company, Ltd.	Delaware
* Reymet Insurance Company Limited	Bermuda
* Reynolds Aluminium Deutschland, Inc.	Delaware
* Reynolds Aluminium France	France
* Reynolds Aluminium Holland B. V.	The Netherlands
* Reynolds Aluminium Deutschland Internationale Vertriebsgesellschaft mbH	Germany
* Reynolds Australia Alumina, Ltd.	Delaware
* Reynolds Australia Metals, Ltd.	Delaware
* Reynolds Becancour, Inc.	Delaware
* Reynolds Consumer Europe, S. A.	Belgium
* Reynolds Consumer Products, Inc. (formerly Presto Products, Inc.)	Delaware
* Reynolds (Europe) Limited	Delaware
* Reynolds International Holdings, Inc.	Delaware
* Reynolds International, Inc.	Delaware
* Reynolds International (Panama) Inc.	Panama
* Reynolds Kansas City Can Company	Delaware
* Reynolds-Lemmerz Industries	Ontario
* Reynolds Wheels-Holding S.p.A.	Italy
* Reywest Development Corporation	Arizona
* RMC Holdings, Inc.	Delaware
* RMC Properties, Ltd.	Delaware
* Reynolds Metals Development Company	Delaware
* Reynolds Metals European Capital Corporation	Delaware
* Reynolds Yilgarn Gold Operations Limited	Australia
* Societa Lavorazioni Industriali Metalli S.p.A.	Italy
* Southeast Vinyl Company	Delaware
* Southern Gravure Service, Inc.	Kentucky
* Southern Reclamation Company, Inc.	Alabama

The names of a number of subsidiaries and associated companies have been omitted because considered in the aggregate they would not constitute a significant subsidiary.

*   Consolidated subsidiaries

Glossary

Accountants (used interchangeably with the terms *auditor, independent accountant, independent auditor, or accounting firm*). A firm that audits financial statements contained in an SEC filing.

Accredited investor. In general, an institutional investor thought to be able to assess investment risk without the full measure of protection provided to the public at large in a registered 1933 act offering.

American Institute of Certified Public Accountants (AICPA). The professional organization to which certified public accountants (CPA) belong. In addition to providing educational and lobbying services on behalf of its members, the AICPA is responsible for promulgating auditing standards.

Basic information package (BIP). A set of company-specific disclosures required in 1933 act and 1934 act filings and, in certain circumstances, in glossy annual reports to stockholders.

Bed-bugging. A registration statement that has been so poorly prepared that SEC staff will not review it.

Beneficial owner. In general, one who has the right to vote or transfer securities or the ability to control such voting or transfer and who has the ability to directly or indirectly receive income from the securities and proceeds from their disposition.

Best-efforts offering. A form of underwriting arrangement in which an underwriter acts as an agent for an issuing company.

Blue-sky laws. Securities laws of individual states.

Comfort letter. A letter, written by an accountant to an underwriter and others having liability under the 1933 act, that provides certain assurances regarding the financial statements included in a registration statement.

Corporate insiders. Individuals who by virtue of their relationships with an entity are aware of material information that has not been made available to the public.

Defensive tactic. A measure adopted by a company to prevent a hostile takeover attempt from being successful or to discourage an unfriendly suitor from making a bid.

Division of Corporation Finance. The division of the SEC primarily responsible for reviewing filings by public companies.

Due diligence. The process performed by parties having liability under the 1933 act to determine that a registration statement is accurate when it becomes effective.

Efficient market hypothesis (EMH). The term used to describe the relationship between movements in security prices and information.

Electronic data gathering, analysis, and retrieval (EDGAR). The SEC's system whereby 1933 and 1934 act documents are filed electronically. When fully operational, investors will have on-line access to the data.

Exemption from registration. Offerings of securities that do not require registration under the 1933 act.

Expertized portion of a registration statement. A part of the registration statement included upon the authority of an expert.

F–1–2–3 scheme. A three-tier registration system for foreign issuers under the 1933 act. All three forms have the same disclosure requirements; the main difference among the forms is the manner in which information is disseminated.

Financial Accounting Standards Board (FASB). The primary private-sector body responsible for promulgating accounting principles.

Firm commitment. A form of underwriting arrangement in which an underwriter buys securities from an issuing company and resells them to the public.

Form 8–K. The current reporting form under the 1934 act whose need for filing is triggered by one or more specified events.

Form 10–K. The annual reporting form under the 1934 act.

Form 10–Q. The quarterly reporting form under the 1934 act.

Fraud on the market theory. A theory of presumptive reliance whereby a misleading statement will defraud all investors even though they have not directly relied on the error or omission.

Generally accepted accounting principles (GAAP). A set of accounting standards for the preparation and presentation of financial statements.

Generally accepted auditing standards (GAAS). A set of standards of conduct for an audit of financial statements.

Global offering. In general, the combination of an international offering of securities with an offering in the issuer's home country.

Going public. The process of transforming a company whose ownership rests with a relative handful of individuals or entities to one whose stock is held by the public at large.

Incorporation by reference. The process of referring readers of a 1933 act registration statement to 1934 act documents already containing the same information.

Independence. An accountant's ability to act with integrity and objectivity when conducting an audit.

Initial public offering (IPO). An offering of securities to the public for the first time.

Integrated disclosure system (IDS). A system whereby virtually the same information about a company is required in 1933 act and 1934 act filings.

International offering. In general, an offering of securities outside the United States by a U.S. company.

Institutional investor. An institutional investor is distinguished from an individual investor. Examples include pension funds, insurance companies, and mutual funds.

Letter of comment. A formal communication from SEC staff to an issuer's attorneys that contains inquiries and suggestions about a registration statement.

Management consulting services (MCS). In general, nonaudit and nontax services performed by accounting firms.

Management's discussion and analysis (MD&A). A part of the basic information package that provides investors with management's own analysis of various aspects of a company's financial situation.

Materiality. The omission or misstatement of an item to which a reasonable investor would attach importance in determining whether to purchase or sell securities.

Merit regulation. The process by which regulators judge whether an offer of securities is fair, just, and equitable. Merit regulation is used by state securities regulators, in contrast to disclosure regulation, the basis for the federal securities laws.

Multijurisdictional disclosure system (MJDS). A system that permits large U.S. and Canadian public companies to conduct offerings in both jurisdictions on the basis of home country rules.

Peer review. A quality-control review of one accounting firm by another.

Preliminary prospectus (or red herring). The prospectus filed with the SEC that contains the same required information as the final prospectus, except for the market price at which the securities will be offered when the registration statement becomes effective.

Private offerings, resales, and trading through automated linkages (PORTAL). A market system for trading privately placed securities, usually those of foreign issuers.

Prospectus. The portion of the registration statement provided to investors that contains information about (1) the company issuing the securities, (2) the securities being offered, and (3) the method of distribution of the securities.

Proxy. The votes of stockholders on matters requiring authorization or consent.

Public float. The aggregate market value of an entity's outstanding common stock.

Qualified institutional buyer (QIB). In general, a bank or other financial institution that owns and invests on a discretionary basis at least $100 million of securities.

Quiet period. The period from the time a registration statement is filed with the SEC to the time it becomes effective. Activities of the issuing company, its management, and the underwriter are restricted during the quiet period.

Racketeer Influenced and Corrupt Organizations Statute (RICO). A federal law that prohibits acquiring or maintaining an interest in an entity through a pattern of racketeering.

Reasonable care defense. A defense against 1933 act liability if, after a reasonable investigation, a party had reasonable grounds to believe and did believe that a registration statement was not defective.

Registration statement. The document filed with the SEC by a company issuing securities to the public under the 1933 act.

Regulation A offering. The small-offering exemption under the 1933 act.

Regulation D offering. The limited-offering exemption under the 1933 act.

Regulation S-K. The principal regulation setting forth the requirements for nonfinancial statement disclosures contained in SEC filings.

Regulation S-X. The principal regulation setting forth the requirements for the form and content of financial statements contained in SEC filings.

Restricted securities. Securities acquired in an offering exempt from registration under the 1933 act. Such securities may not be resold without registration unless another exemption is available.

Rights offering. An offer by a foreign company to existing shareholders to purchase additional shares.

Rule 10b-5. The 1934 act rule that prohibits intentional deceit in connection with the sale of securities.

S-1-2-3 scheme. A three-tier registration system under the 1933 act. The three forms all require essentially the same information, but the information is disseminated differently under each form.

Scienter. The intention to commit fraud.

Secondary offering. An offering of previously unregistered securities of an entity held by its owners. This is in contrast to the typical offering of securities by the issuing company itself.

Securities Act of 1933. The act that regulates the registration and distribution of securities to the public by the issuing company.

Securities and Exchange Act of 1934. The act that regulates continuous reporting by already-public companies.

Securities and Exchange Commission (or, simply, the commission). The agency of the U.S. government primarily responsible for administering the federal securities laws.

Security. Stocks, bonds, or variations thereof or derivatives therefrom. Two essential elements of a security are (1) the purchaser is led to expect a profit on the investment and (2) the actual profit to be earned is largely in the hands of the issuing company.

Short sale. The sale of stock not owned in hopes of buying it at a lower price before delivery.

Short-swing profit. The profit earned by an officer or director of an entity from buying and selling stock in that entity within a six-month period.

Small business issuer. An issuing company whose sales and public float each do not exceed $25 million.

Sophisticated investor. An investor having sufficient knowledge and experience in financial and business matters to be capable of evaluating the merits and risks of an investment opportunity.

Suitor. An entity seeking to acquire another in a takeover attempt.

Takeover bid. An attempt to capture control of another company.

Target. An entity sought to be acquired in a takeover attempt.

Testing the waters. The process of providing information to prospective investors in a Regulation A offering before an offering circular is filed with the SEC.

Tipping. The act by a corporate insider of giving inside information to a third party.

Tombstone ad. An advertisement in the financial press announcing that a public offering is in process.

Underwriter (or investment banker). An intermediary between a company issuing securities (the seller) in a public offering and the purchasers of the securities.

Selected Additional Readings

The following publications should be helpful in learning more about the SEC and the federal securities laws.

AFTERMAN, ALLAN B. *Handbook of SEC Accounting and Disclosure* (1994 ed.). Boston: Warren, Gorham and Lamont, 1994.

AFTERMAN, ALLAN B., AND ROWAN H. JONES. *Securities Regulation of Foreign Issuers.* Chicago: Commerce Clearing House, 1994.

HAFT, ROBERT J. *Liability of Attorneys and Accountants for Securities Transactions* (1994–1995 ed.). Deerfield, Ill.: Clark Boardman Callaghan, 1994.

LOSS, LOUIS. *Fundamentals of Securities Regulation,* 2d ed. Boston: Little, Brown, 1988.

SODERQUIST, LARRY D. *Understanding the Securities Laws,* 3d ed. New York: Practicing Law Institute, 1993.

WATERS, MICHAEL D. *Proxy Regulation.* New York: Practicing Law Institute, 1992.

Index